Turning revolt into style

To buy or to find out more about the books currently available in this series, please go to:
https://manchesteruniversitypress.co.uk/series/studies-in-design-and-material-culture/

general editors
SALLY-ANNE HUXTABLE
ELIZABETH CURRIE
LIVIA LAZZARO REZENDE
WESSIE LING

founding editor
PAUL GREENHALGH

Turning revolt into style
The process and practice of punk graphic design

Russ Bestley

Manchester University Press

Copyright © Russ Bestley 2025

The right of Russ Bestley to be identified as the author of this work has been asserted in accordance with the Copyright, Designs and Patents Act 1988.

Published by Manchester University Press
Oxford Road, Manchester, M13 9PL
www.manchesteruniversitypress.co.uk

British Library Cataloguing-in-Publication Data
A catalogue record for this book is available from the British Library

ISBN 978 1 5261 5132 2 hardback
ISBN 978 1 5261 9604 0 paperback

First published 2025

The publisher has no responsibility for the persistence or accuracy of URLs for any external or third-party internet websites referred to in this book, and does not guarantee that any content on such websites is, or will remain, accurate or appropriate.

EU authorised representative for GPSR:
Easy Access System Europe, Mustamäe tee 50, 10621 Tallinn, Estonia,
gpsr.requests@easproject.com

Typeset
by Cheshire Typesetting Ltd, Cuddington, Cheshire

Contents

	List of figures	vi
	Acknowledgements	xi
	Introduction	1
1	Pretty vacant: punk graphic themes	24
2	Material interventions: punk graphic processes	62
3	Design it yourself: the punk diaspora	103
4	Your generation: punk designers and the art departments	123
5	New sounds, new styles: design and technology	154
6	A different kind of tension: industry and the individual	181
7	Parallel lines: into the eighties	200
8	Retro-spective: influence and legacy	233
	Bibliography	250
	Index	264

List of figures

Every effort has been made to identify and contact the original copyright holders or creators of the material used in this work. In cases where the originator remains untraceable despite these efforts, the material has been included in good faith. Should any copyright holder wish to make themselves known, we are happy to rectify the situation accordingly.

1.1 Satan's Rats (1977), 'In My Love For You', 7" single, United Kingdom: DJM Records. Front cover with 'PUNK' promotional sticker. 29
1.2 Plastic Bertrand (1977), 'Ça Plane Pour Moi', 7" single, Portugal: Vogue Records. Front cover. 30
1.3 'Can you show you're PUNK enough?' advertisement for copper bracelet, *Melody Maker*, 17 September 1977. 31
1.4 Front cover of *Trick* newspaper/fanzine, November 1977. 33
1.5 Jamie Reid, *Never Mind the Bollocks* album cover colour print specification 1977. 35
1.6 Original Sex Pistols logo designed by Helen Wellington-Lloyd, 1976. 36
1.7 Buzzcocks (1978), *Another Music in a Different Kitchen*, vinyl album, United Kingdom: United Artists. 38
1.8 The Damned, 'New Rose' promotional poster, 1976. Design by Barney Bubbles. 39
1.9 Outtake from photo session for *Damned Damned Damned*, 1977. 41
1.10 The Cortinas (1977), 'Fascist Dictator', 7" single, United Kingdom: Step Forward Records. 42
1.11 Blitzkrieg Bop (1977), 'Let's Go', 7" single, United Kingdom: Lightning Records. 43

List of figures   vii

1.12 Headache (1977), 'Can't Stand Still', 7" single, United Kingdom: Lout Records.   44
1.13 Chron Gen (1981), *Puppets of War*, 7" vinyl EP, United Kingdom: Gargoyle Records.   45
1.14 *Sideburns* fanzine no.1, December 1976. 'Play'in in the Band' full page illustration.   47
1.15 The Desperate Bicycles (1977), 'Smokescreen' / 'Handlebars', 7" single, United Kingdom: Refill Records.   48
1.16 The Desperate Bicycles (1977), 'The Medium Was Tedium' / 'Don't Back the Front', 7" single, United Kingdom: Refill Records. Front cover.   49
1.17 The Desperate Bicycles (1977), 'The Medium Was Tedium' / 'Don't Back the Front', 7" single, United Kingdom: Refill Records. Back cover.   50
1.18 Buzzcocks (1978), 'Love You More', 7" single, United Kingdom: United Artists. Back Cover.   56
2.1 'New Wave Gear' advertisement, *New Musical Express*, November 1977.   63
2.2 The Mekons (1978), 'Never Been in A Riot', 7" single, United Kingdom: Fast Product. Front cover.   65
2.3 The Mekons (1978), 'Never Been in A Riot', 7" single, United Kingdom: Fast Product. Back cover.   66
2.4 Gang of Four (1978), *Damaged Goods*, 7" vinyl EP, United Kingdom: Fast Product. Front cover.   67
2.5 Gang of Four (1978), *Damaged Goods*, 7" vinyl EP, United Kingdom: Fast Product. Back cover.   68
2.6 Gang of Four, *Entertainment!* US tour poster, 1980.   69
2.7 Scritti Politti (1978), *Skank Bloc Bologna*, 7" vinyl EP, United Kingdom: St. Pancras Record. Inside cover.   70
2.8 *Sniffin' Glue*, fanzine, 3, September 1976.   72
2.9 Fifty Fantastics (1980), 'God's Got Religion', 7" single, United Kingdom: Dining Out.   74
2.10 The Atoms (1979), 'Max Bygraves Killed My Mother', 7" single, United Kingdom: Rinka Records. Screen printed picture sleeve and inserts.   76
2.11 Victim (1977), 'Strange Thing By Night', 7" single, Northern Ireland: Good Vibrations.   79
2.12 Jamie Reid, Sex Pistols *God Save The Queen* poster 1977.   81
2.13 Crass (1984), 'You're Already Dead', 7" single, United Kingdom: Crass Records.   83
2.14 Crass (1980), 'Bloody Revolutions', 7" single, United Kingdom: Crass Records. Fold-out poster.   85
2.15 Das Schnitz (1979), *4AM*, 7" vinyl EP, United Kingdom: Ellie Jay.   86

2.16	Linder, Pretty Girls, 1977. Photomontage.	89
2.17	The Pigs (1977), *Youthanasia*, 7" vinyl EP, United Kingdom: New Bristol Records.	90
2.18	The Cortinas (1977), 'Defiant Pose', 7" single, United Kingdom: Step Forward Records.	91
2.19	The Partisans (1982), '17 Years of Hell', 7" single, United Kingdom: No Future.	92
2.20	Poster promoting the compilation album *New Wave*, released by Vertigo Records, 1977.	93
2.21	Press advert for The Clash, *The Clash*, *New Musical Express*, 19 November 1977.	96
2.22	Press advert for The Stranglers, 'Something Better Change', *New Musical Express*, 23 July 1977.	97
3.1	Various Artists (1979), *Earcom 3*, double 7" EP, United Kingdom: Fast Product.	107
3.2	The Rings (1977), 'I Wanna Be Free', 7" single, United Kingdom: Chiswick Records. Photography by Pete Kodick/Peter Gravelle.	117
3.3	Label design, Clay Records, Stoke 1980.	120
4.1	*Chainsaw* fanzine, 2, September/October 1977.	125
4.2	Stiff Records identity, 1977. Original artwork.	127
4.3	Theatre of Hate (1980), 'Original Sin', 7" single, United Kingdom: SS Records. Original artwork.	129
4.4	Theatre of Hate *Westworld* promotional poster, 1982.	130
4.5	Buzzcocks (1977), *Spiral Scratch*, 7" vinyl EP, United Kingdom: New Hormones. Front cover.	131
4.6	Buzzcocks (1977), *Spiral Scratch*, 7" vinyl EP, United Kingdom: New Hormones. Back cover.	132
4.7	Buzzcocks logo.	133
4.8	Buzzcocks (1978), 'I Don't Mind', 7" single, United Kingdom: United Artists. Back cover.	133
4.9	Bob Last, *Photo-Montage!*, 1977.	137
4.10	Cocteau Twins (1982), *Lullabies*, 12" vinyl EP, United Kingdom: 4AD.	139
4.11	Killing Joke (1979), *Turn To Red*, 10" vinyl EP, United Kingdom: Malicious Damage.	140
4.12	Killing Joke (1980), *Killing Joke*, vinyl album, United Kingdom: Malicious Damage.	141
4.13	Killing Joke (1990), *Extremities, Dirt and Various Repressed Emotions*, vinyl album, Germany: Aggressive Rockproduktionen. Original artwork.	142
4.14	Siouxsie and the Banshees (1978), 'Hong Kong Garden', 7" single, United Kingdom: Polydor.	145

4.15	The Cure (1979), *Three Imaginary Boys*, vinyl album, United Kingdom: Fiction Records.	149
4.16	Siouxsie and the Banshees (1979), *Join Hands*, vinyl album, United Kingdom: Polydor.	150
5.1	Steve Averill, pencil roughs for Radiators From Space logo, 1977.	160
5.2	Radiators From Space (1977), 'Television Screen', 7" single, United Kingdom: Chiswick.	161
5.3	Killing Joke (1980), *Killing Joke*, vinyl album, United Kingdom: Malicious Damage. Track titles.	162
5.4	Letraset Shatter dry transfer lettering (1973).	163
5.5	Letraset Walbaum Fraktur dry transfer lettering (c.1960).	163
5.6	Letraset Old English dry transfer lettering (c.1960).	164
5.7	Buzzcocks (1977), 'Orgasm Addict', 7" single, United Kingdom: United Artists. Front cover.	168
5.8	Stiff Records lettering, 1977. original artwork.	171
5.9	*Kill Your Pet Puppy* fanzine, 1, 1979. Inner page.	176
5.10	*Kill Your Pet Puppy* fanzine, 3, 1980. Front cover.	177
6.1	Halftone image, inner cover of Siouxsie and the Banshees (1979), *Join Hands*, vinyl album, United Kingdom: Polydor.	182
6.2	National Graphical Association (NGA) union stamp on rear of artwork.	184
7.1	*Home Taping is Killing Music* logo, 1980.	202
7.2	Discharge (1980), *Realities of War*, 7" vinyl EP, United Kingdom: Clay Records.	203
7.3	Blondie, 'Wouldn't you like to rip her to shreds?' advertisement, *New Musical Express*, November 1977.	205
7.4	The Adverts (1977), 'One Chord Wonders', 7" single, United Kingdom: Stiff Records.	206
7.5	Siouxsie and the Banshees (1988), *Peepshow*, vinyl album, United Kingdom: Polydor. Original artwork.	213
7.6	Siouxsie and the Banshees (1988), 'Peek-A-Boo', 7" single, United Kingdom: Polydor. Original artwork.	214
7.7	Various Artists (1978), *A Factory Sample*, double 7" vinyl EP, United Kingdom: Factory Records.	216
7.8	Letraset figures, dry transfer sheet AA130.	218
7.9	The Normal (1978), 'T.V.O.D.', 7" single, United Kingdom: Mute. Back cover.	219
7.10	The Normal (1978), 'T.V.O.D.', 7" single, United Kingdom: Mute. Front cover.	220
7.11	Letraset figures, dry transfer sheet AA115.	221
7.12	The Human League (1978), 'Being Boiled', 7" single, United Kingdom: Fast Product. Front cover.	222

7.13	The Human League (1978), 'Being Boiled', 7" single, United Kingdom: Fast Product. Back cover.	223
7.14	Cabaret Voltaire (1978), *Extended Play*, 7" vinyl EP, United Kingdom: Rough Trade. Back cover.	224
7.15	Cabaret Voltaire (1980), 'Seconds Too Late', 7" single, United Kingdom: Rough Trade.	225
7.16	Thomas Leer (1978), 'Private Plane', 7" single, United Kingdom: Oblique.	226
8.1	AMID logo, 1988.	241

Acknowledgements

I have been writing about the relationship between punk and graphic design for more than thirty years. During that time, I have written about punk in the provinces, satire and humour, the mythology of a do-it-yourself ideal, punk fandom, cover versions, novelty records, fanzines and the history of punk graphics from the late 1960s to the early 2000s. Some sections of this book draw upon that previous work, though this is more specifically an attempt to map the intersection between two independent but related themes: the visual styles and approaches particular to punk and post-punk graphic design and the relationship between a new group of punk-inspired or punk-aligned designers and the established music graphics and printing professions during a period of radical change.

    I have had the good fortune to meet and to interview some of my graphic design heroes. Jamie Reid, Malcolm Garrett, Richard Boon, Linder Sterling, Gee Vaucher, Mike Coles, Vaughan Oliver, Bill Smith, Rob O'Connor, Jill Mumford, Jon Langford, John Hyatt, Arturo Vega, Winston Smith, Steve Averill, Chris Morton, Neville Brody and many others helped to shape my visual consciousness as a music fan over the past fifty years. Many of them inspired me to eventually become a graphic designer through engaging with their work at a time in my life when I had no idea what the terms 'graphic design' or 'visual communication' meant. I was also inspired to pursue a path in design by a few record labels I followed obsessively: Fast Product, Malicious Damage and CNT Records never put a foot wrong (though Stiff Records, Small Wonder, Beggars Banquet, Refill, Good Vibrations, Factory and Mute also played a significant part in my design education).

    I have also worked alongside notable graphic design historians, practitioners and theorists who have informed my approach to our shared practice. Rick Poynor, Ian Noble, Andrew Howard, Jan van Toorn, Mark Pawson,

Karel Martens, Adrian Shaughnessy, Tony Brook, Paul McNeil, Hamish Muir, Jonathan Barnbrook, Tony Pritchard, John Bateson, Tony Credland and my colleagues at the London College of Communication (formerly London College of Printing) – particularly Roger Sabin and Angus Carlyle – have helped me develop a richer understanding of the histories, practices, processes and critical contexts of graphic design. My good friend Paul Harvey has been a constant source of inspiration, both as a brilliant Stuckist artist and as a fellow punk graphic design enthusiast.

Dozens of fans, musicians, artists, journalists, collectors and archivists have generously allowed me access to their collections and insights into their experience. Notable among these, Alex Ogg, Paul Burgess, Peter Gravelle, Pete Holidai, Joly MacFie, Pauline Murray, Gaye Black, Graham Fellows, Mark Perry, Tom Vague, Mike Diboll, Tony Drayton, Tony Fletcher, Alan Rider, Kevin Lycett, Neil Horgan, Kevin Shepherd, Gary Loveridge, Garry Bushell, Mike Malignant, Josef Loderer, Luk Haas, Ian Glasper, Greg Bull, Niall McGuirk, Ged Babey, Rich Levene, Barry Phillips, Steve Pescott, Rich Hassall, Chris Low, Tim Wells, Nicky Forbes, Helen McCallum and Chuck Warner have given me a greater comprehension of punk's rich and diverse history.

I would also like to offer my heartfelt thanks to the brilliant designers, artists and photographers who have generously contributed images to this project, along with numerous fanzine producers, DIY and independent labels. I had intended to also include images of some of the significant 'big name' examples featured in the text, but twenty-first century global entertainment corporations are less than forthcoming in response to requests for permission to reproduce artwork. As such, readers unfamiliar with any of the designs mentioned should adhere to the salient words of The Snivelling Shits, and 'look that one up'.

I also owe a debt of gratitude to my three daughters – Zowie, Chris and Nikita – who were ~~forced~~ encouraged to 'listen and learn' throughout their formative years, and to my wife Sarah, who has been my constant companion, indispensable collaborator, inspiring fellow researcher and emotional sounding-board. Sarah's cogent questioning and unvarnished critique has always kept my feet on the ground and helped me strike a balance between the two, sometimes conflicting, worlds of punk and academia.

I was appointed Reader in Graphic Design and Subcultures at the London College of Communication in 2012, offering me a unique opportunity to bring together my research interests and to develop a body of work encompassing history, theory and practice that, I hope, can be drawn upon and extended by other researchers in the future. Since that time, we have witnessed an exponential growth in what is loosely termed punk studies, moving beyond relatively limited histories of the early scene in New York or London to reflect a much deeper critical analysis of punk music, fashion, politics, philosophy and aesthetics around the globe over a period of more than fifty years. This is clearly evidenced through the work of the interdisciplinary journal *Punk & Post-Punk*, now in its fourteenth year of publication,[1] the international Punk Scholars Network[2] and the Global Punk book series.[3] I am proud to have played a central role in each of these developments, while I am indebted to the work of many others, particularly Mike Dines, Matt Grimes, Matthew Worley, Alastair Gordon, Ellen Bernhard, Daniel Makagon, Paul Fields, Laura Way, Francis Stewart, Phil Kiszely, Paul Hollins, Jessica Schwartz, Michael Mary Murphy, John Dougan, Anita Raghunath, Pete Dale and Rich Cross. Valuable insights into punk art and design have come from my academic colleagues in the (punk) arts: Maria Elena Buszek, Marie Arleth Skov, Ian Trowell, Becky Binns, Ana Raposo, Simon Strange and Gavin Butt.

Turning revolt into style: The process and practice of punk graphic design embodies all this work over more than three decades, together with my lived experience and passion for punk and graphic design that goes back much further – to my early involvement in the scene as a teenage punk rocker in the 1970s and the ways it shaped my approach to life thereafter. Graphic design is traditionally a collaborative practice, while punk participation and academic research share similar values – each requires a sense of communal engagement and the sharing of knowledge, values or experience. This book is an attempt to bring those disparate themes together.

Notes

1 https://intellectdiscover.com/content/journals/punk (Accessed 13 February 2025).
2 www.punkscholarsnetwork.com (Accessed 13 February 2025).
3 www.intellectbooks.com/global-punk-series (Accessed 13 February 2025).

If you're going to reminisce, then you need to do it properly.
(The Mekons, 1982, '1st Guitarist', *The Mekons Story*)

Introduction

Turning revolt into style: The process and practice of punk graphic design takes a close look at the complex relationship between punk and the graphic design profession, from the innovations of DIY pioneers to radical changes in the commercial design industry. These changes reflected not just the influence of an emerging cohort of young designers who aligned themselves with the new subculture, but also the advent of new technologies and working practices, particularly in the printing industry during the early days of photocomposition and digital reproduction. While punk history spans more than five decades and myriad global scenes, this book attempts to capture a relatively brief time frame and centres on the United Kingdom. Its focus ranges from Helen Wellington-Lloyd, Nils Stevenson and Jamie Reid's first attempts to graphically visualise punk in the early days of the Sex Pistols, through dramatic changes in technology and labour relations in the printing industry during the early 1980s, culminating in the responses by music graphics professionals to the Copyright, Designs and Payments Act of 1988.

Punk's visual language was formed in response to the cultural moment in which it was situated. This book draws upon interviews with leading punk and post-punk designers including Malcolm Garrett, Bill Smith, Chris Morton, Steve Averill, Mike Coles, Bob Last, Rob O'Connor, Jill Mumford and Neville Brody, together with print production expertise from Murray Arbiter at ArbiterDrucken and Tim Milne of Artomatic. Along with a close analysis of punk and post-punk record covers, fanzines and other artefacts, it charts the story of a seismic cultural shift that was to have a lasting impact for decades to come. The text centres on two key questions: how did a new generation of young, punk-inspired graphic designers navigate the music graphics profession in the late 1970s and early 1980s? And how did significant changes in printing technology, labour relations and working practices in the design profession impact their work during that period?

The visual styles of the emerging punk subculture (graphics, fashion, dress, photography) were formed not just from historical antecedents but also in relation to contemporary conditions. While several high-profile books, exhibitions and articles in recent years have focused on punk graphics,[1] they have not usually situated punk's visual aesthetic within the technological, cultural, professional and political contexts that directly impacted its look, style and material qualities. These 'punk art' collections have tended to showcase objects, sometimes naming the designer and adding a few art historical references to provide design inspiration or context, but they rarely if ever consider the design process – the actual *practice* of making designed artefacts. This book is an attempt to join the dots, to map the connections between amateur producers, punk-related or affiliated design practitioners, the mainstream music industry and its allied music graphic design professionals and studios. It also considers the impact of craft skills, design and print technologies and the social and political landscape within which those designers turned revolt into style (to borrow a phrase from the late, great, George Melly) and created a set of innovative, powerful and long-lasting subcultural visual codes that would impact the mainstream for many years to come.

The initial punk explosion in the United Kingdom happened at a time of significant social, political and technological change. Graphic designers contributed to, and were deeply affected by, those changes. Punk's back to basics ideology brought a sense of urgency to a stagnant and complacent music industry, while many established design professionals took the opportunity to contribute positively to the new movement. In practice, surprisingly little attention has been paid to the commercial and professional relationship between popular culture and punk, particularly the role of the music industry and the business model that operates behind the creation of new styles and markets.[2] This includes not only the investors, managers, critics and journalists, marketing teams, promoters, manufacturers, distributors and retailers, but also the art directors, typographers, illustrators, photographers and branding and identity designers who created its visual aesthetic.

While this book can never hope to be comprehensive, the focus is on graphic design and typography, rather than illustration and photography as distinct, separate disciplines. Professional rock photographers who helped shape a punk aesthetic deserve recognition, however, not least because their work was closely integrated with the design of some notable punk and post-punk album covers. Among these, an older group of professional photographers including Michael Beal, Keith Morris, Derek Ridgers, Rik Walton, Sheila Rock,[3] Jill Furmanovsky, Adrian Boot, Pennie Smith, Peter Gravelle,[4] Kate Simon, Chris Gabrin and Brian Griffin[5] predated the punk explosion. Many had experience working with design teams at the major record labels, while relative newcomers such as Janette Beckman, Ray Stevenson, Erica Echenberg and Mick Mercer established a photographic practice through their documentation of the new subculture from the inside.

Like photography, illustration is mentioned only lightly. This book is about the design practice and process, which often entailed an art director or graphic designer working with an illustrator, photographer or type designer as commissioned contributors to a larger, more complex project. In this model, the graphic designer might be seen as the concept originator, project manager and coordinator leading the construction of a visual identity, with the image – photograph or illustration, for instance – one component of the bigger whole. Obviously, such definitions are messy, complicated and flawed, particularly in those instances where a photographer or illustrator took on the design brief in its entirety, or where the image constituted a significant part of the final design. Russell Mills, Ian Wright or Linder Sterling might be important examples here, particularly in Mills' work for Penetration, The Skids and Wire, or his collaboration with Brian Eno, *More Dark Than Shark* (1986),[6] along with Wright's illustrations for *The Face* and *New Musical Express* and Sterling's drawing, collage and photomontage work for Magazine and her own post-punk band, Ludus. Gee Vaucher's work also spans a similar range of professional roles as Mills and Sterling, working primarily as an illustrator but also taking responsibility for much of the graphic design output of the anarcho-punk group Crass, along with her own tabloid format illustrated journal, *International Anthem* (1977–84).[7]

The evolution of a new form of punk-inspired visual communication also enabled a generation of young, innovative designers to gain a foothold in the profession, or at least to contribute to a rapidly developing and dynamic new set of styles. These ranged from those with art school experience or design training who became closely linked to a particular group or label – Jamie Reid, Chris Morton, Malcolm Garrett, Linder Sterling, Bob Last, Gee Vaucher, Peter Saville, Vaughan Oliver – to up-and-coming music graphics specialists including Phil Smee, Neville Brody, Mike Coles (Malicious Damage), Rob O'Connor (Stylorouge) and Alex McDowell (Rocking Russian). At the same time, a new generation of punk-inspired amateurs struggled against the odds without any clear historical or contextual reference points. These included Mark Perry, Tony Moon, Charlie Chainsaw, Tony Fletcher, Mike Diboll, Tom Vague, Alan Rider, Tony Drayton and hundreds of others, particularly in the burgeoning punk fanzine market. Punk graphics also owed an obvious debt to a cohort of experienced art directors and designers who could utilise their skills in the marketing and branding of the new style, such as Barney Bubbles, George 'God' Snow, Bill Smith, Jo Mirowski, Jill Mumford, Paul Henry, Nicholas de Ville and David Jeffery.

A punk visual aesthetic

With a history now spanning fifty years or more, punk is a phenomenon that is difficult to define in simple terms. As a social, cultural, philosophical and aesthetic movement, it has always covered a wide assortment of practices, styles and expressions. Recent popular accounts have at times sanitised punk history and attempted to shoehorn it into a retrospectively 'progressive' narrative that belies its original complexity and inherent contradictions.[8] Some punk participants are considered, reflective and socially or politically engaged. Others care about hedonism more than activism, with punk functioning as a stylistic backdrop to their greater desire to have fun. Still more are happy to fit in to the scene as fans and followers, without a desire to actively contribute to the wider 'punk community'. Core values are, therefore, hard to pin down, though a few simple codes and conventions receive support across many punk scenes: a call for autonomy, authenticity and empowerment alongside a rejection of authority, tradition and commercial exploitation.

None of these values are unique to punk, nor did the subculture set a precedent anything like as powerful and dramatic as some sections of the media would go on to portray. That is not to say, however, that punk did not embrace and facilitate new opportunities and codes of practice that deeply affected a range of institutions, from the music business to film, photography, art, design, journalism, publishing and the wider entertainment industry. It is not the intention here to narrow punk to a tightly bound set of principles or a particular historical narrative, though the focus is largely on its impact in the United Kingdom. This book attempts to investigate the intersection between subculture, media, the music industry, design, technology and the wider social, cultural, political and economic environment of the late 1970s and early 1980s. At the same time, it makes the case for punk art and design as an act of *making*, embodying practice, craft, technology, materials and labour, and for the dissemination and reception of punk through objects and artefacts – records, fanzines, flyers, posters, magazines, badges and other graphic ephemera – alongside clothing, music and performance.

As an early London Weekend Television documentary on the UK punk rock phenomenon, first broadcast on 28 November 1976, indicated, part of the new subculture's philosophy revolved around the idea of participation and the levelling of hierarchies between performer and audience. Presenter Janet Street-Porter's narration attempted to get to grips with the basic principles of punk as a do-it-yourself model of subcultural participation: 'There's also a new feeling that you don't have to be a special sort of person to pick up a guitar or stand in front of a mic and sing. In punk rock, anyone can have a go'.[9] In practice, such hierarchies were harder to budge, particularly outside the realm of punk performance, although even here the mythology only briefly outweighed the brutal reality that some musicians were simply more capable, or more interesting, than others.

Just over a year later, LWT revisited the subculture with a longer programme entitled *The Year of Punk*, drawing on some of the same footage as the original feature, but now accompanied by clips of bands performing live at the Roxy and Vortex punk clubs in London over the previous year. Street-Porter once again highlighted punk's anyone can do it philosophy, although with the benefit of hindsight she also offered something of a critical reflection: 'Another fundamental part of punk's attraction was the belief that anyone could be a musician. This was exciting for the punk fans, but it naturally led to some rather basic performances'.[10]

By now, punk and new wave music was becoming a big business, and the down-to-earth, street-level narrative was perhaps more of a mechanism for selling commodities through a sense of supposed authenticity than a practical manifesto for wider participation. There is, of course, a tension here between punk as attitude and ideology and punk as a new and distinct form of popular music, between a philosophical approach to the subculture and the commercial priorities of a music industry that saw an opportunity to access emerging markets and new audiences. Certainly, when it came to punk products – records, clothing, promotional material – the more traditional business-led operations of branding, marketing, professional design and copyright held sway. Punk clothes, always displaying a tension between the high fashion of Vivienne Westwood and Malcolm McLaren in their King's Road boutique and the charity shop adaptations and homemade, do-it-yourself outfits of early fans, also witnessed a boom in copycat items sold by smaller traders and mail order sellers advertising in the back pages of the music press.

Early punk graphics in the United States, United Kingdom, Europe and Australia ranged from the Situationist-inspired détournement of the Sex Pistols to the everyday street style of The Ramones, The Saints, The Undertones and The Lurkers, the minimalist sophistication of Talking Heads and Wire, the comic irreverence of The Damned, the ironic visual identity of Stiff Records and their roster of oddball, leftfield artists, the retro styling of The Jam, The Rezillos and Generation X, the overt DIY call to arms of The Desperate Bicycles, Television Personalities and Scritti Politti, the quirkiness of Buzzcocks, XTC and Magazine, or the gritty, urban rock'n'roll street gang image of The Clash, Sham 69 and countless others that followed in their wake. In the United Kingdom, Jamie Reid's work for the Sex Pistols led the way, leaking out through the music press and mainstream media even before the group had recorded their first single. Reid's deliberately rough and ready, agit-prop style was mirrored to an extent by the early punk fanzines, though the symbiotic relationship was largely coincidental – many of the fanzine producers were creating graphics that were primarily driven by (the lack of) available technology and limited skill sets, while Reid (a highly experienced artist and graphic designer) was making a conscious choice of visual strategy. Some years earlier, Reid had developed a rough and ready sense of agitprop visual style at Suburban Press, after the collective acquired a Multilith 1250 offset press. He brought these graphic strategies to the table in the creation of a punk aesthetic, utilising methods and at times reusing older work for a new purpose.[11]

> As the members of Suburban Press did much of their own servicing, they learned the capabilities of the machine through trial and error, also finding that bolder designs with marker pen, ripped edges and less finesse would reproduce with more attack than finer images.[12]

Perhaps as much by serendipity as by choice, punk's do-it-yourself graphic underground aesthetic closely mirrored the developing styles and conventions of the punk mainstream and vice versa. Professional designers could emulate some of the rough and rudimentary styles that were bubbling up from below to project a sense of grass-roots authenticity, while many of the amateur punk DIY creatives attempted to fit their work within emerging punk visual styles, much of it residing in the mainstream music industry. The dissemination and reach of punk 'product', usually a direct result of the marketing and distribution power of the major labels and their (temporary, at least) investment in the new wave, meant that many of these examples set the tone more widely. In the process, punk record covers and features in the traditional music press contributed directly to a received notion of punk fashion and graphic style across the regions of the United Kingdom, particularly among younger audiences with little direct experience of live gigs or the London-centric punk clubs.

Once punk became more widely recuperated and stylised, by the record industry and fans alike, visual conventions began to narrow, leading to a more generic set of punk graphic conventions that persist today. Harder visual boundaries were put in place between punk and what became known as new wave, for instance, though the two terms had been largely interchangeable when the scene was in its infancy. Different factions subsequently diversified and fragmented from punk's original broad umbrella to create more tightly focused scenes and subgenres, including hardcore, anarcho-punk, Oi! and post-punk, each developing its own visual conventions in the process.

Music graphics

The relationship between the fine arts and the applied or commercial arts is long and complex. The creation of visual work in response to a brief or on behalf of a client is widely viewed as distinct from, and sometimes inferior to, those practices where the artist is attributed with concept, content and form, without external input or influence. Meanwhile, graphic design for the popular music industry, or music graphics, occupies a somewhat elevated position within the design profession, at least for its more celebrated exponents, separated from the murky world of more mainstream, commercial creative practice such as branding and identity, packaging, information and editorial work. In part, this is due to the long-established cultural cachet afforded certain sections of the popular music industry, where notions of counterculture still hold sway. A legacy of the 1950s and 1960s rock'n'roll and beat booms, rock music has long been associated with the popular avant-garde, with notions of authenticity, rebellion and independence from the mainstream.[13]

Elements of rock and pop music have achieved a level of critical acclaim that has resonated with the public, situating both the recording artists and their associated partners (producers, designers, illustrators, photographers, record labels) in a nebulous space somewhere between 'high' and 'low' culture. Album cover art (a term that is equally problematic in its ambiguous connotations) in many cases plays an intrinsic part in the cultural significance of 'iconic' albums. From *Abbey Road* to *Led Zeppelin*, *Dark Side of the Moon* to *Aladdin Sane*, the record cover is often inseparable from the songs, embedded in the mind of the listener as the image that directly reflects the content of the music and offers some special insight into the philosophy and character of the artist. Meanwhile, the designers and creative teams behind much of this work often go unrecognised, beyond perhaps a minor credit in the sleeve notes. Those few designers and studios that did manage to achieve a level of public recognition at the height of the popular music boom of the 1970s and 1980s – Roger Dean, Storm Thorgerson and Aubrey Powell at Hipgnosis,[14] Barney Bubbles,[15] Jamie Reid,[16] Peter Saville[17] – often did so through the critical and commercial status of the artists and albums they packaged as much as the intrinsic qualities of the visual work they created.

There were a few rare instances where public acknowledgement and appreciation of the creator of the cover design approached that of the musicians, often due to the existing profile or status of an acclaimed guest artist, rather than a recognition of the work of an anonymous graphic designer commissioned to create a visual identity. The critical high praise surrounding, for instance, Peter Blake and Jann Haworth's physical montage for The Beatles' *Sgt. Pepper's Lonely Hearts Club Band*, Richard Hamilton's embossed, plain white cover for The Beatles' *The Beatles* (popularly known as *The White Album*), or Andy Warhol's artwork for the Rolling Stones' *Sticky Fingers* and The Velvet Underground's *The Velvet Underground & Nico* muddy the water further, with the notion that *some* album designs may even stand alone as venerated examples of visual art. Those covers seem to hold a resonance separate from the music, superseding the core principles of branding and identity design that apply more generally to record packaging. In practice, for many listeners, fans, readers and viewers, a balance is always struck between the group or artist who created the music, the sound of the recorded songs, the design of the cover and the cultural status or desirability of the manufactured product.

Art vs design

Graphic design occupies a unique position within the creative arts. It is an applied art, rather than a form of independent artistic practice – it marries creative practices with batch (usually print) production for commercial or cultural ends. Much graphic design work is also anonymously produced, with the artefact and message embodying its central purpose and its creator left uncredited.[18] At the same time, graphic design objects are often viewed as ephemeral: the 'design' is the conduit to access the event, product, or content (poster, package, book, magazine), rather than an object with cultural or commercial value in and of itself. Seldom would a buyer purchase a book or record purely for its cover. A book may be beautifully designed, and its functionality may be seamless and harmonious, but its primary purpose is to package the text in an appropriate form to be read by a reader. While a poster for an event may have aesthetic qualities that lead to its display on the wall beyond the time frame of its message or content (as a beautiful, desirable or collectable object), its core function is to communicate – not simply to act as a visual artefact in and of itself. Graphic designers are usually commissioned to handle the form of a piece of visual communication, while content is authored by someone else: the client, the brief. Design may offer an aesthetically pleasing or appropriately functional window to content, but it is seldom the focal point: books are to be read, records to be listened to, posters to communicate information – the packaging simply a vehicle to guide the reader or listener to the content.

The punk subculture, in its mid- to late 1970s incarnation, significantly affected the graphic design profession, from the impact of pioneering – and often independent – designers disrupting traditional practices and career patterns to their embrace of new and innovative methods and technologies. Punk's desire to demystify and enable a close relationship between the artist and spectator, to break down barriers with the audience and encourage others to 'do it themselves' is also reflected in design strategies and methods that offer a sense of authenticity, autonomy and personal connection. This projection of grass-roots authenticity and a connection between artist and audience is exemplified not only in the design and production of fanzines and independent DIY punk records, but also in much of the work produced by professional designers at the major record labels to fit the contemporary zeitgeist.

The design of record sleeves and other graphic ephemera associated with popular music relates directly to a range of wider fields: the design and print industry, technologies for reproduction, cultural conventions, materials, economics, audiences and readers or buyers.[19] The design of punk and post-punk visual material in the United Kingdom is little different in this respect, though rapid changes in technology along with a radical restructuring of the print industry through the early 1980s did have a material effect on the way designers worked and the kinds of work that they created. While punk graphic design has been a subject of some interest to historians and curators, it has often been situated in the context of social history or as a subsidiary area of subcultural studies, itself a field largely centred in the humanities and social sciences.

This book takes a wider critical approach, positioning punk and post-punk graphic design within a range of contemporaneous social, cultural, economic and technological contexts. These include the established music graphics industry and professional design studios in the 1970s and 1980s, the evolving punk mantra of independence and do-it-yourself, the impact of new technology and the social, political and economic conditions of the design and print industry at a critical juncture in its history. During a period when aspiring new artists and designers were engaging with the opportunities afforded by punk's social and cultural schism, technological upheavals were heavily affecting the design and print industries. Wholesale changes in pre-press techniques significantly disrupted the labour market and led to the axing of jobs embedded in specialist crafts, particularly in composition and hot metal typesetting in the national newspaper industry. In turn, this impacted the power of the print unions and forced major changes to long-standing working practices throughout the graphic design and print professions.

A punk design historiography

The election of a new Conservative administration under Margaret Thatcher in May 1979 led to a new era in industrial relations. Long-stablished working practices were now under threat and the dominance of the trade unions that had reached its pinnacle in the Winter of Discontent of 1978/79 was to swiftly become a focus of media and government attention. Traditional industries centred on manufacturing and engineering (such as steel, coal mining, shipbuilding and car making) faced radical restructuring or closure, leading to a series of high-profile industrial disputes between 1981 and 1987 and increasingly acrimonious battles between the government and unions.[20] This period has been highlighted as significant in contemporary British history, though many of the books published on the subject have tended to blend journalism with academic research. In part, this may reflect the increasing centrality of popular culture to our understanding of historical narrative, along with a deeper public interest in the recent past. At the same time, as Lucy Robinson notes, it has inspired a range of alternative interpretations of events.

> Popular journalism and academic work blurred around the eighties, with journalists writing many of the histories that have ended up on university reading lists, and with academics producing narrative accounts for the trade market ... If there is a consensus in these histories of the eighties, it is that there is *no consensus* over the history of the 1980s.[21]

After a period of two or three decades had passed and the 1970s and 1980s shifted into the rearview mirror, writers began to produce narrative accounts of each decade, focusing primarily on social, cultural and political change. Central themes ranged from the global crises and industrial strife of the early 1970s to the impact of Margaret Thatcher's Conservative administration between May 1979 and November 1990. Andy Beckett's *When the Lights Went Out: Britain in the Seventies* (2009),[22] along with Alwyn W. Turner's *Crisis? What Crisis? Britain in the 1970s* (2008)[23] and *Rejoice! Rejoice! Britain in the 1980s* (2010),[24] perhaps best capture this drive to slice historical events into temporally delineated thematic critiques. Turner in particular employs popular culture as a lens through which to comment on changes in British society: notable examples taken from pop music, television drama, comedy and film are juxtaposed with bigger questions relating to industrial relations, race, the environment, women's rights, violence, the Cold War and globalisation. Meanwhile, Dominic Sandbrook's popular histories *State of Emergency: Britain, 1970–1974* (2010),[25] *Seasons in the Sun: Britain, 1974–1979* (2012)[26] and *Who Dares Wins: Britain, 1979–1982* (2019)[27] focus on even narrower temporal and societal shifts, while adopting broadly similar approaches to historical narrative.

Andy McSmith's *No Such Thing as Society: A History of Britain in the 1980s* (2011)[28] also draws on pop cultural references to construct a grand narrative of what the publisher's cover blurb describes as 'the revolutionary decade of the twentieth century', though the author places social, political and economic change (the Thatcher government, feminism, the miners' strike, race relations, unemployment, the Falklands War) front and centre. Examples from television, pop music and media are employed by McSmith as a reference point rather than a driver of events. Similarly, Graham Stewart's *Bang! A History of Britain in the 1980s* (2013)[29] offers a few nods to prominent pop stars and events (Wham, Frankie Goes to Hollywood, Live Aid) but the core focus is on national politics, foreign policy, the media and the economy.

Andy Beckett's *Promised You a Miracle: UK 80–82* (2015)[30] and David Elliott's *1984: British Pop's Dividing Year* (2020)[31] both move beyond the notion of historical shifts arranged by decade to focus on brief periods of radical change: in Beckett's case largely centring on the economy and political ideology during the first term of the Thatcher government, while Elliott looks more explicitly at pop music from Prince and Michael Jackson to Mark E. Smith. Intriguingly, Elliott also dedicates a chapter in the book to graphic design, offering a broad summary of some of the key players in the early 1980s and the emerging aesthetic tropes of post-punk, synth-pop and the New Romantics, though the author doesn't attempt to map these in relation to professional practice or technological developments.

A recent history of the 1980s by Lucy Robinson, *Now That's What I Call a History of the 1980s: Pop Culture and Politics in the Decade That Shaped Modern Britain* (2023),[32] takes a slightly different approach. The author doesn't seek to avoid inevitable overlaps when exploring green activism, the peace movement, militarism, racism, employment rights and the unions, terrorism, the news media, censorship, sexuality, AIDS and consumerism. Robinson deftly leads the reader through these topics while offering parallels in the music and visual style of such disparate pop culture figures as Adam Ant, Smiley Culture, Bananarama, Princess Diana and Roland Rat. Using the *Now That's What I Call Music!* series of compilation albums launched by Virgin Records and EMI in 1983 as a metaphor for the contemporaneous interplay between a multitude of themes, events and institutions, the book invites readers to think beyond simple chronologies and to embrace complexity.

In the late 1990s and early 2000s, a resurgence of interest in the history of punk in the United Kingdom (inspired by anniversaries of several prominent dates in the original punk calendar) resulted in a flurry of activity. In 1999, Roger Sabin edited the first serious collection of academic essays on the history of punk, *Punk Rock: So What?*,[33] an attempt to reconsider punk in a cultural and sociological framework, questioning the value of persistent myths and often repeated histories. As Sabin records in his introduction, a great deal of writing had been done on the subject, but objective studies based on the application of a rigorous academic methodology were uncommon, with a plethora of personal, subjective documentaries holding sway in the market:

> but the problem with all this debate around punk is that history is being rewritten. There'd be no need to worry if the discussions were making the correct historical connections; if the parameters of the debate were sound; if, ultimately, the commentators were 'getting it right'. But unfortunately, in general, they haven't been, and some serious errors of emphasis have been made.[34]

September 2001 saw the first British academic conference solely concerned with punk rock – No Future? Punk 2001, a week-long series of events, presentations and discussions at Wolverhampton University, timed to coincide with the twenty-fifth anniversary of the 100 Club Punk Festival of September 1976. This academic review of punk as an important element in contemporary cultural history reflected a growing trend through the 1990s towards a reappraisal of its impact since 1976. Jon Savage had set the standard for narrative histories of the early punk scene back in 1991 with the justifiably acclaimed *England's Dreaming: Sex Pistols and Punk Rock*,[35] and many other journalists and former punk musicians joined the rush to publish their own version of events. In a frenzy of hyperbolic marketing blurb, several purported (and failed miserably) to tell the 'definitive' history of punk, often accompanied by little-known or previously unpublished photographs and memorabilia,[36] while others went back to musicians from the era and conducted retrospective interviews to create punk 'oral histories' that varied from insightful and informative to rose-tinted nostalgia.[37]

A popular narrative among critics and music historians suggests a lineage from successful British groups of the 1960s, through progressive rock and glam in the early 1970s, to punk in the late 1970s in the form of the Sex Pistols and The Clash. The early 1980s are usually represented by post-punk groups such as Joy Division and later New Order, with popular music again splintering and diversifying to embrace funk, disco and the New Romantic movement. Some of these aspects of what has been termed post-punk came under wider critical attention in the early 2000s. Music journalist Simon Reynolds' narrowly framed history of post-punk, *Rip it Up and Start Again*,[38] was published in March 2005 to widespread critical acclaim, prompting several features in the mainstream press.

In parallel to these broad social histories of Britain in the 1970s and 1980s and retrospective critical analyses of punk through the lens of sociology, ethnography and cultural history, numerous books have been published about punk and post-punk art and design. Like the popular histories, there was something of an acceleration of publishing after the turn of the Millennium, with the original punk movement by that time largely recuperated and institutionalised more than two decades after its perceived demise. Punk's highly charged visual aesthetic was ripe for exploitation and commentators seized the opportunity to get in on the act. There were, of course, precursors. *Melody Maker* journalist and punk advocate Caroline Coon had attempted to contextualise the early punk scene in an image-heavy book, *1988: The New Wave Punk Rock Explosion*,[39] first published in 1977, though most contemporary reportage was conducted through the music press and the punk fanzines.

Meanwhile, early collections of visual material, such as Ray Stevenson's *Sex Pistols File* (1978),[40] were aimed at fans and collectors, serving more as catalogues of memorabilia than critical appraisals of graphic artefacts. Jamie Reid and Jon Savage's *Up They Rise: The Incomplete Works of Jamie Reid* (1987)[41] focused on the artist's portfolio to date and included some contextual commentary from both Reid and Savage, though there was still little sense of reflective critique regarding the *how* and *why* of the work.

By this time, however, Reid's work for the Sex Pistols – and punk graphics more broadly – was beginning to receive at least some wider attention. Brian Cannon's *Going Nowhere: The Art and Design of Punk and New Wave* (1989)[42] attempted to summarise some of the conceptual themes behind punk's visual language, though the author did not attempt to unpack the practical processes at work behind the chosen graphic examples. Rock music journalist Greil Marcus got in on the act with his deeply flawed – and unfathomably influential – account of punk's artistic precursors, *Lipstick Traces*, in 1989.[43] Marcus cited solid philosophical and aesthetic connections between Dada, the Situationists and punk, helping to substantiate a broader mythology that was set to endure in subsequent writing on punk art and design. He also dramatically overstretched the narrative to include medieval heretics and mythological characters that seemed to reflect Malcolm McLaren's deliberate appropriations of the French Revolution and the Gordon Riots as a statement of fact, rather than a tongue-in-cheek, quasi-Situationist stunt.

In the broader field of modern graphic design history, expanding beyond a focus purely on punk graphics, Catherine McDermott's *Street Style: British Design in the 80s* (1987) framed a significant element of then-contemporary design in relation to punk's catalysing effect, though she linked it to a longer tradition of non-conformity in British culture.

> There is, however, an alternative British tradition which is essentially non-conformist and slightly eccentric. It has its origins in a working-class way of life which has always expressed itself by using irony, dissidence and poking fun at the establishment.[44]

Though it offers a broad critical reflection on fashion and textiles, graphic design, interior design and furniture, McDermott's book focuses on a small group of high-profile key players, with punk graphics largely reduced to the work of Jamie Reid, Malcolm Garrett and Barney Bubbles along with a nod to fanzines via Mark Perry's *Sniffin' Glue*. This brief history leads the reader seamlessly on to post-punk stylists Peter Saville, Russell Mills, 23 Envelope (Vaughan Oliver and Nigel Grierson), Terry Jones and Neville Brody, all seemingly engaged in auteur-like isolation from the graphic design profession and the traditional art departments behind the scenes in the music industry. There are numerous errors and omissions (crediting Barney Bubbles with early work for The Clash, for instance, while a lengthy section attributes the collective visual output of Throbbing Gristle to Genesis P. Orridge and Cosey Fanni Tutti, with no mention of Peter 'Sleazy' Christopherson). This lack of specific detail is, sadly, typical of punk design history at what was then a nascent time in its development. However, McDermott does present a cogent case that sets the template and establishes the core narrative for many punk design histories to follow, though her emphasis is on the new generation of successful practitioners who moved into high-profile professional roles, with little acknowledgement of either the far larger cohort of punk amateur makers or the experienced professionals behind the scenes in the traditional music industry art departments.

Four years after the publication of McDermott's book, journalist Cynthia Rose published *Design After Dark* (1991),[45] a picture-based overview of what the author describes as 'fresh design' in the field of contemporary popular culture and brief profiles of 'eleven dancefloor designers' including Ian Wright, Paul Elliman and Ian Swift. Much of the work featured strays some way beyond punk and post-punk design, mainly centring on dance music, jazz, soul and funk-related branding and identity or illustration work, though Rose does attempt to link styles back to punk-era designers including Jamie Reid, Alex McDowell and Terry Jones. Less successfully, she attempts to wrap in visual references to Mayakovsky and Constructivism, which are treated simply as examples of 'Soviet style' to be cross-referenced and namechecked, shorn of any guiding philosophy or historical context.

Another book that touched on the impact of punk in the fields of art, design and visual communication of the 1980s, John A. Walker's *Cross-Overs: Art into Pop and Pop into Art* (1987),[46] paralleled Simon Frith and Howard Horne's *Art into Pop*, published the same year.[47] Whereas Frith and Horne focused on the interrelationship between art schools and pop performers, Walker examined how pop draws upon art movements like Dada, Futurism and Surrealism in the design of album covers and in live performance, while at the same time contemporary artists use pop music for inspiration. Both books offer a broad overview of their subject spanning more than three decades, though the impact of punk – and particularly the work of the many visual communicators in the scene who had never been anywhere near an art school and knew little if anything of the early twentieth century European avant-garde – is described in very limited terms. Journalist and commentator Jon Savage had offered a more critical account of these relationships in two articles for *The Face* magazine some five years earlier,[48] aligning punk's radical deployment of appropriation with a subsequent era of art historical referencing as a commercial strategy centred on nostalgia. Savage's scathing critique of the 'age of plunder' also suggested that 1980s pop's pillaging of its own visual past was playing into the hands of contemporary right-wing politics in the first term of Margaret Thatcher's government.

In 2012, Russ Bestley and Alex Ogg's *The Art of Punk*[49] attempted to examine the intention behind a broader range of punk-related graphic material from the early 1970s to the early 2000s, with a stronger emphasis on the voices of the artists and designers involved. The book features interviews with notable punk designers including Arturo Vega, Jamie Reid, Malcolm Garrett, Peter Gravelle and John Holmstrom, along with key contributors to the early punk scene such as Mick Farren, Andrew Matheson and Marc Zermati. In the same year, Johan Kugelberg's *Punk: An Aesthetic*[50] covered similar ground, though the book was more of a showcase of rare and unseen punk graphics with limited critical analysis: brief contributions from Gee Vaucher, Linder Sterling, Jon Savage and William Gibson obfuscate rather than illuminate a reading of the accompanying images. A year later, Jon Savage and Stuart Baker's *Punk 45: The Singles Cover Art of Punk 1976–80* (2013)[51] focused on the reproduction of a selection of seven-inch single sleeves from the United Kingdom, United States and further afield, though again it worked as a coffee table picture book rather than a critical study. Featuring some interesting choices of punk singles from the United Kingdom, United States and Europe, images of the front (and sometimes back) covers are simply captioned with the name of the band, song titles, label, release date and band members – with few designers credited and no analysis or reflection on the design or production process. Beyond a coherent introduction by Jon Savage, setting out some of the contextual history and citing some well-chosen examples of punk singles from the period, there is no critique or exegesis. The book revolves around the background to the material, leaving the images of record sleeves to somehow 'speak' for themselves without explanation, with very little writing on the 'art' that its title purports to be about.

The official '40th anniversary of punk' was commemorated in the United Kingdom in 2016, with exhibitions and events in London and other major cities along with yet another raft of publications on the history of the subculture. More archives and collections were raided for previously unseen artefacts, with some of the higher profile, wealthier collectors delving into their vaults, taking advantage of the resurgence of interest (along with corporate and government funding) to jump on the bandwagon. Johan Kugelberg, Jon Savage and Glenn Terry's huge, luxurious volume *God Save Sex Pistols* (2016)[52] omitted any captioning or explanation of the visual material featured, beyond a chronology of the Sex Pistols alongside quotes from members of the band and their entourage. One high-profile book did at least begin to engage with some of the designers behind the artwork that was lavishly reproduced in full colour. Toby Mott's *Oh So Pretty: Punk in Print 1976–1980* (2016)[53] featured a short essay by leading graphic design historian Rick Poynor, who attempted to introduce the importance of design and print technology and the nature of craft in visual communication, disaggregating visual style from (perceived) intention, though the overarching theme of the book was as a simple showcase of the rare and expensive items in Mott's collection, functioning more like an auction catalogue than an exegesis of the design, aesthetics and print production of punk graphic material.

Meanwhile, Tony Brook and Adrian Shaughnessy's *Action Time Vision: Punk and Post-Punk 7" Record Sleeves* (2016) featured a selection of single sleeves from the late 1970s and early 1980s taken from the collections of Tony Brook and Russ Bestley, with accompanying analysis by Brook and Bestley and interviews with Malcolm Garrett, Mark Perry and Daniel Miller.[54] The featured material in this case was selected for its visual style and interest to designers, rather than for its rarity or value on the collectors' market. Jamie Reid once again occupied the foreground in punk's emerging graphic history in 2018, with a retrospective exhibition, *XXXXX: Fifty Years of Subversion and The Spirit* at Humber Street Gallery, Hull, accompanied by a hardback book that catalogued fifty years of the artist's work.[55] That book was followed three years later by another collection of Reid's lo-tech and photocopied graphics, *Rogue Materials: 1972–2021* (2021).[56]

Other designers also utilised the growth in independent publishing to reflect on their own careers. Notable among these, Gee Vaucher's *Crass Art and Other Pre Post-Modernist Monsters*,[57] Mike Coles' *Forty Years in the Wilderness*,[58] Bill Smith's *Cover Stories*[59] and Rob O'Connor's *Delicious: The Design and Art Direction of Stylorouge*[60] provided a highly personal, illustrated history of the designers' work. More punk DIY in nature, Graham A. Rhodes – who had worked as a designer for The Police and Miles Copeland's Faulty Products group of independent labels in the late 1970s – produced an autobiographical account of his career in art and design, *The View from Inside the Punk Monster*, in 2016.[61] While Rhodes' book is entirely text-based and lacks the visual exuberance of Vaucher, Coles et al., and relies heavily on anecdotes, he does at least outline some details regarding the design and print processes used in his work, from Letraset to the PMT (photomechanical transfer) camera.

A more recent fascination with punk fanzines as a source for archival research – and as sometimes fetishised visual artefacts – led to several retrospective compendiums of specific titles along with edited collections and at least some critical commentary. Notable among these, Mark Perry's *Sniffin' Glue: The Essential Punk Accessory* (2000)[62] led the way, followed by Tony Drayton's *Ripped & Torn: 1976–79: The Loudest Punk Fanzine in the UK* (2018),[63] Alan Rider's *Adventures in Reality: The Complete Collection* (2021),[64] Tony Fletcher's *The Best of Jamming! Selections and Stories from the Fanzine That Grew Up, 1977–86* (2021)[65] and Pete Webb and Tom Vague's *Vague Volume One: 1979–1984* (2023).[66] Eddie Piller and Steve Rowland provided a broader contextual history in *Punkzines: British Fanzine Culture from the Punk Scene 1976–1983* (2021),[67] with further detailed critique and analysis provided by an academic collection from the Subcultures Network, *Ripped, Torn and Cut: Pop, Politics and Punk Fanzines from 1976* (2018)[68] and Matthew Worley's archival history, *Zerox Machine: Punk, Post-Punk and Fanzines in Britain, 1976–88* (2024).[69]

2020 saw the first of two extensive hardback volumes by another collector, Andrew Krivine. *Too Fast to Live Too Young to Die: Punk & Post Punk*

Graphics 1976–1986[70] included not only a vast collection of visual material spanning a full decade, from the initial punk explosion to its fragmentation into a diverse collection of competing subgenres, but also the voices of several prominent designers and design historians (Steven Heller, Rick Poynor, Russ Bestley and Malcolm Garrett) who attempted to dig a little deeper into the work on display. Krivine published a second volume, *Reversing into the Future: New Wave Graphics 1977–1990*,[71] the following year, shifting the emphasis a little to include more commercial and popular material spanning new wave, synth-pop and the New Romantics. The book also featured in-depth commentary and articles by two of the leading designers featured, Malcolm Garrett and Chris Morton, along with essays by cultural historian Matthew Worley and design historians Andrew Blauvelt and Rick Poynor. Blauvelt's essay, 'Riding a new wave', outlines a rounded historical and cultural context for the graphics on show, positioning styles, techniques and technologies in relation to the incursion of a 'new wave design' within the wider graphic design industry that 'would challenge the profession's conventions and, in particular, the hegemony of corporate-style Swiss design of the era'.[72] As a notable graphic design historian and curator, rather than a punk specialist, Blauvelt cites celebrated professional designers Rosmarie Tissi, Wolfgang Weingart, Willi Kunz and Hans-Rudolf Lutz, along with US designers April Greiman and Dan Friedman, as pioneers of 'new wave' design. However, the specific connections between graphics created for new wave artists (particularly in the United Kingdom, e.g. by Garrett, Saville, Morton and others) and a developing postmodern design style within the wider industry in the United States and Europe (Weingart, Greiman, Friedman) is harder to justify beyond visual or aesthetic similarities (we will return to this theme in Chapter 7, 'Parallel lines: into the eighties').

More recently, art and design historians have made steps to interrogate specific aspects of punk art history and practice, with a focus on individual designers and the broader social and cultural context through which certain individuals came to prominence. *Gee Vaucher: Beyond Punk, Feminism and the Avant-Garde* (2022)[73] by Rebecca Binns situates Vaucher's work in the context of art history, politics and the counterculture. *Blank Canvas: Art School Creativity from Punk to New Wave* (2022)[74] by Simon Strange charts the relationship between British art school education and a generation of punk and post-punk musicians in the late 1970s, while Gavin Butt's *No Machos or Pop Stars: When The Leeds Art Experiment Went Punk* (2022)[75] examines a close-knit community of artists and post-punk musicians that emerged from the University of Leeds and Leeds Polytechnic in the late 1970s. Meanwhile, Marie Arleth Skov's *Punk Art History: Artworks From the European No Future Generation* (2023)[76] examines punk as an art movement, combining archival research and personal interviews with artists from London, New York, Amsterdam, Copenhagen and Berlin, and

Ian Trowell's *Throbbing Gristle: An Endless Discontent* (2023)[77] focuses on the early history of avant-garde art/music collective Throbbing Gristle, from their countercultural roots in the art collective COUM Transmissions to their first steps into the punk and post-punk milieu.

Action, time and vision

This book is an attempt to cover a broad area of this historical and contextual ground within a single volume, to span both the cultural, political and economic history of the United Kingdom and the range of visual material associated with punk and post-punk in the late 1970s and early 1980s. It is a study of punk graphics in print, encompassing the *how* and *why* of a wide range of visual material, together with a critical reflection on design as *process* as well as *product*. It offers an overview of the dynamic relationships at play during a particular period in modern British history, centred on the ways punk and post-punk designers embraced alternative ways of making and navigated rapid and significant changes in the music industry and the design and print professions. Concepts that have become closely engrained in discussions of punk art and design – do-it-yourself, autonomy, a rejection of tradition or authority – are subject to question, while we will also analyse the way punk 'designers' (from amateur to professional) employed materials, tools and techniques to respond practically to those developing, but often rather nebulous, ideals.

This book also seeks to acknowledge the many anonymous artworkers and pre-press operators who were an essential part of the chain of print production and whose vital roles and craft skills have been lost to historical record through rapidly changing technologies. It aims to cover different aspects of the design process, from the tools that designers could access (which drove much of the graphic style of punk) to their engagement with the design and print industries (a particularly problematic issue for untrained amateurs and new designers who didn't follow traditional routes into the profession). In the process, it reflects on the expansion of the design and print industries to accommodate a new generation of punk-inspired designers along with a reduction in the power of the print unions and the breakdown of closed shop practices. This leads us to an important question: how did design and print technologies – and access to those technologies – influence the development of a particular visual style for punk and post-punk graphics? Unlike many other studies of punk visual communication, the emphasis here is less about purely the 'look' of the objects and more about the way the social, technological and economic conditions of their manufacture led to stylistic approaches that, ultimately, became established as a punk visual aesthetic.

The chapters in *Turning revolt into style* are not intended to be comprehensive – references and citations linking to other in-depth studies

Introduction 19

are provided throughout to facilitate further reading. However, the intersection between a newly emerging punk-inspired design aesthetic, the promise of a kind of do-it-yourself autonomy for a new generation of designers, changing technologies in the print industry and the ensuing radical shake-up in industrial relations does merit investigation. This is an attempt to provide an overarching narrative concerning the various cultural, professional and commercial interests at play.

> Punk graphic design filled the gap between the advent of the photocopier and the advent of the computer.[78]

The following volume is divided into eight chapters. Chapter 1, 'Pretty vacant: punk graphic themes', introduces the notion of punk graphic design, the use of visual communication to promote the early punk scene and core themes that emerged. These include a rejection of standard pop music conventions, do-it-yourself, a wide range of radical and performative politics, the machine aesthetic, art school and art historical references. Chapter 2, 'Material interventions: punk graphic processes', then interrogates the range of design methods that were utilised in response to these punk thematic ideals and the ways in which punk concepts were visually materialised. These practical strategies include the use of DIY tools and technologies as a rhetorical call to arms, appropriation, repetition, collage, distortion and wear and tear.

Chapter 3, 'Design it yourself: the punk diaspora', reflects on the take-up of punk-inspired styles in different regions of the United Kingdom, along with the adoption of locally specific images and iconography, together with changing post-punk styles associated with a range of distinct sub-genres that emerged over time. Chapter 4, 'Your generation: punk designers and the art departments', outlines the relationship between the new, punk-inspired designers entering the music graphics profession in the late 1970s and the senior art directors and design professionals who had been working for many years to create visual identities for rock and pop bands in the established industry. Chapter 5, 'New sounds, new styles: design and technology', focuses on design and print reproduction, ranging from the increased use of lo-tech, analogue tools by punk fanzine writers and DIY, independent record producers to photomechanical processes and the emerging digital pre-press tools that would become ubiquitous a decade later. The 1970s saw a gradual shift away from design as a process of specification to a more holistic model of planning, construction and pre-press artwork preparation on the part of the individual designer or studio.

Chapter 6, 'A different kind of tension: industry and the individual', then centres on industrial and labour relations within the printing industry. Radical changes in design were reflected in a significant reconstitution of the print professions due to the impact of new technologies. These were led, in turn, by a complete overhaul of the national newspapers that met significant resistance from the print unions and resulted in widespread industrial action. Government interventions, in particular new legislation on secondary picketing and closed shop agreements, heightened the degree of antagonism on both sides, ultimately shifting the balance of power in favour of the employers and weakening the power of the trade unions. While the impact of this industrial relations battle was most evident in the national and local press, its effects rippled down throughout the industry, weakening the stranglehold the unions had held over print production for more than a century. Consequently, however, at least some independent, punk-inspired graphic designers were able to make further inroads to a design profession that had previously restricted access through closed shop working practices. Chapter 7, 'Parallel lines: into the eighties' explores the new design aesthetic of the 1980s, the 'new wave' styles associated with the emerging street style and fashion magazines and the apparent visual overlap with the 'new wave of graphic design' and emerging philosophies of postmodernism in design schools and the profession. Finally Chapter 8, 'Retro-spective: influence and legacy', looks at the contemporary legacy of punk aesthetics, from youth branding and marketing to retro nostalgia, critiquing punk as both a heritage project and an ongoing global subculture. This reflective chapter also considers the nature of the contemporary graphic design industry in contrast to the design and print professions of the 1970s and 1980s.

Notes

1. Johan Kugelberg (2012), *Punk: An Aesthetic*, New York: Rizzoli; Russ Bestley and Alex Ogg (2012), *The Art of Punk*, London: Omnibus Press; Toby Mott (2016), *Oh So Pretty: Punk in Print 1976–1980*, London: Phaidon; Andrew Krivine (2020), *Too Fast to Live Too Young to Die: Punk & Post Punk Graphics 1976–1986*, London: Pavilion; Andrew Krivine (2021), *Reversing into the Future: New Wave Graphics 1977–1990*, London: Pavilion.
2. A recent publication by Michael Mary Murphy and Jim Rogers offers an interesting perspective on a specific part of the industry and a useful model for others to follow. Michael Mary Murphy and Jim Rogers (2023), *Sounds Irish, Acts Global: Explaining the Success of Ireland's Popular Music Industry*, Sheffield: Equinox.
3. Sheila Rock (2020), *Young Punks*, London: Omnibus Press.
4. Peter Gravelle (2016), *The Death of Photography: The Shooting Gallery*, London: Carpet Bombing Culture.
5. Brian Griffin (2017), *Pop*, London: GOST Books.
6. Brian Eno and Russell Mills (1986), *More Dark Than Shark*, London: Faber & Faber.
7. Gee Vaucher (2018), *International Anthem*, London: Exitstencil Press.
8. See Russ Bestley (2015), '(I want some) demystification: Deconstructing punk', *Punk & Post-Punk*, 4:2/3, pp. 117–127, and Robin Ryde and Russ Bestley (2016), 'Thinking punk', *Punk & Post-Punk* 5:2, pp. 97–110.
9. *Punk Rock* (1976), dir. Bruce Macdonald, episode of *The London Weekend Show* (28 November, London Weekend Television).
10. *The Year of Punk* (1978), dir. Bruce Macdonald, episode of *The London Weekend Show* (1 January, London Weekend Television).

11 Early work for the Sex Pistols was printed out of hours at Rye Express in Peckham, a print studio set up by one of Reid's former colleagues at Suburban Press, Nigel Kershaw.
12 John Marchant in Jamie Reid (2021), *Rogue Materials: 1972–2021*, London: L-13 Light Industrial Workshop, p. 2.
13 Hugh Barker and Yuval Taylor (2007), *Faking It: The Quest for Authenticity in Popular Music*, London: Faber & Faber.
14 See Aubrey Powell (2017), *Vinyl. Album. Cover. Art: The Complete Hipgnosis Catalogue*, London: Thames & Hudson; and Aubrey Powell (2014), *Hipgnosis Portraits*, London: Thames & Hudson.
15 Paul Gorman (2010), *Reasons to be Cheerful: The Life and Work of Barney Bubbles*, London: Adelita Ltd.
16 Jamie Reid (2018), *XXXXX*, London: L-13 Light Industrial Workshop.
17 Emily King (ed.) (2003), *Designed by Peter Saville*, London: Frieze.
18 This fact can, of course, create problems for design historians, particularly in areas of graphic design where the work never had a high cultural or artistic value in the first place.
19 Russ Bestley and Paul McNeil (2022), *Visual Research*, London: Bloomsbury, pp. 70–71.
20 See David Goodhart and Patrick Wintour (1986), *Eddie Shah and the Newspaper Revolution*, London: Coronet; Alwyn W. Turner (2008), *Crisis? What Crisis?: Britain in the 1970s*, London: Aurum Press; Alwyn W. Turner (2010), *Rejoice! Rejoice!: Britain in the 1980s*, London: Aurum Press; Andy McSmith (2011), *No Such Thing as Society: A History of Britain in the 1980s*, London: Constable; Graham Stewart (2013), *Bang!: A History of Britain in the 1980s*, London: Atlantic Books.
21 Lucy Robinson (2023), *Now That's What I Call a History of the 1980s: Pop Culture and Politics in the Decade That Shaped Modern Britain*, Manchester: Manchester University Press, pp. 2–3, original emphasis.
22 Andy Beckett (2009), *When the Lights Went Out: Britain in the Seventies*, London: Faber & Faber.
23 Turner, *Crisis? What Crisis?*
24 Turner, *Rejoice! Rejoice!*
25 Dominic Sandbrook (2010), *State of Emergency: Britain, 1970–1974*, London: Allen Lane.
26 Dominic Sandbrook (2012), *Seasons in the Sun: Britain, 1974–1979*, London: Allen Lane.
27 Dominic Sandbrook (2019), *Who Dares Wins: Britain, 1979–1982*, London: Allen Lane.
28 McSmith, *No Such Thing as Society*.
29 Stewart, *Bang!*
30 Andy Beckett (2015), *Promised You a Miracle: UK 80–82*, London: Allen Lane.
31 David Elliott (2020), *1984: British Pop's Dividing Year*, London: York House Books.
32 Robinson, *Now That's What I Call a History of the 1980s*.
33 Roger Sabin (ed.) (1999), *Punk Rock: So What?*, Abingdon: Routledge.
34 Sabin, *Punk Rock: So What?*, p. 2.
35 Jon Savage (1991), *England's Dreaming: Sex Pistols and Punk Rock*, London: Faber & Faber. See also Jon Savage (2009), *The England's Dreaming Tapes*, London: Faber & Faber.
36 See, for instance, Adrian Boot and Chris Salewicz (1996), *Punk: The Illustrated History of a Music Revolution*, London: Penguin Studio; Stephen Colegrave and Chris Sullivan (2001), *Punk*, London: Cassell & Co.; Henrik Bech Poulsen (2005), *'77: The Year of Punk and New Wave*, London: Helter Skelter; Mark Blake (ed.) (2006), *Punk: The Whole Story*, London: Dorling Kindersley.

37 Alex Ogg (2006), *No More Heroes*, London: Cherry Red; John Robb (2006), *Punk Rock: An Oral History*, London: Ebury Press.
38 Simon Reynolds (2005), *Rip it Up and Start Again: Post Punk 1978–84*, London: Faber & Faber.
39 Caroline Coon (1977), *1988: The New Wave Punk Rock Explosion*, London: Hawthorn.
40 Ray Stevenson (1978), *Sex Pistols File*, London: Omnibus Press.
41 Jamie Reid and Jon Savage (1987), *Up They Rise: The Incomplete Works of Jamie Reid*, London: Faber & Faber.
42 Brian Cannon (1989), *Going Nowhere: The Art and Design of Punk and New Wave*, London: Omnibus Press.
43 Greil Marcus (1989), *Lipstick Traces: A Secret History of the Twentieth Century*, Cambridge, MA: Harvard University Press.
44 Catherine McDermott (1987), *Street Style: British Design in the 80s*, London: Design Council, p. 19.
45 Cynthia Rose (1991), *Design After Dark*, London: Thames & Hudson.
46 John A. Walker (1987), *Cross-Overs: Art into Pop and Pop into Art*, London: Routledge.
47 Simon Frith and Howard Horne (1987), *Art into Pop*, London: Routledge.
48 See Jon Savage (1983), 'The age of plunder', *The Face*, January, pp. 44–49; and Jon Savage (1983), 'Guerilla graphics: The tactics of agit prop art', *The Face*, October, pp. 26–31.
49 Bestley and Ogg, *The Art of Punk*.
50 Kugelberg, *Punk: An Aesthetic*.
51 Jon Savage and Stuart Baker (eds) (2013), *Punk 45: The Singles Cover Art of Punk 1976–80*, London: Soul Jazz Records.
52 Johan Kugelberg, Jon Savage and Glenn Terry (2016), *God Save Sex Pistols*, New York: Rizzoli.
53 Mott, *Oh So Pretty*.
54 Tony Brook and Adrian Shaughnessy (eds) (2016), *Action Time Vision: Punk and Post-Punk 7" Record Sleeves*, London: Unit Editions.
55 Reid, *XXXXX*.
56 Reid, *Rogue Materials*.
57 Gee Vaucher (1999), *Crass Art and Other Pre Post-Modernist Monsters*, Edinburgh: AK Press.
58 Mike Coles (2016), *Forty Years in the Wilderness: A Graphic Voyage of Art, Design & Stubborn Independence*, London: Malicious Damage.
59 Bill Smith (2021), *Cover Stories: Five Decades of Album Art*, London: Red Planet.
60 Rob O'Connor (2001), *Delicious: The Design and Art Direction of Stylorouge*, Berlin: Die Gestalten Verlag.
61 Graham A. Rhodes (2016), *The View from Inside the Punk Monster*, Scarborough: Templar Publishing.
62 Mark Perry (2000), *Sniffin' Glue: The Essential Punk Accessory*, London: Sanctuary.
63 Tony Drayton (2018), *Ripped & Torn: 1976–79: The Loudest Punk Fanzine in the UK*, London: Ecstatic Peace Library.
64 Alan Rider (2021), *Adventures in Reality: The Complete Collection*, Krakow: Fourth Dimension.
65 Tony Fletcher (2021), *The Best of Jamming!: Selections and Stories from the Fanzine That Grew Up, 1977–86*, London: Omnibus Press.
66 Pete Webb and Tom Vague (2023), *Vague Volume One: 1979–1984*, Bristol: PC Press.
67 Eddie Piller and Steve Rowland (2021), *Punkzines: British Fanzine Culture from the Punk Scene 1976–1983*, London: Omnibus Press.
68 Subcultures Network (ed.) (2018), *Ripped, Torn and Cut: Pop, Politics and Punk Fanzines from 1976*, Manchester: Manchester University Press.

69 Matthew Worley (2024), *Zerox Machine: Punk, Post-Punk and Fanzines in Britain, 1976–88*, London: Reaktion Books.
70 Krivine, *Too Fast to Live Too Young to Die*.
71 Krivine, *Reversing into the Future*.
72 Krivine, *Reversing into the Future*, p. 103.
73 Rebecca Binns (2022), *Gee Vaucher: Beyond Punk, Feminism and the Avant-Garde*, Manchester: Manchester University Press.
74 Simon Strange (2022), *Blank Canvas: Art School Creativity from Punk to New Wave*, Bristol: Intellect.
75 Gavin Butt (2022), *No Machos or Pop Stars: When the Leeds Art Experiment Went Punk*, Durham, NC: Duke University Press.
76 Marie Arleth Skov (2023), *Punk Art History: Artworks from the European No Future Generation*, Bristol: Intellect.
77 Ian Trowell (2023), *Throbbing Gristle: An Endless Discontent*, Bristol: Intellect.
78 Neville Brody (2024), online interview with the author, 5 March.

1
Pretty vacant: punk graphic themes

Punk's original premise embraced several ideological positions: a self-effacing rejection of celebrity, particularly in the rock and pop music industry, the notion that expertise is unnecessary ('anyone can do it'), a call to arms for direct action and independence ('do-it-yourself') and a questioning of authority. These were married to a focus on individuality, creativity and personal expression that set itself in opposition to the norm. Punk's initial success led to an explosion of new sounds and styles, from music to fashion, art, graphic design, film, writing and publishing. Punk, or new wave, was at that time simply an umbrella term that could be applied to an eclectic and disparate range of activity and this was equally clear in relation to punk's visual and graphic languages.

Lyrically and musically, punk was an attempt to move away from what were seen as the conventional practices of the mainstream music industry. The clichéd rhetoric that situates punk as a grass-roots musical rebellion against the excesses of the rock music industry has been overplayed and exhausted, though there is some truth in the mythology. The notion of some kind of punk year zero has also been largely debunked – punk drew upon all kinds of antecedents and influences. Some punk conventions do hold up, however, despite many examples to the contrary. David Laing, in *One Chord Wonders: Power and Meaning in Punk Rock* (1985), suggested that punk lyrical themes offered a counterpoint to the standard conventions of the pop song. Themes of love and romance were replaced by more aggressive narratives and an overt rejection of popular music tradition – The Clash directly inverted the 1960s hippie cliché of love and peace into 'Hate & War', for instance, while many other popular punk groups emphasised what Laing describes as 'first person feelings' and 'social and political comment.'[1]

Laing's sample was, however, very limited, largely centring on a few high-profile British punk bands (the Sex Pistols, The Clash, The Damned, The Vibrators and The Stranglers), and there are myriad examples of the author's stereotypical pop themes – love songs, novelty songs and songs about 'music and dancing' – by punk groups that could offer a counter-claim to his argument (including, ironically, in the wider repertoire of the groups cited). Equally, many earlier rock and pop songs were political, angry and 'unromantic', though Laing's generic approach to lyrical stereotypes still has at least some merit. It can be asserted that as a stylistic convention, much punk music was fast, loud and simple, and lyrics tended towards the abrasive, angry, frustrated, antagonistic or apathetic. Songs about boredom and frustration were common, as was an aggressive assertion of self-identity or subjective angst. 'I Wanna Be Me' by the Sex Pistols, 'I Just Wanna Be Myself' by The Drones, 'I Don't Wanna' by Sham 69, 'I Don't Care' by The Boys and 'I Hate School' by Suburban Studs all followed a similar pattern of (often negative) statements in the first person. Many designers who were closely aligned with the new movement adopted a similarly individualist stance, expressing a desire for autonomy and complete control of the creative process. Such a position reflected an attempt to project a sense of authenticity and a level of independence away from established rock music conventions.

Alongside acerbic comments on the music industry and the conventions of contemporary pop music, there was also always a strand of reflexive critique within the developing punk scene. Some amounted to little more than inter-band rivalries and personal abuse, between the Sex Pistols and The Heartbreakers or The Clash and The Jam (or The Stranglers and everyone else), for instance, but others were more concerned with the commercialisation and recuperation of punk's original brief flash of inspiration. Punk's fanzine writers engaged in lengthy debates about the purpose and value of the new musical revolution, balancing ethics, politics, provocation and critical self-reflection. Lyrics referenced the development of a recognised punk scene. The Adverts asked rhetorically where the movement was headed in 'Safety in Numbers' on their debut album, *Crossing the Red Sea*, while Alternative TV asked, 'How Much Longer?' would punk – and other subcultures – last in practice.

> How much longer will people wear
> Nazi armbands and dye their hair?
> Safety pins and spray your clothes
> Talk about anarchy, fascism and boredom[2]

Like the music, at this point unsullied by the self-imposed stereotyping that was to dog punk as soon as an identifiable commercial entity (or uniform) could be milked for all it was worth, early visual approaches reflected punk's core themes of provocation, individuality, novelty, directness, honesty and authenticity. Instant, homemade and handmade graphic styles – whether genuine or mimicked for effect – mirrored, whether intentionally or otherwise, a long line of twentieth-century artistic traditions, from Dada to Surrealism, the Lettrists and Situationists and the late 1960s counterculture. Punk's key watchwords of autonomy and authenticity were reflected in visual design strategies that self-consciously revealed their origins and their construction – 'anyone' could, indeed, do the same and here was a clear, or at least implied, set of instructions to follow. Even the fact that in many cases the actual artefacts were far more complex than they appeared to the unsuspecting viewer, having been created by professional graphic designers along with teams of pre-press artworkers and reproduced on expensive printing presses in commercial studios, doesn't completely undermine the message.

Plastic passion

The range of physical, designed objects produced in reaction to punk's call to arms included gig flyers, posters, photographs, clothing, badges, fanzines and record covers. The domination of the seven-inch single sleeve as the definitive artefact in punk graphic design did not arise by chance. Early UK punk espoused an ideology that set itself in opposition to the contemporary fashion in popular music towards heavily produced, musically complex arrangements and concept albums. Punk songs tended to be short, fast and aggressive, and the widely repeated credo that 'if it can't be said it three minutes, it's not worth saying' was adopted as standard practice. The seven-inch 45rpm single, a mainstay of earlier rock'n'roll, pop and glam rock, was widely adopted by punk groups as a cheap, accessible, effective and ultimately disposable format for the quick dissemination of musical ideas. Many punk groups wanted to project their message out to the public as a matter of urgency – punk celebrated a lack of musical prowess and the dedication and discipline necessary to rehearse and record enough material to produce an album was beyond the reach of many participants in the movement. Records, along with media reports, were a key factor in the ways in which regionally based aspiring punks could hear, interpret and re-enact a punk identity. While it could be argued that punk was essentially a live phenomenon, recorded material reached far beyond any immediate access at gigs and helped to shape the wider punk subculture across the UK.

The punk (or new wave) seven-inch single also inspired the return to popularity of the picture sleeve – a graphic marketing convention which was to become increasingly important to the developing genre. A popular concept for extended play (EP) formats and special releases during the 1950s (when a range of music, from classical to jazz, was widely available on seven-inch records) and the early 1960s, the picture sleeve was a graphic identity and packaging device that had subsequently fallen out of fashion. Unlike fanzines and flyers, which were usually produced by fans or local promoters, record sleeves were often directly commissioned and approved by the group or their management, or in the case of many DIY punk records were originated by the group themselves. This does lend the sleeve design some authority in the way that a particular group is represented – even in the case of punk groups signed to major labels, where an in-house design team might have been responsible for the design and production of the record sleeve, there would usually be some indication of an official group visual style or brand identity. The record sleeve was often the first point of contact for fans and followers of the group – and the graphic message would be the first thing a prospective buyer would encounter in a record shop.

The diversity of punk graphic design styles and aesthetics needs to be understood in relation to three loosely defined groups of visual practitioners: 'pure' DIY amateur enthusiasts inspired by punk to create visual work; up-and-coming designers (often emanating from art schools) who embraced the contemporary scene; and established design professionals who were commissioned by managers, PR firms and record labels to create material that reflected the look, style and visual vocabulary of an evolving new subculture. As the media hype around this dangerous, deviant and/or exciting new movement generated interest, demand outstripped supply, with many of the major labels scrambling to sign up groups who were jumping the new wave bandwagon to hitch a ride to stardom. However, the journey from nascent punk scenes and small-scale gigs to the manufacture of physical products – in the form of vinyl records in particular – took some time. For many bands that did get as far as recording two tracks for a seven-inch single release, the step up to production of a full album proved too great a leap.

At the same time, the demand for punk product helped stimulate an underground economy of bootleggers. The first Sex Pistols single was released in November 1976, but it took nearly a year (and three record contracts) before the much-anticipated album, *Never Mind the Bollocks*, made it to vinyl. By that time the group was close to self-immolation, with limited other new material forthcoming, opening the field for shady manufacturers to tap into an open market with a variety of live and demo recordings of varying quality. Perhaps the most famous, *Spunk*, was widely credited as a deliberate behind-the-scenes provocation by Sex Pistols manager Malcolm McLaren and found its way into circulation just a few days before the official release of the band's debut album by Virgin Records in the Autumn of 1977. *Spunk* featured a plain white cover, with some outlets stencilling or painting their own titles. Subsequent Sex Pistols bootlegs – *No Future U.K.?*, *Indecent Exposure* – adopted visual approaches in keeping with the generic punk fanzine style. The critical and commercial interest in punk led to dozens of other unlicensed albums by some of the scene's leading players, including The Clash *Take It Or Leave It!*, The Stranglers *London Ladies*, Buzzcocks *Time's Up* and a compilation of demos and John Peel radio session recordings by the as-yet unsigned Siouxsie and the Banshees, *Love in a Void*, all of which offered punk fans a visual punk aesthetic halfway between the amateur fanzines and the official releases that were slowly trickling onto the market and into the charts.

It was the simplicity of the lo-tech, handmade flyers produced by Helen Wellington-Lloyd and Jamie Reid for the Sex Pistols, along with an underground revolution in homemade fanzines and other printed ephemera produced by inspired and enthusiastic fans – from raw, amateur mark-makers to avid collectors and scrapbook compilers – that kickstarted a punk design aesthetic.[3] By contrast, however, it was the hugely influential work of professional art directors and designers including Barney Bubbles,[4] Chris Morton,[5] George 'God' Snow, Jo Mirowski, Bill Smith,[6] Michael Beal, Malcolm Garrett and Jill Mumford that helped it reach a mainstream audience.

Punk visual conventions

The relationship between punk and visual aesthetics has been an evolving area of discussion over the past forty years. Early attempts to theorise – or at least contextualise – punk styles and dress codes often centred on the more shocking and disruptive elements that had already found infamy in the mainstream media: swastikas, safety pins, razor blades, chains, piercings, ripped and torn clothing. While nearly all of these applied largely to dress codes, visual symbols of the new punk subculture were shared widely through press photos and began to appear as graphic devices on early punk flyers, fanzines, record covers and other ephemera. They also presented a blunt but instantly recognisable visual device for marketing beyond already captive audiences, particularly as record labels attempted to commercialise the new scene internationally. Stylised razor blades sat alongside stickers and attention-grabbing decals announcing 'PUNK' content for the curious (or unsuspecting) potential buyer (Figure 1.1). The fact that this promotional technique could be used to entice purchases by less knowledgeable or experienced music fans did lead to a broad spectrum of attributions of the 'punk' tag, from pub rockers The Hammersmith Gorillas to Cock Sparrer, Suburban Studs and Plastic Bertrand (Figure 1.2). Many of these visual devices were short-lived, however: the punk subculture's self-professed quest for autonomy and a desire to avoid stereotyping by the media and record industry led to many symbols being quickly dropped as soon as they became widely recognised. Some (safety pins, razor blades) became visual clichés to denote 'punk' in newspaper cartoons, comedy sketches and parodies,

Pretty vacant: punk graphic themes 29

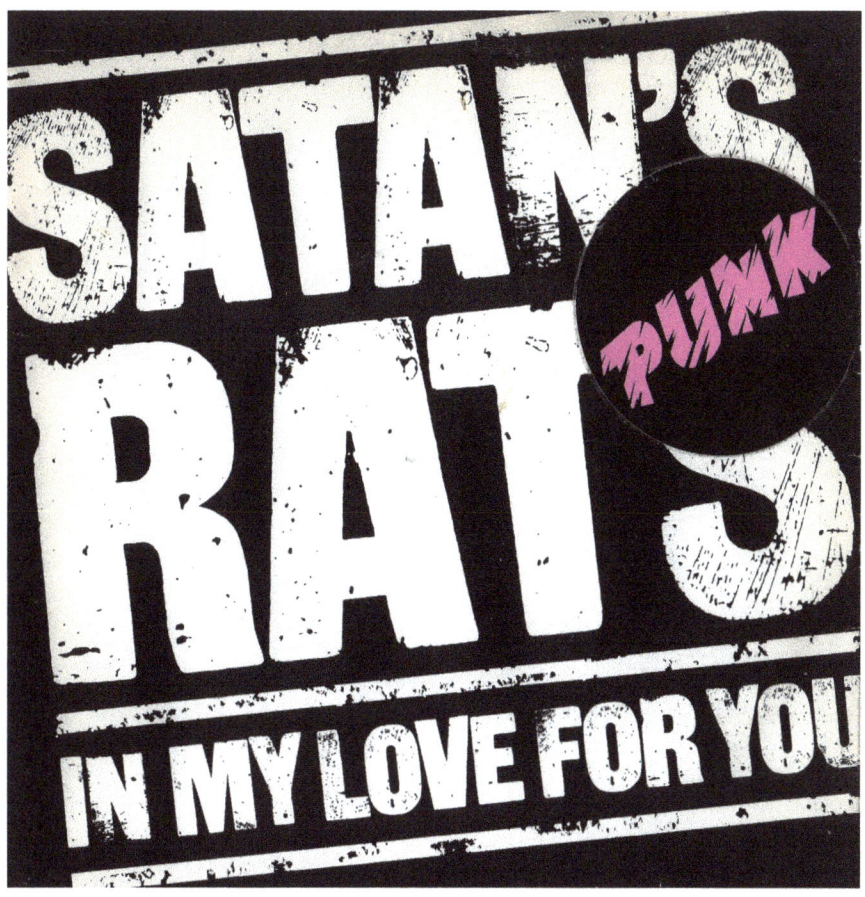

1.1 Satan's Rats (1977), 'In My Love For You', 7" single, United Kingdom: DJM Records. Front cover with 'PUNK' promotional sticker. Courtesy of Steve Eagles, collection of the author.

accelerating their demise as useful symbols for the subculture, while the term itself quickly became co-opted for a diversity of cash-ins by unscrupulous manufacturers (Figure 1.3).

As punk matured and became more widely recognised and accepted, by fans and critics alike, a kind of reflective metanarrative began to take shape, in the music press and the national media as well as the punk fanzine underground. Journalists saw the opportunity to develop a critical commentary on the developing subculture, while publishers identified a potential new market – punk readers. Several publications attempted to capture the scene in real time. Julie Davis published *Punk* at the end of 1977, a fanzine-style large format paperback featuring photographs by Erica Echenberg and brief essays by Lucy Toothpaste and Charlie Chainsaw.[7] The former management of the Roxy club in Covent Garden,

1.2 Plastic Bertrand (1977), 'Ça Plane Pour Moi', 7" single, Portugal: Vogue Records. Front cover. Collection of the author.

London (Andrew Czezowski, Susan Carrington and Barry Jones) also collaborated with author Michael Dempsey and several photographers including Derek Ridgers, Humphrey Murray, Richard Braine and Peter Gravelle on a publication that commemorated the short life of the iconic punk club in the first half of 1977. The resulting book, *100 Nights at the Roxy* (1978),[8] featured photographs of bands and audience members, though by the time the book was published many of the fashion styles had moved on from distressed school uniforms and reappropriated second-hand clothes to a more generic punk look reflecting the widespread availability of bespoke 'punk fashion', from band t-shirts to bondage trousers, leather jackets and boots.

Ironically, given the stated impetus behind the punk fanzine boom lay in the slow uptake by mainstream music journalists to report on the

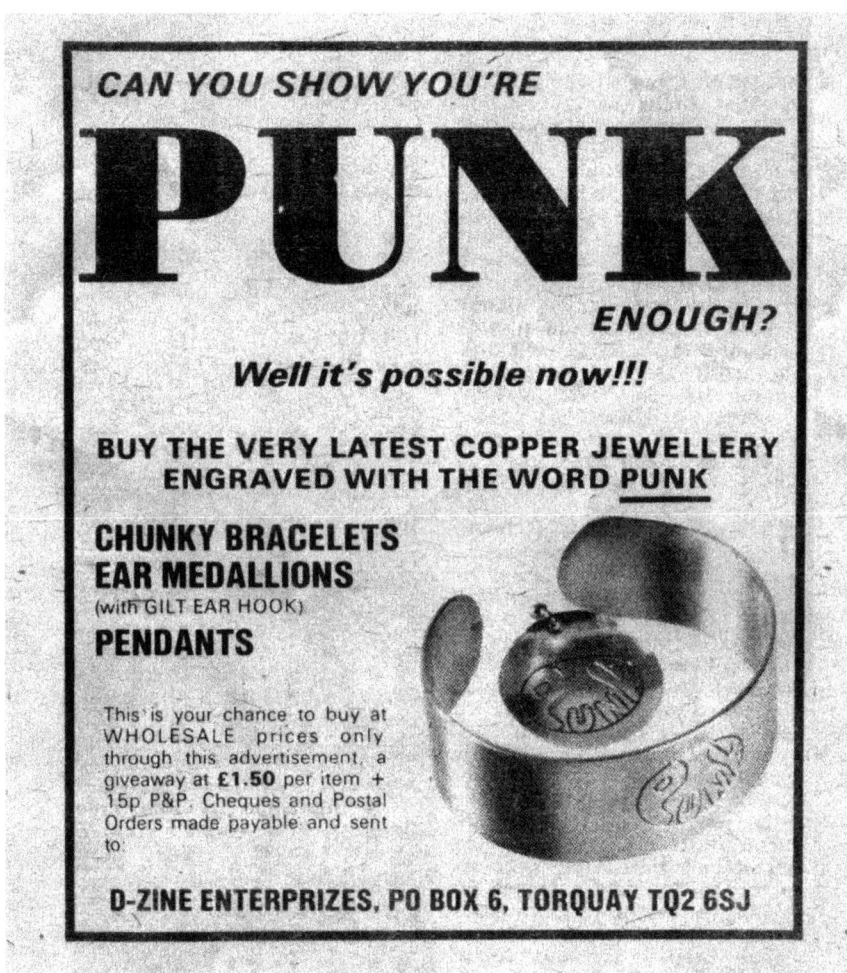

1.3 'Can you show you're PUNK enough?' advertisement for copper bracelet, *Melody Maker*, 17 September 1977. Collection of the author.

scene in the national music press – the *New Musical Express*, *Sounds*, *Melody Maker* and *Record Mirror* – November 1977 saw the launch of a new monthly music paper specifically dedicated to punk. Adopting a full-size tabloid newspaper format, rather than the standard A4, Letter or Legal dimensions of most punk fanzines, *Trick* was produced by a team of former fanzine writers – including the creator of one of the more visually sophisticated early fanzines, *Shews* – along with the ex-managers of the short-lived Vortex club in Wardour Street, London. Production and distribution, along with the creation of editorial content and advertising, was supported by record labels including Island, Virgin, Step Forward and Polydor.[9]

Employing a curious mix of fanzine-style graphics and standard newspaper formatting, *Trick* sat awkwardly in the space between the do-it-yourself fanzines and the traditional music press (Figure 1.4). High Street retailers WH Smith and John Menzies agreed to sell copies nationally, but the project was ultimately forced to close after just two issues. The tabloid format was also adopted by Gee Vaucher for her illustrated journal *International Anthem* (1977–84),[10] with some of the content overlapping her work for Crass, while four issues of the similarly styled *Impossible Dream* were produced by closely aligned anarcho-punks Poison Girls between 1979 and 1986.[11]

Some writers attempted to engage with the evolving punk visual aesthetic and to draw parallels with historical examples that appeared, on the surface at least, to share similar themes. Journalist Val Hennessy's 1978 photobook, *In the Gutter* (1978),[12] juxtaposed press photographs of punks in London with images of primitive tribes in remote parts of Africa and South America, though the author's critical position was unclear and the visual comparison rather clumsy, to say the least. The same year, former *Vogue* art director Terry Jones teamed up with journalist Isabelle Anscombe to produce a visual thesis on contemporary punk style. Printed in two colours (black and red) with a bright pink typographic cover strongly reminiscent of *Blast*, Wyndham Lewis and Ezra Pound's Vorticist manifesto first published in 1914, *Not Another Punk Book* (1978)[13] featured brief essays on clothing, style and the philosophy of the evolving scene juxtaposed with street photographs of punk fans in the King's Road by Steven Johnston. *Not Another Punk Book* pre-empted the editorial approach and street-style fashion photography of Jones' next venture, *iD* magazine, which launched in 1980 and was initially printed at Joly MacFie's Better Badges.[14] MacFie's street-smart commercial operation was already at that point making inroads into large-scale print production for several other successful punk-related fanzine titles, as a parallel concern to its core badge-making business.

A year later, Dick Hebdige attempted to deconstruct punk politics, aesthetics and philosophy in his ground-breaking cultural studies book, *Subculture: The Meaning of Style*.[15] Hebdige linked punk's graphic output – particularly the newly evolving punk fanzine culture – with an attempt 'to provide an alternative critical space within the subculture itself to counteract the hostile or at least ideologically inflected coverage which punk was receiving in the media'.[16] As such, Hebdige argued, punk fanzines provided a communal voice and helped to bring the subculture together in the face of wider media criticism and a lack of representation in the traditional music press. This does make some sense in respect to the writing within the fanzines, presenting a critical overview – or at least a sympathetic public voice and promotion of – an evolving scene, but Hebdige's argument is less convincing in relation to the visual language

Pretty vacant: punk graphic themes

1.4 Front cover of *Trick* newspaper/fanzine, November 1977. Collection of the author.

of these underground punk publications.[17] He goes on to make some broad assumptions about the design of punk fanzines and record sleeves, suggesting direct connections between punk ideology and visual form.[18]

> Even the graphics and typography used on record covers and fanzines were homologous with punk's subterranean and anarchic style. The two typographic models were graffiti which was translated into a flowing 'spray can' script, and the ransom note in which individual letters cut up from a variety of sources (newspapers, etc) in different typefaces were pasted together to form an anonymous message. The Sex Pistols' 'God Save The Queen' sleeve ... for instance incorporated both styles: the roughly assembled legend was pasted across the Queen's eyes and mouth which were further disfigured by those black bars used in pulp detective magazines to conceal identity (i.e., they connote crime or scandal).[19]

While this attempt by Hebdige to define punk typography has some merit, his suggestion that there were 'two typographic models' adopted by designers is not supported by an examination of a range of punk records from the period. Hebdige seems to be referring to record covers by Jamie Reid for the Sex Pistols – the 'God Save The Queen' and 'Pretty Vacant' singles and the *Never Mind the Bollocks* album cover (Figure 1.5) – and perhaps to some of the other promotional material produced by Reid, such as posters and press advertisements, which sometimes used these typographic styles.[20] The use of handwritten text (which Hebdige suggests is based on graffiti) is common in the broader range of punk-related visual material, though it could be argued that this was often a case of necessity driving the design decisions, as Rick Poynor later argued.

> Punk's telltale devices – rough photocopied images, hand-drawn letters, ransom note lettering, crudely cut and torn edges – have become a category in the history of graphic style, where they are seen to represent a deliberate flouting of the rules of professional practice. For the punks who put together fanzines and flyers, this categorisation may be highly questionable. Some of these raucous 'sites of resistance' (as academics have dubbed them) may have looked as they did, not in order to make any particular point, but because that was all that could be achieved using limited reprographic resources. Their makers cared about the subject matter – the bands and the music – rather than the relatively arcane question of the meaning of graphic style.[21]

The need to produce lines of text quickly without access to a commercial studio or compositor meant that handwriting would seem to be an obvious course of action for the fanzine writer or amateur sleeve designer attempting to create headlines and text at a larger size than the otherwise widely used manual typewriter or Letraset. However, the second style of typography Hebdige cites – ransom note – was almost unique to Reid's work in music packaging and promotion for the Sex Pistols and was not commonly used on record covers for other punk artists. The ransom note style did occur in punk fanzines, however, where there was obviously less

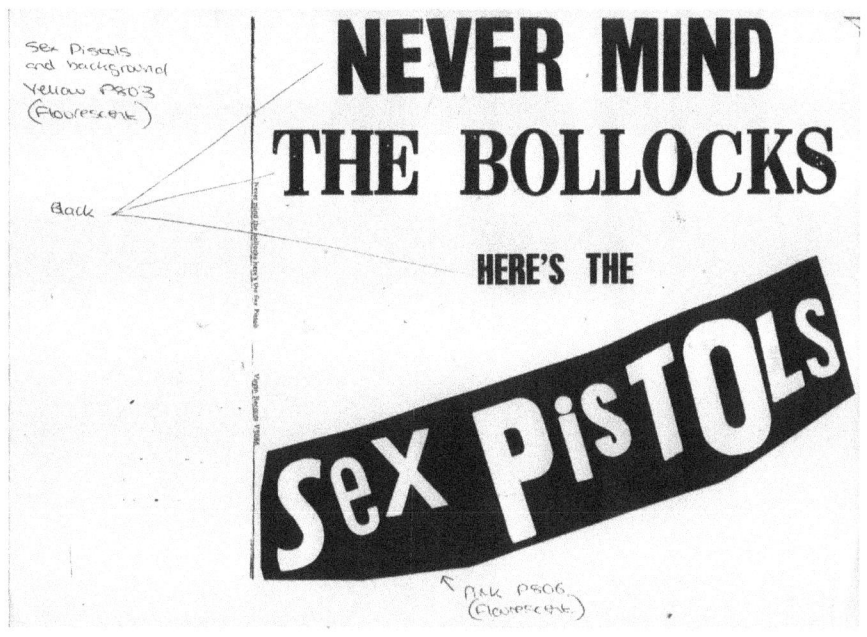

1.5 Jamie Reid, *Never Mind the Bollocks* album cover colour print specification 1977. Courtesy John Marchant Gallery.

control of branding and identity in relation to individual bands or artists and the aesthetic was simply chosen as a visual shorthand to denote 'punk' more broadly. This also marks a clear distinction between different modes of punk graphic practice, along with the skill sets of the designers and production values of the final object: successful punk groups often wanted to show clear markers of difference to their competitors, whereas punk fanzines were usually more homogenous and less focused on a unique visual identity.

Like the safety pins and razor blades worn by punk fans for a brief period, the ransom note style became something of a cliché within punk graphics. While there were obvious connections to earlier art movements, notably Dada artists Raoul Hausmann and Kurt Schwitters who had combined letters in different sizes and typefaces to create striking visual collages in the 1920s, the punk interpretation deliberately revealed the unevenly cut-out background as well as the individual characters themselves, further emphasising the construction process. Though he had employed relatively standard typesetting, Reid had used this technique to roughly cut out single words and paste them on top of a halftone[22] image for his 'Keep Warm This Winter – Make Trouble' posters at Suburban Press back in 1974.[23] Malcolm McLaren, interviewed in 2006, attempted to place some personal ownership on the new punk typographic style,

1.6 Original Sex Pistols logo designed by Helen Wellington-Lloyd, 1976. Courtesy Paul Burgess Archive, Brighton.

while at the same time giving it a rather unusual retrospective justification as an artistic statement: 'look at the Sex Pistols' ransom note lettering – classic example of how you make something ugly become beautiful'.[24] More recent punk histories have also attributed the origins of the visual style not to Jamie Reid, but to Helen Wellington-Lloyd,[25] an early associate of McLaren who produced graphic material with Nils Stevenson during the summer of 1976, prior to Reid's direct involvement with the group (Figure 1.6). Interviewed many years later by John Robb, Stevenson suggested that the design was born of necessity.

> The punk aesthetic was simple. Me and Helen Wellington-Lloyd were doing the handouts for the Pistols, and we ran out of Letraset so we cut up a newspaper and pasted it. If we hadn't run out of the Letraset there wouldn't have been the blackmail lettering. We made things from what was available.[26]

This version of events contradicts earlier statements, including those of Reid himself, who attributes the first use of the ransom note style in the Sex Pistols camp to a flyer he produced for a gig at the 100 Club on 31 August 1976.[27] Paul Stolper and Andrew Wilson also note that the design of flyers changed radically in the autumn of 1976, when Reid took over full design direction for the group.[28]

The success – and notoriety – of the Sex Pistols as the figureheads of the new movement was reflected in the wider public acknowledgement of a set of visual stereotypes that sat alongside media clichés and commonly held assumptions about punk music, fashion and behaviour. In terms of graphic design, this was a double-edged sword: on the one hand, punk was beginning to develop a recognisable set of visual styles, largely centred on Reid's work for the Sex Pistols (the 'Anarchy in the U.K.' promotional poster and press ads, together with gig flyers and the iconic record sleeve and posters for the group's most notorious single, 'God Save the Queen'). However, the sheer power and dominance of that aesthetic coupled with the subculture's self-professed focus on individuality, autonomy and authenticity meant that other up-and-coming punk bands were conscious of the need to avoid being seen as copying the Sex Pistols and to stand out on their own from the pack. At the same time, largely due to its powerful visual impact, ransom note typography – along with safety pins, razor blades, and, more problematically, swastikas – quickly became symbolic of early UK punk in the mainstream media and therefore a cliché to be best avoided unless the designer's intention was to make a parodic comment on the commercial exploitation of the new subculture.[29]

Punk's graphic conventions can be broken down into three separate but interconnected stages in the creative process: themes, methods and practices. First, we might consider common approaches that were adopted by designers to reflect the values and principles of the new movement. These included a rejection of common visual practices associated with the pop music industry, the promotion of a do-it-yourself punk ideal, political posturing, an embrace of machine aesthetics and the employment of art historical references.

Industry standards

The inclusion of a photograph of the group – standard practice in the pop music market going back to the 1950s – is prevalent in many early punk record sleeves, though the convention was rejected by some groups, including the Sex Pistols, Siouxsie and the Banshees, Magazine, Wire and The Fall, precisely because of its association with the mainstream music industry. Jamie Reid made a conscious choice when commencing work with the Sex Pistols that record covers would not feature group photographs. Instead, he relied heavily on a combination of collage, typography and détournement – appropriating and disrupting found images from the media and advertising. While offering a complete contrast to Reid's rough, agit-prop approach, Malcolm Garrett's designs for singles by Buzzcocks also avoided group photographs, instead bringing a hard-edged but playful visual style to the fore utilising simple, geometric shapes, flat colours and sans serif typography. The first two albums by Buzzcocks, *Another Music in a Different Kitchen* (1978) (Figure 1.7) and *Love Bites* (1979), retained the geometric style and typographic quirks of the singles, though they each featured a group photograph. However, the style of photography

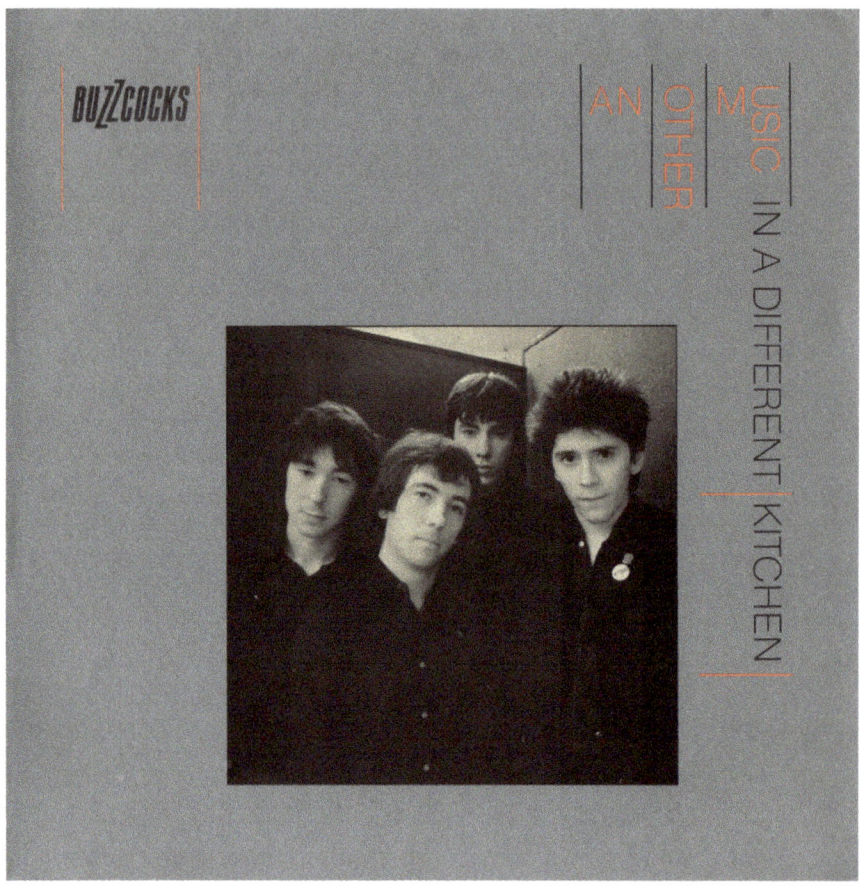

1.7 Buzzcocks (1978), *Another Music in a Different Kitchen*, vinyl album, United Kingdom: United Artists. Design by Malcolm Garrett, photography by Jill Furmanovsky. Courtesy Malcolm Garrett/Assorted Images.

and the composition and visual hierarchy of both album covers still set them apart from what might be seen as standard industry practice.

Meanwhile, others such as The Damned, The Stranglers, The Clash and The Jam displayed no such qualms and cover shots of these groups helped to establish some common tropes in the sleeve design of the punk and new wave bands that followed (Figure 1.8). An image of the group standing in a street, backed by a grubby and decaying brick wall, became an archetype for punk portraiture which would last well into the next decade. This pose, together with the style of photography and reproduction, can be traced to the cover of the first album by US punk progenitors The Ramones, released by Sire Records in July 1976. The cover featured a high contrast, black and white photograph of the group by Roberta Bayley (an amateur

Pretty vacant: punk graphic themes

1.8 The Damned, 'New Rose' promotional poster, 1976. Design by Barney Bubbles, photography by Chris Gabrin © Stiff Records Art Department – All Rights Reserved.

photographer and regular contributor to *Punk* magazine) standing in front of a rough, graffiti-strewn brick wall. The album was highly influential on the nascent UK punk scene, sartorially and graphically as well as musically, and the cover stance has been replicated by countless other groups since. In December 1977, the cover of the third Ramones album, *Rocket to Russia*, repeated the same design process, featuring a raw, halftone black and white photograph of the group taken by manager Danny Fields in the street behind CBGBs nightclub in New York, only this time with coloured (pink) titles.

The opportunities for intervention relate to the style of photograph and stance of the musicians at the initial shoot, or in the graphic treatment of the image once selected at the design stage. Key examples of initiatives by the photographer include, for instance, the cover shoot for the debut album by The Damned, *Damned Damned Damned*, which took place in the autumn of 1976. Peter Gravelle (a.k.a. Peter Kodick), a fashion and advertising photographer in London, was married at the time to US artist and musician Patti Palladin. Palladin's collaborator in the group Snatch, Judy Nylon, was in a relationship with Damned guitarist Brian James and asked Gravelle if he could do the shoot pro-bono, since they had no budget. Gravelle agreed, so long as he could art direct himself. Displaying a high degree of irreverence towards the canon of 'serious' rock music photography, he subsequently chose to picture the group covered in custard pies, in homage to classic stage and screen physical comedy. The team couldn't find a supplier for the kind of custard pies required, so they used ketchup, shaving foam and mustard along with flan bases to mimic the visual effect (Figure 1.9). The resulting album cover, designed by Barney Bubbles, centres on a close-up colour image of the four group members, with little further graphic intervention beside the group's name in large, bright yellow capital letters at the top edge. The Damned employed an equally ridiculous photograph for the cover of their second single, 'Neat Neat Neat' (1977). Shot by celebrated rock photographer Keith Morris, who had previously worked with Nick Drake, T. Rex, Dr. Feelgood and others, and again designed by Barney Bubbles, the black and white image shows the four members of the band with paper bags over their heads and holes cut out for their eyes. The covers of both *Damned Damned Damned* and 'Neat Neat Neat' reflect the slapstick, cartoonish image of the band, undermining the seriousness of much rock music of the time.

As a set of generic visual conventions, the photographic portrait of the group, suitably framed in an urban location and graphically treated to render a high contrast, distressed or distorted image, was to become one of the core signifiers of punk graphic style. In many cases the standard format for rock and pop music album covers would have involved a professional, high-quality, colour photograph of the artist or band. Since most punk and new wave albums were released by major labels that would

Pretty vacant: punk graphic themes 41

1.9 Outtake from photo session for *Damned Damned Damned*, 1977. Courtesy Peter Kodick Gravelle.

have suitable budgets and access to facilities to produce conventionally sophisticated cover artwork, punk designers made a conscious choice to utilise lo-tech approaches, distressed images and typography and reduced colour palettes as deliberate punk graphic signifiers. Punk singles, by contrast, were usually produced on more limited budgets and there was a clear tendency towards one- or two-colour sleeves and simple graphic treatments, in part due to economic and technical constraints as well as the conventions of an emerging punk visual aesthetic.

As punk became commodified and commercialised, by far the most common visual trope in the depiction of the punk rock group is the band line-up against a brick or concrete wall or a similarly gritty urban background. This can be seen in the cover of the debut single by The Cortinas, 'Fascist Dictator' (1977), which features a black and white photograph

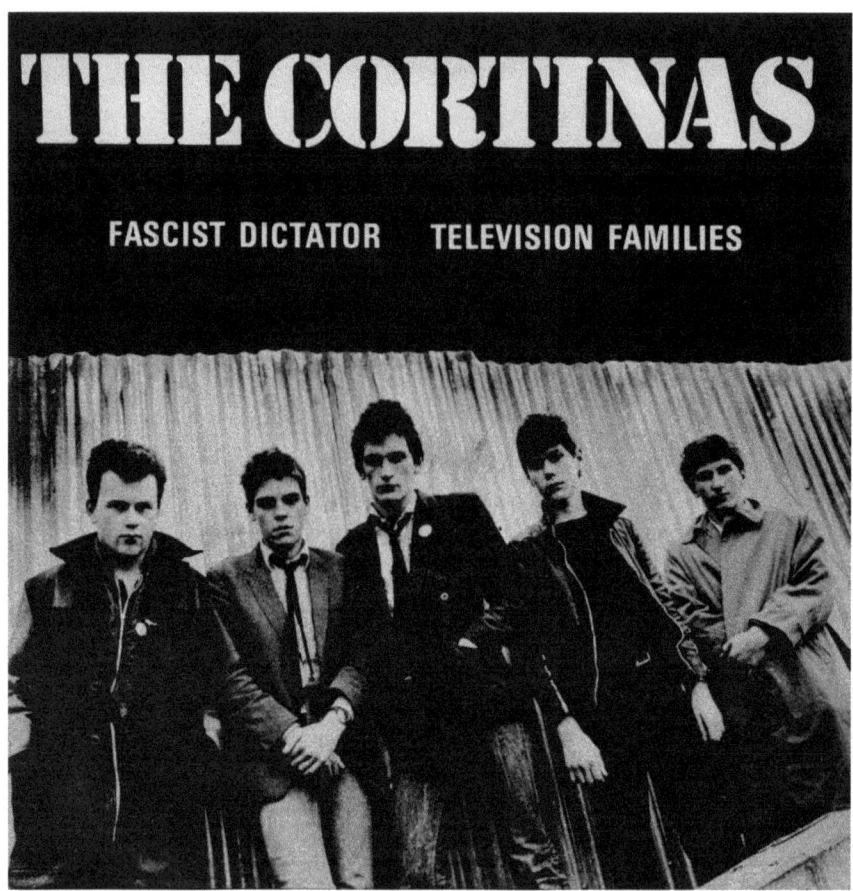

1.10 The Cortinas (1977), 'Fascist Dictator', 7" single, United Kingdom: Step Forward Records. Photography and design Jill Furmanovsky © Mark Perry. Collection of the author.

of the band in front of a corrugated iron fence, by professional rock photographer Jill Furmanovsky (Figure 1.10),[30] as well as in numerous later sleeves, from Blitzkrieg Bop (Figure 1.11) and Headache (Figure 1.12) in 1977 to Chron Gen (Figure 1.13), The Partisans, Blitz and Anti-Social in the early 1980s. While some punk groups chose to be photographed in front of widely recognisable local locations, the visual style of the 'band against the wall' image was generic and non-specific – a decaying urban environment which could be anywhere.

Dress codes of the group members photographed on the record covers were also very important, as they helped to establish common visual and sartorial connections and reflected the fashion styles of developing punk subgenres. Given that the group photograph had become a

1.11 Blitzkrieg Bop (1977), 'Let's Go', 7" single, United Kingdom: Lightning Records. Collection of the author.

well-used cliché on record sleeves since the 1960s and that there is little other visual information contained in a photograph with a flat plane as a background, these codes were of central importance in communicating with potential buyers of the record and in establishing or supporting communal punk identities. Some of these fashion tropes became formalised during the early 1980s – from the boot boy styles and codes of street punk and Oi! to the studded leather jackets, bondage trousers and mohican hairstyles of hardcore punk. Glossy, full-colour and high-quality picture sleeves didn't fit the narrative and early punk examples are quite scarce, although some later hardcore and new punk groups did take on some of the full-colour fashion styling associated with pop stars since the 1960s.[31] At the same time, the commercial new wave boom and chart success of artists such as Blondie, The Police, The Jam, The Pretenders

1.12 Headache (1977), 'Can't Stand Still', 7" single, United Kingdom: Lout Records. Photography Box Brownie. Collection of the author.

and Elvis Costello & The Attractions brought greater prominence and bigger marketing and promotion budgets onto the scene, along with a return to more traditional promotional techniques centred on the image of the performer.

DIY in principle

Punk's do-it-yourself mantra was perhaps best exemplified by the glut of fanzine producers who followed in the footsteps of Mark Perry's pioneering *Sniffin' Glue*.[32] Absolved of the technical constraints and expense associated with creating music, fanzine writers and editors could contribute to the emerging punk scene as commentators and citizen journalists, cementing their (sub)cultural credentials while gaining access to bands

1.13 Chron Gen (1981), *Puppets of War,* 7" vinyl EP, United Kingdom: Gargoyle Records. Design by Chron Gen. Collection of the author.

and publicity by association, though for his part Perry did acknowledge that punk DIY needed to go much further.

> This 'new-wave' has got to take in everything, including posters, record-covers, stage presentation, the lot![33]

Fanzines were relatively cheap to produce, though a significant part of their retrospective mythology has become overly narrow, their apparent immediacy and back to basics authenticity disguising the production processes behind their creation. Punk's rough and ready style took work, it took *effort*, not just in construction but in reproduction and distribution. Over time, something of a support network evolved among punk fanzine producers, though they often had to strike a careful balance between citizenship and idiosyncratic individuality. We will return to the punk fanzine revolution in the next chapter, but for now our discussion of punk DIY is centred on the creation of records and physical artefacts by punk groups, labels and promoters.

Tony Moon's classic three-chord diagram entitled 'Play'in in the Band', published in *Sideburns* fanzine in December 1976 (Figure 1.14), has become something of a visual cliché in relation to DIY and punk. While Mark Perry was encouraging others to write about the new scene in the pages of *Sniffin' Glue*, Moon set out to recruit a new generation of active participants and musicians under the punk banner. A month later, Buzzcocks released their debut EP, *Spiral Scratch*. The record was funded through a series of loans, including £250 from guitarist Pete Shelley's father, and a deal was arranged by manager Richard Boon for the pressing of the record at Phonogram. *Spiral Scratch* was the first UK independent punk record and the widespread critical acclaim it received ensured both the record's success and the broader circulation of a punk do-it-yourself idea. *Spiral Scratch* quickly sold out its initial pressing of one thousand copies and went on to eventually sell sixteen thousand, before being officially deleted when the band signed to United Artists in August 1977.

While Buzzcocks communicated DIY principles, others such as The Desperate Bicycles went one stage further, encouraging others to action through a deliberate call to arms. Five hundred copies of their debut single, 'Smokescreen' / 'Handlebars', were released on their own Refill label in April 1977, with both songs pressed on each side of the record, apparently due to the proscriptive cost of cutting a master for two separate sides (Figure 1.15). The run-out for record at the end of 'Handlebars' features a sole shouted voice – 'It was easy, it was cheap, go and do it!' The first pressing sold out within four months, resulting in a profit of £210. Using this money, a second pressing of one thousand was made, which sold out in a fortnight. The profit from that was used to finance the pressing of their second release, 'The Medium Was Tedium' / 'Don't Back the Front', in July 1977 (Figure 1.16). Again, both tracks were pressed on each side of the record and it featured a lyrical continuation from their debut – the words 'It was easy, it was cheap, go and do it!' formed the chorus of the first song. During the final verse, vocalist Danny Wigley voices his frustration with the hesitance of others to become involved and to form their own bands.

> I'm sick of telling people that they're capable too
> They don't want to believe me and there ain't just a few[34]

The song goes on to make Wigley's ambitions to inform, educate and spur others to action clear, communicated now more as a form of instruction to the listener.

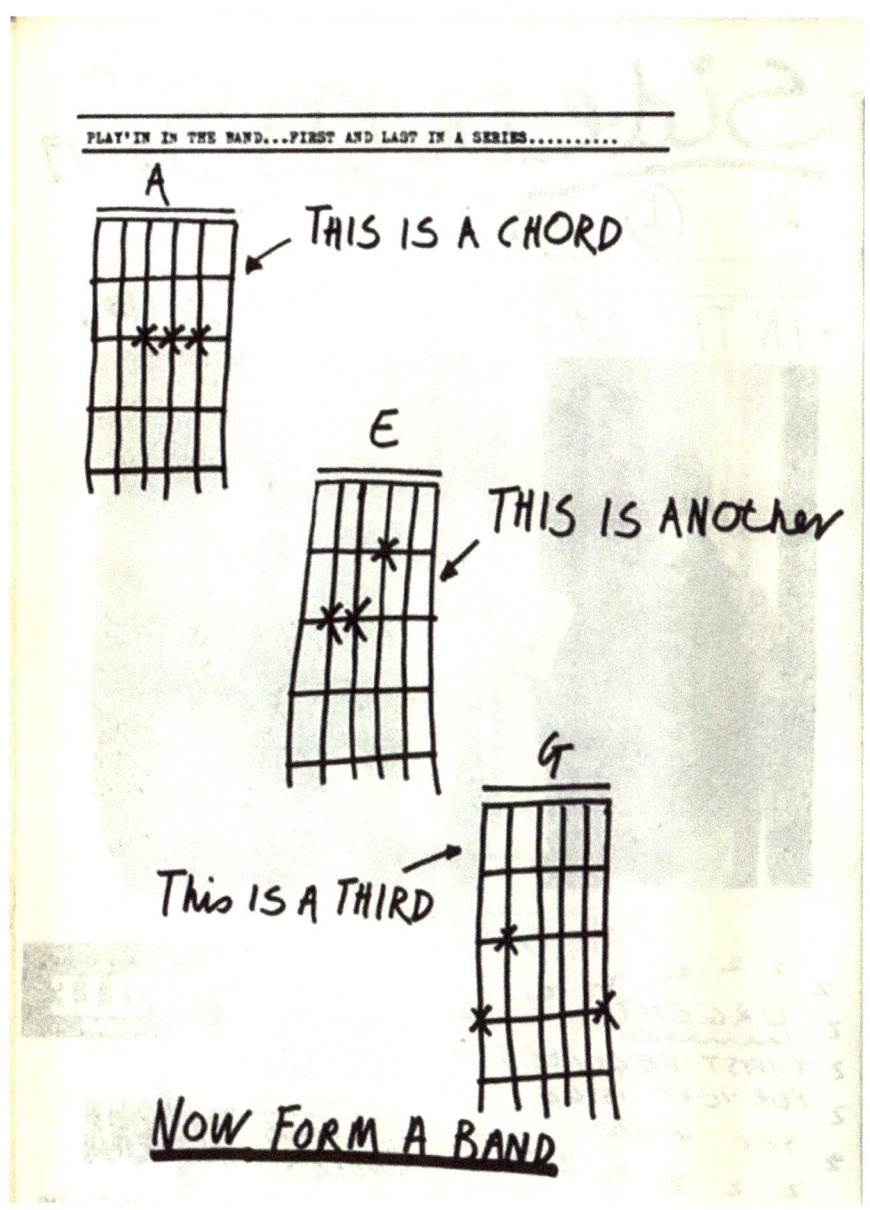

1.14 *Sideburns* fanzine no.1, December 1976. 'Play'in in the Band' full page illustration. Design by Tony Moon.

1.15 The Desperate Bicycles (1977), 'Smokescreen' / 'Handlebars', 7" single, United Kingdom: Refill Records. Design by Diana Fawcett, collection of the author.

> So, if you can understand
> Go and join a band
> It was easy, it was cheap, go and do it![35]

The typewritten text on the back sleeve – created by Diana Fawcett, an illustrator who also worked as an assistant to Barney Bubbles – provide further encouragement (Figure 1.17).

> They'd really like to know why you haven't made your single yet … So, if you can understand, go and join a band. Now it's your turn ….[36]

1.16 The Desperate Bicycles (1977), 'The Medium Was Tedium' / 'Don't Back the Front', 7" single, United Kingdom: Refill Records. Front cover. Design by Diana Fawcett, collection of the author.

Defiant pose

The first wave of punk in the United Kingdom presented mixed messages in relation to politics, at least in relation to established parties and activist organisations. Historian Matthew Worley suggests that 'a rejection of traditional and hierarchical political organisation found expression through punk-associated claims to autonomy'.[37] In part, this reflected the nascent ideals of what was generally a youthful new scene, with many participants barely of voting age, together with a wider sense of dissatisfaction with national politics during a period of significant industrial unrest and a collapsing economy under a Labour administration. Some journalists in the music press attempted to corral punk's incoherent rage towards broadly leftist political positions, while activists on both the far left and far right,

1.17 The Desperate Bicycles (1977), 'The Medium Was Tedium' / 'Don't Back the Front', 7" single, United Kingdom: Refill Records. Back cover. Design by Diana Fawcett, collection of the author.

from the Socialist Workers Party to the National Front, tried to establish closer relationships to bolster their own numbers. Journalist and fanzine writer Garry Bushell championed punk in the pages of *Socialist Worker*, calling for closer involvement in the developing new scene among his comrades, though punk's (dis)organised resistance was hard to contain and political calls-to-arms were not widely reciprocated.[38]

> Punk Rock worked *tactically*. When the Pistols were vibrant and relevant was when no one could label them. The media couldn't label them. I mean you were National Front one day, Reds under the Bed another, and Anarchists the next.[39]

Although political groups from both right and left had been initially reluctant to become closely associated with the often unruly and unfocused punk insurrection, by mid-1977 the movement had achieved such a groundswell of interest nationally that activists saw an opportunity to become more involved. However, it was largely the left-wing groups that gained national publicity for their links with punk and the new wave, through a sympathetic music press. Journalists who held political agendas through which they wrote about the punk movement included Nick Kent, Julie Burchill and Tony Parsons at the *New Musical Express*, Caroline Coon at *Melody Maker* and Jonh Ingham and Jon Savage at *Sounds*, all of whom saw punk as a potential vehicle for a radical cultural revolution. The battle for the hearts and minds of punk audiences was played out across the political spectrum. The Anti-Nazi League and Rock Against Racism held close allegiances with left-wing parties and campaign groups, including sections of the Labour Party, trade union groups and the Socialist Workers Party. The strong bonds between Rock Against Racism and the Socialist Workers Party did raise objections from punk and new wave performers and fans who were deeply distrustful of left-wing activism and political parties of all stripes, with some groups choosing to pursue their own anti-racist agendas outside the auspices of the organisation. Rock Against Racism did, however, embrace sections of the movement, promoting gigs and publishing newspapers and a dedicated fanzine, *Temporary Hoarding*, featuring punk articles and interviews.[40]

Despite the introduction of the term 'anarchism' to mainstream British pop culture by the Sex Pistols in November 1976,[41] most punk discourse was rhetorical and performative, centring on themes spanning teenage frustration, boredom, novelty, mischief-making and a criticism of the contemporary music industry rather than an attack on government or state. Punk was no erudite ideological critique: talk of anarchy, along with autonomy and individuality, nestled next to calls for personal freedom and liberty, though few punks took these loose notions any further towards a concrete plan for action. Sex Pistols manager Malcolm McLaren, alongside Vivienne Westwood and Bernie Rhodes, played a key role in providing the new movement with an appropriately antagonistic visual vocabulary, drawn from a curious mixture of late sixties underground manifestos, early twentieth century political art movements and more recent cultural commentators from media, film and literature. Clothes sold in Westwood and McLaren's shop in the Kings Road, London, bore slogans drawn from Marxist theory and more recent countercultural manifestos. Westwood and McLaren's Only Anarchists Are Pretty shirts bore slogans such as 'Be Reasonable, Demand the Impossible' (from 'Soyez réalistes, demandez l'impossible!', anonymous graffiti in Paris, 1968), 'Try Subversion, it's Fun' and 'Believe in the Ruins', while the Anarchist Punk Gang muslin shirt featured anarchy symbols alongside a skull and crossbones and the legend 'As You Were I Was, As I Am You Will Be' (from Hunter S. Thompson's *Hell's Angels*, published in 1967).[42] In practice, the use of the anarchy symbol by Westwood and McLaren bore no more importance than other graphic elements such as the skull and crossbones, swastika, the union flag or images of the Queen, Karl Marx, Marilyn Monroe or Mickey Mouse (who in turn featured an anarchy 'A' on his right ear). McLaren also updated his classic Vive Le Rock t-shirt design in 1977, adding images taken from William Powell's *The Anarchist Cookbook* – a countercultural text first published in the USA in 1971 and widely circulated within the late hippie underground. This montage-like approach, mixing symbols of insurrection and revolution with images of authority, religion and popular culture, was largely aesthetic, or at least lacking in a clear focus or specificity of political intent. Anarchy was a threatening term, but its value within the early UK punk scene was rhetorical – a device to vaguely suggest freedom from restrictions or convention, rather than a disciplined call to social and political reorganisation.

McLaren, Westwood and Rhodes' obsession with both historical and contemporary radicalism, drawing on images and quotes from both right- and left-wing intellectuals, was largely centred on an attempt to provoke and shock rather than a clear form of ideological positioning or political allegiance, and others among UK punk's early pioneers soon evolved a similar distaste for organised politics and the doctrines of the past. A loose interpretation of the anarchist position – rebellious but unfixed, sceptical, antagonistic, critical of political organisation and centred on the ideology of the individual (at least in terms of its punk definition) – was a relatively easy one to take, particularly for a young and less than studious subcultural group. Interviewed by Nick Kent for the *New Musical Express* in November 1976, McLaren stated that the use of the term 'anarchy' provided a perfect slogan for his new prodigies: 'I just see it as a reaction against the last five years of stagnation'.[43] The version of anarchism adopted by early punks was, then, partly based on a loosely informed historical concept but more broadly adopted as a philosophical position invoking a sense of liberty, personal freedom, individualism and anti-authoritarianism, not totally dissimilar to the sentiments of earlier generations of rock'n'roll rebels. As Worley asserts, 'boiled down, "anarchy" encapsulated punk's allusions to "be yourself", "think for yourself" and "do what you want to do"'.[44]

Punk's sartorial flirtation with taboo also introduced contentious, and contested, political symbols to the emerging scene. McLaren and Westwood's playful appropriation of the iconography of both left and right, including the swastika – perhaps the most shocking symbol for an older generation of the British public – had its roots in the late 1960s counterculture and an at least partially informed critique of national values and history.[45] Hebdige gives a great deal of emphasis to the use of the swastika as a form of subcultural exotic display. His assertion that the symbol was made available to punks via David Bowie and Lou Reed's Berlin phase, reflecting 'punks' interest in a decadent and evil Germany – a Germany which had no future'[46] – labours the point a little, ignoring a range of other precursors.

More influential perhaps, at least sartorially, were the films *Cabaret*, directed by Bob Fosse and starring Liza Minnelli, released in 1972, and *The Night Porter*, directed by Liliana Cavani and starring Charlotte Rampling and Dirk Bogarde, released in 1974. Both films depict a mixture of sexually charged imagery alongside the decadence of pre-war Germany and the threat of Nazism. The mid-1970s also saw several high-profile films and books about former Nazi leaders in hiding long after the end of the war. Ira Levin's fictional thriller, *The Boys from Brazil*, the story of a Jewish Nazi hunter searching for war criminals, was published in 1976 and made into a film in 1978. Meanwhile, *Marathon Man*, a thriller starring Dustin Hoffman released in 1976, centred on the story of a young man's encounter with a former Nazi war criminal. Wartime Nazi defector Rudolph Hess also featured heavily in the British media in the late 1970s. Eugene Bird, a former American Commandant at Spandau Prison, where Hess was serving a life sentence for his part in Hitler's administration, had written a book about his famous prisoner, *The Loneliest Man in the World*, in 1976, and a widespread media campaign had highlighted his physical and mental deterioration, with politicians and media figures calling for his compassionate release on the grounds of poor health.

Hebdige also excludes other first-hand references from within punk's own direct musical lineage. New York group The Ramones had released their eponymous debut album in July 1976, playing their debut UK show at the London Roundhouse around the same time. Songs such as 'Blitzkrieg Bop' and 'Today Your Love, Tomorrow the World' made direct lyrical reference to Germany and Second World War themes.

> I'm a shock trooper in a stupor, yes I am
> I'm a Nazi schatze, y'know I fight for the Fatherland[47]

Ramones bassist and songwriter Dee Dee Ramone had spent most of his childhood in Germany, his father working at several US military bases there before returning to the USA in the late 1960s, and it appears that at least some of the interest in the Second World War stems from his teenage experiences. Fellow US punks The Dead Boys also adopted Nazi imagery in their dress codes, even going so far as to wear German uniforms, swastikas and SS military insignia. In fact, besides the swastika itself, militaria – and especially German regalia such as the peaked caps of SS officers – was to become a common fashion accessory within punk on both sides of the Atlantic. The lyrical reference to Nazism, either as a cartoonish mock salute or as an overt statement against racism and fascism, was carried through by a number of early British punk groups – notably in songs such as The Spitfire Boys 'Mein Kampf' (1977), The Cortinas 'Fascist Dictator'

(1977), The Valves 'For Adolfs' Only' (1977), The Nosebleeds 'Fascist Pigs' (1977) and The Vibrators '(I'm Gonna Be Your) Nazi Baby' (1978), as well as in group names such as Stormtrooper, Warsaw, The Stukas and Martin & The Brownshirts.

Hebdige's interpretations of punk's flirtation with Nazi iconography are also challenged by Stacy Thompson in a flawed overview of the relationship between punk and commerce, *Punk Productions: Unfinished Business*.

> Punks did not want their surfaces to be legible; they did not want their surfaces to contain them within traditional categories of sexuality, class, and politics ... punk style raises the question of what forces construct identity besides style, and where does the negation of style leave identity as a construct?[48]

Although this notion of punk as intellectual critique of the dominant social order might be attractive to cultural theorists such as Thompson, the young ages of many punk followers who bought into these dress codes go some way to counter this position. Simply put, this was the first post-war generation without any direct experience of the conflict – many of their grandparents fought in the Second World War and their parents were affected by immediate family involvement and disrupted childhoods. The war with Germany was still fresh in the minds of many of the older generation (i.e. those who the punks wished to rebel against), war films were commonplace at the cinema and on television and historical militaria was widely available. Popular children's toys and comics reflected the theme – Action Man, sold in the United Kingdom by Palitoy Ltd, was a British version of the American GI Joe figure and was a common feature in many young lives.[49] In London, army surplus stores such as Silvermans and Laurence Corner stocked a range of military surplus uniforms and combat wear, and smaller stores across the country sold similar goods as heavy-duty workwear. This widespread availability of military uniforms, together with the nature of the Second World War as central to the identity of the older generation, meant that the ability to shock through the adoption of German military insignia was a relatively easy stance to take. In the way that the black clothes of the bad guys in cowboy films filtered into rock'n'roll styles in the 1950s, the demonised SS officers in films such as *The Desert Rats* (1953), *The Longest Day* (1962) and *The Great Escape* (1963) bore some rebellious attraction for a generation of disenfranchised youth.

The machine aesthetic

Several early punk groups had explored the theme of consumerism and the tensions brought about by the marketing and selling of punk music and fashion. X-Ray Spex, fronted by former Kings Road boutique assistant

Poly Styrene, produced a string of singles and an album, *Germ Free Adolescents*, with lyrics reflecting the developing punk scene in London and satirising consumer culture. Album tracks included 'Identity', 'Warrior in Woolworths', 'The Day the World Turned Day-glo' and 'Art-I-Ficial', the latter of which featured lyrics which revolved around the theme of modern consumerism and domestic appliances.

> I know I'm artificial
> But don't put the blame on me
> I was reared with appliances
> In a consumer society[50]

Similarly, Buzzcocks explored themes of musical and lyrical repetition. Songs such as 'Boredom', on their debut *Spiral Scratch* EP featured deadpan vocal phrasing and simple, repetitive musical themes – in the case of 'Boredom' a two-note guitar solo which builds tension 'in its fixated refusal to go anywhere melodically'.[51] Guitarist Pete Shelley, who took over the lead vocal role after the departure of original singer Howard Devoto in February 1977, had a long-standing interest in electronic music and Krautrock by the likes of Can, Neu! and Kraftwerk and his songwriting for Buzzcocks explored both melodic pop punk and repetitive rhythmic structures. 'Moving Away From The Pulsebeat', 'Why Can't I Touch It?' and 'I Believe' (which repeats the staccato phrase 'there is no love in this world anymore' fourteen times in succession during the final verse) played with the notion of mechanical music and the removal of the pretence of artistic individuality, and the theme was continued within some of the graphic design approaches for the group's sleeves, designed by Malcolm Garrett under a series of pseudonyms.[52] Early copies of the debut Buzzcocks album *Another Music in a Different Kitchen*, released in March 1978, were packaged in a silver carrier bag printed with the word PRODUCT in bold, orange, sans serif type.

Many others set out to explore the concept of machine music and themes of robotics, science fiction and computers became popular. Early punk songs such as The Valves 'Robot Love' (1977) and The Saints 'Do the Robot' (1977) tied the concept neatly to certain trends in punk clubs for robotic dancing, blank stares and a rejection of human emotions, perhaps best encapsulated in the debut single by Welsh group The Table with 'Do the Standing Still' (1977). The punk fanzine aesthetic, incorporating simple collage and photocopier reproduction, was also reflected in the music and song lyrics: Adam and the Ants recorded a song entitled 'Zerox' in 1979, and The Desperate Bicycles declared 'Xerox music's here at last!' on their second single, released in February 1978. Manchester avant-garde pioneers The Fall included a song on their debut single entitled 'Repetition', which included a caustic self-reflection on the groups' musical approach.

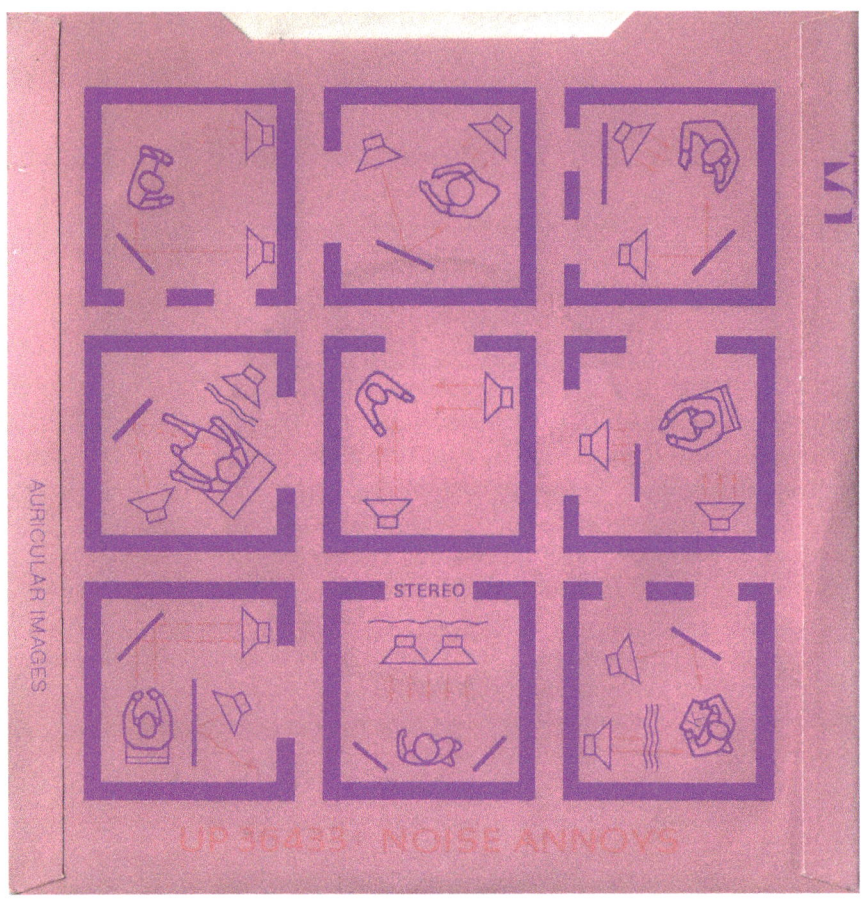

1.18 Buzzcocks (1978), 'Love You More', 7" single, United Kingdom: United Artists. Back Cover. Design by Malcolm Garrett/Auricular Images, courtesy Malcolm Garrett/Assorted Images.

> We dig repetition
> Repetition in the drums
> And we're never going to lose it
> This is the three R's
> The three R's:
> Repetition, Repetition, Repetition[53]

These mechanical themes were influential on the graphic styles adopted by sleeve designers. Garrett utilised a range of geometrical forms and flat colours for the early Buzzcocks single sleeves, adding simple visual elements including figures from the Letraset architectural catalogue (Figure 1.18). Wire utilised technical drawing on several sleeves, including 'I Am the Fly' (1978) and 'Dot Dash' (1978), and a similar graphic approach was developed across a range of avant-garde DIY releases by groups such as Spizzoil, The Mekons and Cabaret Voltaire.

I don't want to go to art school

Contested histories of specific graphic techniques aside, the relationship between punk and its varied visual manifestations continued to be a source for both academic debate and journalistic commentary as the historiography of the subculture expanded through the 1990s and early 2000s.[54] Two books published a decade after Hebdige's *Subcultures* placed greater emphasis on earlier art movements as a source of inspiration for punk performers, artists and designers. In *Lipstick Traces* (1989),[55] Greil Marcus attempted (and largely failed) to make connections between the Sex Pistols, Dada, Surrealism and the philosophies of much earlier political agitators, while in *England's Dreaming* (1991),[56] Jon Savage emphasised Situationist International precursors along with the centrality of women's and gay rights within the early punk movement. However, while Malcolm McLaren and Jamie Reid had indeed caught the late 1960s zeitgeist and attempted to engage with the then current ideas of the Situationists and the student protest movement while at art college during the previous decade, the suggestion of substantive links between participants in the wider punk scene and the work of earlier art groups is less convincing.

The direct impact of art school education on punk visual aesthetics is a well-trodden narrative that often fails to convince when placed under critical scrutiny. There has long existed a connection between art school students and pop music, as captured by Simon Frith and Howard Horne in their 1987 publication *Art into Pop*.[57] Frith and Horne noted that a significant number of British pop artists from the 1960s on had attended art schools, though as with the art historical connections applied previously, a quantitative survey of artists and groups that fell at some stage beneath the banner of punk and post-punk would almost certainly place that significant number in the minority.

Jamie Reid had attended a pre-diploma course in art and design at Wimbledon Art School between 1962 and 1964, which he described as 'very odd. Tweed jackets, brogues, and monocles, still lifes and life classes: very much the old guard's last retreat before everything went pop',[58] before going on to Croydon Art School to take a vocational course in painting. Although political events around 1968 were a strong influence on his work (especially material he produced for Suburban Press in the early 1970s), there is little to suggest that the school, or its curriculum, had a great deal of influence on his later output. This isn't to say that the art school environment – and the opportunity for peer learning and networking afforded creative young people within the proximity of a college building – was not a factor in the careers and visual practices of several punk artists.

Connections between a generation of art students and a post-punk aesthetic among clusters of soon-to-be musicians in Leeds, Manchester, Liverpool and London have been effectively explored in two recent books by Gavin Butt (2022)[59] and Simon Strange (2022),[60] though again we must avoid extrapolating a particular set of personalities and circumstances to describe a much bigger and more diverse punk community of practice nationally, or indeed internationally. That isn't to say that Butt and Strange's theses are wrong: there was indeed a close connection between the experiences of some punk and post-punk musicians at art school and their ensuing musical, lyrical and visual practices.[61] Gang of Four, The Mekons, The Raincoats, Scritti Politti and others reflected their art school backgrounds in their lyrics, interviews and approach to musical composition, though the sheer number of punk-related groups and the diversity of the punk scene across the United Kingdom indicates that the art school bands were in a relatively small minority. In fact, anti-student rhetoric was commonplace within local scenes, particularly in the older university towns and cities. Punk's self-avowed working-class politics and street-level 'authenticity' often exacerbated the perceived divide between town and gown for many participants.

The notion of the art school as a place for free expression was, however, adopted by several early punks, at least rhetorically. Paul Weller, though not a graduate of the system himself, even used the subject as a metaphor for the punk movement in the song 'Art School', on the debut album by The Jam, *In the City* (1977).

> Anything that you wanna do, any place that you wanna go
> Don't need permission for everything that you want
> Any taste that you feel is right
> Wear any clothes just as long as they're bright
> Say what you want, 'cos this is a new art school[62]

Some of the punk and post-punk musicians who had attended art school in the 1970s drew inspiration from fine art history, theory and practice, but many of those who studied graphic design (or the applied arts more generally) had a less positive experience. While a small number of British art schools were experimenting with new approaches to radical pedagogy, particularly in the fine arts, graphic design education remained widely conventional, tied to the vocational training needs of commercial practice. Several designers who went on to prominence in the profession, including Linder Sterling, Malcolm Garrett, Rob O'Connor, Peter Saville, Ian Wright and Neville Brody, had a less than satisfactory experience as students and felt restrained by the often limited and conservative nature of their education. Brody subsequently described his time at London College of Printing as repressive and stultifying, with his work condemned by tutors as 'uncommercial'.[63]

From concept to practice

These loose-knit themes and concepts were to become embedded in the rhetoric of the emerging punk subculture in the late 1970s. The do-it-yourself call to arms extended not just to the pure punk DIY pioneers and fanzine producers but became a regularly voiced punk convention even among many groups and artists signed to major labels and operating in the mainstream music industry. Historical links to the language of rebellion and the avant-garde were also common, along with tongue-in-cheek references to consumerism, the machine-made and non-human.

Notes

1. Dave Laing (1985), *One Chord Wonders: Power and Meaning in Punk Rock*, Milton Keynes: Open University, p. 27.
2. Alternative TV (1977), 'How Much Longer', 7" single, United Kingdom: Deptford Fun City Records.
3. Russ Bestley and Paul Burgess (2018), 'Fan artefacts and doing it themselves: The home-made graphics of punk devotees', *Punk & Post-Punk* 7:3, pp. 317–340.
4. Gorman, *Reasons to be Cheerful*.
5. Russ Bestley (2023), '"Fuck Art, Let's Dance": An interview with Chris Morton', *Punk & Post-Punk* 12:3, pp. 353–377.
6. Smith, *Cover Stories*.
7. Julie Davis (1977), *Punk*, London: Millington.
8. Michael Dempsey and Derek Ridgers (1978), *100 Nights at the Roxy*, London: Big O Publishing Ltd.
9. The paper was published by a company called Wishcastle Limited, London and printed by the Courier Printing and Publishing Company, Tunbridge Wells, Kent – printers of local and regional newspapers.
10. Vaucher, *International Anthem*.
11. *Fallout*, a large format illustrated magazine, adopted a similar approach in the United States. Designed by Winston Smith, its contents merged with the artist's work for hardcore punk group Dead Kennedys.
12. Val Hennessy (1978), *In the Gutter*, London: Quartet Books.
13. Terry Jones and Isabelle Anscombe (1978), *Not Another Punk Book*, London: Aurum Press.
14. Terry Jones (2001), *Smile i-D: Fashion and Style: The Best from 20 Years of i-D*, Los Angeles: Taschen America.
15. Dick Hebdige (1979), *Subculture: The Meaning of Style*, Abingdon: Routledge.
16. Hebdige, *Subculture*, p. 111.
17. A wider range of critiques relating to other aspects of Hebdige's book can be found in Subcultures Network (ed.) (2020), *Hebdige and Subculture in the Twenty-First Century*, London: Palgrave Macmillan.
18. A theme Hebdige would return to and expand in his later book, *Hiding in the Light*, which employed theoretical concepts drawn from semiotic theory and postmodernism to deconstruct punk style. Dick Hebdige (1988), *Hiding in the Light*, London: Routledge.
19. Hebdige, *Subculture*, p. 112. Note that Hebdige also appears to conflate the typographic styles employed by Reid for the 'God Save the Queen' record cover and the accompanying poster campaign. The former utilised the 'ransom note' style, as suggested, but did not feature any hand-rendered text or 'flowing "spray-can" script'.

20 See Reid and Savage, *Up They Rise* and Reid, *XXXXX*.
21 Mott, *Oh So Pretty*, p. 21.
22 A photographic process that converts continuous tone images such as photographs to varying sizes of black and white dots or lines for printing.
23 Reid, *XXXXX*.
24 Paul Rees (ed.) (2006), 'Punk '76', *Q Magazine*, March, p. 73.
25 Bestley and Burgess, 'Fan artefacts and doing it themselves'.
26 Robb, *Punk Rock: An Oral History*, p. 207.
27 Reid and Savage, *Up They Rise*, p. 51.
28 Paul Stolper and Andrew Wilson (2004), *No Future: Sex, Seditionaries and the Sex Pistols*, London: The Hospital Group, p. 32.
29 Russ Bestley (2013), '"I tried to make him laugh, he didn't get the joke …" – taking punk humour seriously', *Punk & Post-Punk* 2:2, pp. 119–145.
30 By this time, Furmanovsky had worked as a commercial rock photographer for several years. She worked with the high-profile design agency Hipgnosis from 1974 and became a regular in-house photographer (and sometimes designer) for Step Forward Records, a label established by Miles Copeland with Mark Perry and Harry T. Murlowski of *Sniffin' Glue* in the summer of 1977.
31 Including Vice Squad, GBH and the UK Subs on record covers, together with a broader range of 1980s punk groups in magazines such as *Punk Lives!*, *Punk's Not Dead* and *Noise!* See Ian Trowell (2017), 'Digging up the dead cities: Abandoned streets and past ruins of the future in the glossy punk magazine', *Punk & Post-Punk* 6:1, pp. 21–40.
32 Worley, *Zerox Machine*.
33 Mark Perry (1976), *Sniffin' Glue* 3, p. 4.
34 The Desperate Bicycles (1977), 'The Medium Was Tedium' / 'Don't Back the Front', 7" single, United Kingdom: Refill Records.
35 The Desperate Bicycles, 'The Medium Was Tedium'.
36 The Desperate Bicycles, 'The Medium Was Tedium'.
37 Matthew Worley (2017), *No Future: Punk, Politics and British Youth Culture, 1976–1984*, Cambridge: Cambridge University Press, p. 141.
38 Worley, *No Future*, p. 35.
39 Jamie Reid, quoted in Savage, 'Guerilla graphics', p. 30.
40 Worley, *No Future*, pp. 142–153.
41 Earlier groups had certainly adopted 'anarchist' political positions, particularly in the early 1970s underground (Gong, Hawkwind, Here & Now, Pink Fairies, Deviants), but the mainstream presence and media impact of the Sex Pistols brought the term to a much wider audience.
42 Stolper and Wilson, *No Future*.
43 Nick Kent (1976), 'Meet the new Col. Tom Parker', *New Musical Express*, 27 November.
44 Worley, *No Future*, p. 159.
45 Others faced more direct condemnation, including a young Sex Pistols fan, Siouxsie Sioux, who was photographed wearing a swastika armband at the 100 Club Punk Festival in September 1976. The symbol was also scrawled on clothing by many other young fans, at least until the media backlash and internal scene opprobrium pushed it beyond the pale.
46 Hebdige, *Subculture*, p. 116.
47 Ramones (1976), 'Today Your Love, Tomorrow The World', *Ramones*, vinyl album, USA: Sire Records.
48 Stacy Thompson (2004), *Punk Productions: Unfinished Business*, New York: State University of New York Press, p. 29.
49 Alex Ogg (2013), 'For you, Tommy, the war is never over', *Punk & Post-Punk* 2:3, pp. 281–304.

50 X-Ray Spex (1978), 'Art-I-Ficial', *Germfree Adolescents*, vinyl album, United Kingdom: EMI International.
51 Reynolds, *Rip it Up and Start Again*, p. 16.
52 Garrett's design studio changed name regularly, employing a variety of aliases, almost always using two words starting with the letters A and I, including Arbitrary Images, Additional Images, Angular Images, Affective Images, Associated Images and Assorted Images. Garrett also played typographic games to insert his initials, as in Assorted iMaGes.
53 The Fall (1978), 'Bingo-Masters Break Out', 7" single, United Kingdom: Step Forward Records.
54 Skov, *Punk Art History*.
55 Marcus, *Lipstick Traces*.
56 Savage, *England's Dreaming*.
57 Frith and Horne, *Art into Pop*. See also Butt, *No Machos or Pop Stars* and Strange, *Blank Canvas*.
58 Reid and Savage, *Up They Rise*, p. 12.
59 Butt, *No Machos or Pop Stars*.
60 Strange, *Blank Canvas*.
61 Many examples are conceptual rather than formal in nature. Musicians drew on the ideas expressed by radical artists from the past, in their lyrics and occasionally in approaches to performance or composition, but few made explicit visual connections to art historical references in record sleeves etc. Examples of the latter might include the second, self-titled album by The Mekons, sometimes known as *Devils, Rats & Piggies: A Special Message from Godzilla* (1980), which featured a cover image of Caspar David Friedrich's Romantic painting *Der Wanderer über dem Nebelmeer* [The Wanderer Above the Sea of Fog] (1818) set against a plain white background, or the same group's 1987 album *Honky Tonkin'*, which featured another Caspar David Friedrich painting, *Das Eismeer* [The Sea of Ice] (1823). The latter album also included academic and art historical references on the inner sleeve.
62 The Jam (1977), *In the City*, vinyl album, United Kingdom: Polydor.
63 Jon Wozencroft (1988), *The Graphic Language of Neville Brody*, London: Thames & Hudson, p. 5.

2
Material interventions: punk graphic processes

This chapter interrogates common methods and practices of graphic communication in relation to punk. DIY features heavily here once again, both as a way of creating and reproducing artwork and as a reflection of its content. Cut and paste, appropriation, détournement and collage are also common tropes, along with wear and tear, roughness and distortion. Following this, we introduce the relationship between punk's visual creatives, the music industry and design technology – in short, the way punk's common themes and methods were manifested in practice. This theme will be explored in greater depth in Chapter 5, 'New sounds, new styles: design and technology'.

DIY in practice

We need to distinguish between genuine punk do-it-yourself producers, notably those engaged in fan-related activities including the creation of fanzines and homemade graphic ephemera (such as badges, scrapbooks, homemade record sleeves etc),[1] and the more official (or semi-official) creative practices associated with the music industry. In many ways this mirrors the separation between homemade punk dress (including, for instance, disfigured school uniforms and second-hand clothing) and the developing punk fashion market that ranged from expensive boutique creations by Vivienne Westwood and punk styles selected by Malcolm McLaren to an emerging mass market led by the likes of Boy and Acme Attractions. In turn, as the punk scene bloomed and became more visible within popular culture and the music industry, these styles cascaded down to knock-off copies in Carnaby Street, Camden and Kensington Market and, eventually, to a host of back page advertisements in the music press for bondage trousers, PVC jeans, bum-flaps and an assortment of unofficial band t-shirts and badges (Figure 2.1).

2.1 'New Wave Gear' advertisement, *New Musical Express*, November 1977. Collection of the author.

However, most punk commodities that were intended to be sold needed to be produced in multiple, from the simplest short-run fanzine to Westwood and McLaren's clothing range at Sex and Seditionaries, or from extremely limited pressings of do-it-yourself records to big selling chart hits at the major labels. In terms of visual style, each side of the equation informed the other and it can sometimes be difficult to unpack a constructed aesthetic centred on simplicity, immediacy and lo-tech methods for origination and reproduction. While punk's do-it-yourself creatives were pushing their limited knowledge of design and print to try to create *something*, it was far easier for experienced professionals to play down to a far less sophisticated visual style.

Some sleeve designers chose to develop a rhetorical visual style for do-it-yourself, either as a direct reflection of the content of the record or in response to the broader punk call to arms. Punk's DIY practice was often deliberately self-referential, revealing its process of creation as a set of instructions to others, following similar principles to the breaking down of barriers between stage and audience attempted by at least some punk performers. With an overt nod to Brecht's distancing effect, the front sleeve for the debut single by The Mekons, 'Never Been in A Riot' (1978), designed by Bob Last, features hand-rendered typography on graph paper and a montaged image of a microphone and stand, while the reverse continues the microphone lead to join a pair of speakers, with directions indicating 'to record' and 'to you' – a simple, and very literal, illustration of the recording and production process and the material relationship between object and listener (Figures 2.2 and 2.3). Some of the limitations of do-it-yourself and lo-tech production within the independent scene were a source of critical self-reflection (or even embarrassment) rather than assertive positioning on the part of producers. While he denies his group wanting to sound or look like the Sex Pistols or The Clash, preferring to forge their own individual punk identity, Kevin Lycett of The Mekons recalls a sense of naivety with respect to the recording process.

> Back in those days no one knew anything about recording, and we thought that just the fact of making a record would result in a record that sounded like a 'proper' record. It was a profound shock to hear such a 'crap' sounding thing and we were all too embarrassed to play it to anyone for a long time. We wanted it to sound like a 'real' record![2]

In retrospect, the record is widely recognised as something of a punk classic because of its simplicity and the impression of a group struggling with their instruments – perhaps something that Last recognised instinctively in their sound that was not apparent to the members of The Mekons at that point. Either way, the distinction between group or individual aspirations and the reality of recording and manufacturing a record is crucial to an understanding of the genre.

Material interventions: punk graphic processes 65

2.2 The Mekons (1978), 'Never Been in A Riot', 7" single, United Kingdom: Fast Product. Front cover. Design by Bob Last © Holdings Ecosse Ltd.

Last also designed the sleeve for the debut EP by Gang of Four, *Damaged Goods*, released shortly afterwards. The band had sent him a photograph, a clipping from a newspaper depicting a female Spanish bullfighter and a bull, along with a typewritten letter specifying a set of instructions. They wanted the matador and the bull to be cut out from the background, with an added dialogue between the two and a caption, 'Olé! The feminine touch from Senorita Maribel'. Two of the four band members were art school students in Leeds and they were interested in a Marxist reading of the image as a dialectic. The concept reflected a critique of corruption in the entertainment industry: the matador and the band each must give the audience what they want. In the group's suggested text, the bull is saying to the matador that there is a point when we must take responsibility for our actions. However, Last chose instead

2.3 The Mekons (1978), 'Never Been in A Riot', 7" single, United Kingdom: Fast Product. Back cover. Design by Bob Last © Holdings Ecosse Ltd.

to create a simple but effective typographic front cover based on the group's name in upper case oriented around three sides, with smaller text labelling the sleeve-as-object: 'the sleeve for a Gang of Four recording of "DAMAGED GOODS", "LOVE LIKE ANTHRAX" and "ARMALITE RIFLE"' (Figure 2.4).[3]

Like Malcolm Garrett's design for 'Orgasm Addict' by Buzzcocks, the visual treatment reflects the notion that there is no single 'way up' for a circular disc and emphasises the fact that this is 'an object in three dimensions'.[4] The typographic treatment is also sympathetic to the structure of the band's name – by placing the conjunctive 'OF' between the first and last word, Last was able to achieve a measure of symmetry, with four letters on each line. The use of a sans serif typeface with circular letter 'O' (Letraset Futura Bold)[5] further emphasises the optically balanced effect.

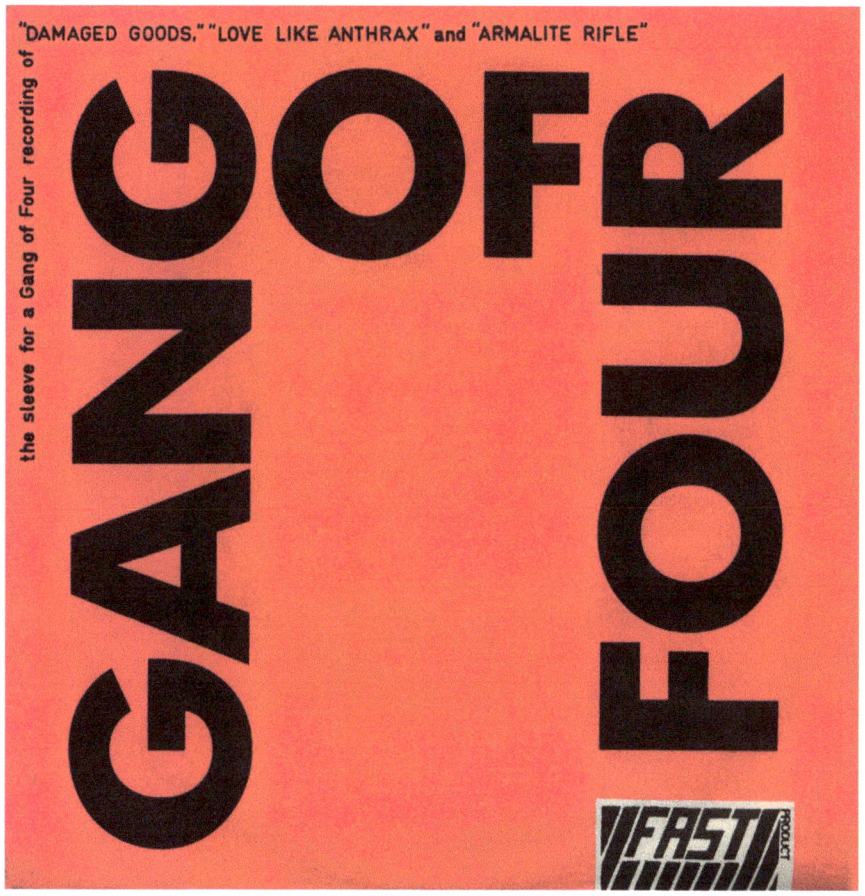

2.4 Gang of Four (1978), *Damaged Goods*, 7" vinyl EP, United Kingdom: Fast Product. Front cover. Reproduced courtesy of Holdings Ecosse Ltd.

Last then simply placed the torn-out photograph alongside the group's typewritten instructions on the back of the cover (Figure 2.5). Like the Mekons sleeve, the cover of *Damaged Goods* is explicit in its reflection of production, though in this case the concept is pushed even further, reflecting the marketing operation between performer and label, as well as between artefact and consumer.[6]

Others were more practical and direct. Inspired by The Desperate Bicycles, Scritti Politti took a proactive approach to punk DIY, openly sharing information on their first two record sleeves detailing the costs of production and producing a fanzine-style guide to making your own record. The debut Scritti Politti EP release, the *Skank Bloc Bologna*, listed details of the costs of each stage of production and service providers utilised by the group for record pressing and packaging (Figure 2.7).

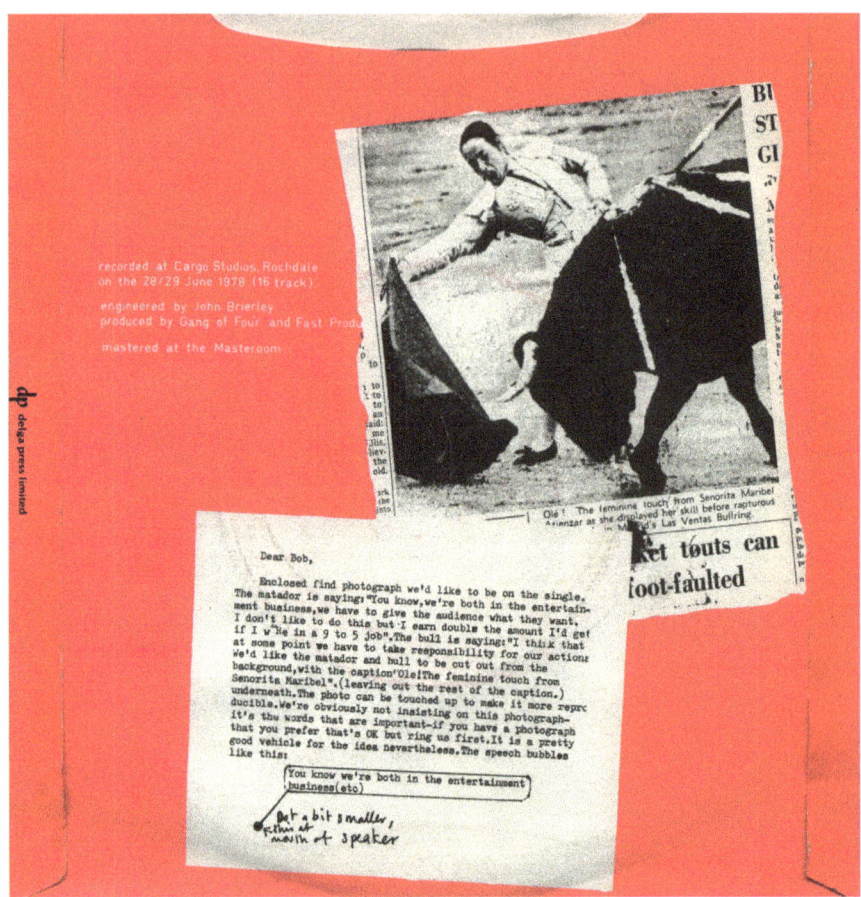

2.5 Gang of Four (1978), *Damaged Goods*, 7″ vinyl EP, United Kingdom: Fast Product. Back cover. Reproduced courtesy of Holdings Ecosse Ltd.

Ironically, the costs of sleeve printing are not included in the listed information. The cover was lithoprinted in two colours (black and red) on the front and one colour (black) on the back. The group's second release, *Work in Progress: 2nd Peel Session*, featured a folded, photocopied sleeve, again detailing costs and contacts for production along with a slightly cryptic note regarding the cover: 'INSERTS – printed cheap by Beattie'.

The Television Personalities released their *Where's Bill Grundy Now? EP* the same month as Scritti's first release (November 1978), with a folded sleeve also detailing the costs and methods of production on the reverse, along with contact details of cutting services, pressing plants and printers. The back cover of the first pressing of *Where's Bill Grundy Now?* details the print production process.

Material interventions: punk graphic processes

2.6 Gang of Four, *Entertainment!* US tour poster, 1980. Design by Jon King, from the collection of Andrew Krivine.

2.7 Scritti Politti (1978), *Skank Bloc Bologna*, 7″ vinyl EP, United Kingdom: St. Pancras Records. Inside cover. Design by Scritti Politti, collection of the author.

> First 2,000 sleeves by DELGA PRESS of Raglan Road, Bromley, Kent. £45 for plate … £65 for sleeves … IF you have the patience you can save time and Money by getting cheaply produced printing. Adresses [sic] in Yellow pages etc.[7]

In both the Television Personalities and Scritti Politti cases, there is also a degree of correlation between concept and form. While some aspects of graphic production were outsourced to professional services (such as cheap lithographic printing and record labelling), at least some parts were taken onboard by the groups themselves, including folding, assembling and stapling covers.[8]

In contrast to the production of records, even for the new independent labels (which often ran to more than one thousand copies), most punk fanzines were printed in very short runs of under fifty copies – often far less. The economics and technical difficulties of writing, design, print, collation, binding and distribution proved too high a hurdle for many producers to stay in the game beyond one or two issues. The rough and ready look of many fanzines was less a deliberate aesthetic choice on the part of the designer and often driven by available tools and skill sets. Mark Perry's extremely raw and simple design for the cover of the first issue of *Sniffin' Glue* fanzine in July 1976 was an attempt to emulate the style of the mainstream magazines that Perry was familiar with: a large masthead and title, a subheading or tagline, typewritten issue number and price, along with a selection of large, typographic band names/article titles filling the space below (The Ramones, Blue Öyster Cult, Punk Reviews). Binding was facilitated through a single staple, a convention that was widely adopted by other fanzine producers. The artwork was created in simple monochrome, partly to allow it to be photocopied, though the limitations of that technology impacted on the design – it took until issue three in September 1976 for the fanzine to start featuring images (Figure 2.8), with halftone reproduction of photographs for lithographic printing coming even later still.

In the United Kingdom at least, photocopier technology produced by companies such as Xerox was still relatively expensive in the mid-1970s, with smaller community groups requiring duplication technologies (such as schools, community centres and youth clubs) still employing ageing hand-cranked Gestetner Cyclographs and other wet ink, stencil-based mechanical systems such as the Banda spirit duplicator.[9] These machines could be used to reproduce text-based documents together with simple line-art illustrations but were incapable of duplicating photographs or more complex continuous tone images.

The relatively hi-tech electronic photocopier technology was a significant business investment at the time, largely seen as a duplication device for financial, corporate and legal services rather than a creative tool. Two types of monochrome photocopier were available. Plain paper copiers used an electrostatic transfer process, where the image would be copied to a drum and then transferred to plain paper sheets. The advantage of this system was that the user could print onto cheap, plain paper and could choose coloured or preprinted stock if desired. The more adventurous creative designer could even make multiple passes with the same sheet of paper, though such experimentation was rare. The second type of machine used a direct electrostatic system, where the image is produced directly onto special paper that has been treated with a light-sensitive coating such as zinc oxide.[10] These machines were more expensive, though they tended to produce deeper tones and stronger contrast than plain paper copiers, which often suffered from greyer solids and dirtier copies as residue from the process affected white areas of the paper. As will be shown later, that greyness and dirtiness could also be embraced by designers as part of the emerging punk aesthetic.

Even where photocopiers could be accessed by budding fanzine producers, they were seen as a tool purely for duplication rather than creative origination or artwork adaptation. The technological capacity for image manipulation was still some way off at this point and even the simple enlargement or reduction of visual elements was a complicated task beyond the ability of most amateur designers. Artwork would usually be constructed at the same size as its intended reproduction – page by page, using paper, Sellotape, felt-tip pens, scissors and glue in the case of

2.8 *Sniffin' Glue*, fanzine no.3, September 1976. Courtesy Mark Perry.

fanzines – and there was rarely a modification or adjustment stage of the process between construction and duplication.

As the punk fanzine market expanded, producers found alternative methods to print longer runs, usually through commercial providers, while at the same time photocopiers were spreading to community centres, schools, libraries and colleges, affording better – if still often surreptitious – access to those starting out or continuing to operate at a lower level. Access to cheap lithographic printers and community print shops enabled higher quality and longer print runs, while in some cases also providing advice on image reproduction and some of the technical aspects of design. Some, like Joly MacFie's Better Badges, set up dedicated print departments to facilitate production, including for the first time the incorporation of coloured inks in the punk fanzine market.

While perhaps any sense of design sophistication in fanzine production was still some way off at this point, the shift to incorporate colour – even if it was crude and rudimentary in practice – was a way to stand out from the competition. In some instances, this came down to using coloured paper for the cover or a few single pages, breaking with the standard punk monochrome aesthetic, or adding an element of colour by hand using felt-tip pens or ink. For issue #5 of *Jamming!* fanzine in October 1978, Tony Fletcher struck upon a novel idea. Fletcher's collaborator Jeff Carrigan secured the services of an offset lithoprinter in Hastings through his father, with one thousand copies printed in black and white and the masthead added afterwards with a stencil and spray paint.

> Jeff's dad dropped 1,000 uncollated copies at my house, some pages printed on yellow paper given we had run other supplies dry. I now had the fun of not only collating and stapling, but spray painting the logo through homemade stencils, an idea lifted from the TRB LP and a mild stroke of marketing genius: the visual effect served as a distinguishing 'fanzine' and 'pop art' factor to offset the otherwise conventional layout.[11]

An attempt to shift the design of the fanzine for the following issue proved disastrous. Following criticism for their conservative typesetting and lack of 'punk' visual flair, Fletcher and Carrigan attempted to break away from a standard grid, while also creating a collaged cover more in keeping with the Xeroxed competition. However, the printer then applied a halftone screen, resulting in a washed-out, grey, and largely unreadable final product a long way from the desired effect. A fortuitous meeting with Joly MacFie at Better Badges led to a far more successful collaboration. MacFie helped Fletcher introduce colour to the process – printing some monochrome pages in single-colour red, green, or blue along with multiple colours for the covers and layered black text over single-colour images on some of the running pages. Collaborations with other fanzine producers reflected this evolving new style, with several successful titles – including

2.9 Fifty Fantastics (1980), 'God's Got Religion', 7″ single, United Kingdom: Dining Out. Design by The Steppes/Fifty Fantastics, collection of the author.

Chainsaw, *Kill Your Pet Puppy* and *Rising Free* – extending print runs into the multiple thousands.

Once photocopier technology became more immediately available, some DIY record sleeve designers chose to design, print and fold their sleeves, taking the entire graphic production process in-house. This strategy led to the creation of some extremely simple sleeves, as in the basic, black and white, one-sided Xerox copies produced for the single 'Hypocrite' by Newtown Neurotics (1979), 'God's Got Religion' by Fifty Fantastics (1980) (Figure 2.9) and *Six Minute War* EP by Six Minute War (1980) (which went one stage further, creatively, by using coloured paper). In comparison, the silkscreen-printed coloured stripes on the Manchester Mekon single 'Not Forgetting' (1979) required access to more technical equipment. Three stripes were screen-printed directly onto standard plain paper record bags, which were already factory folded and glued. The omission of any text or image on the sleeve means that factors such as registration are unimportant – information relating to the group and song titles was included on the centre labels and on a photocopied insert. Other silkscreen-printed sleeves such as the *Lunch with The Adicts* EP by The Adicts (1979), 'Here Come the Buts' by Disco Zombies (1980) and 'We Are Natives' by Blank Students (1980) were all screen-printed in one colour on a piece of card which was then folded to create the sleeve.

Access to silkscreen print technology could lead to more elaborate and sophisticated designs, although the mechanical problems of cutting, folding and gluing sleeves meant that many DIY producers chose to print on a 14" × 7" flat piece of card, folded and wrapped around the record – which was usually housed in a separate white inner bag. One highly elaborate DIY production, a package for the single 'Max Bygraves Killed My Mother' by The Atoms (1979), included two separate seven-inch square, silkscreen-printed front and back cards, together with screen printed sticky centre labels to glue to the record, and a variety of printed, photocopied and handwritten postcards and inserts – all contained in a PVC sleeve (Figure 2.10). This level of detail and handmade material would be extremely difficult, and uneconomical, to achieve with a large-scale release, and such excesses were generally limited to small-scale independent labels.

The impact of do-it-yourself on record manufacturing was mirrored in marketing and distribution. Groups could set up their own label and sell direct to customers either locally at gigs or by mail order, but they were largely at the mercy of a national distribution system, together with long-established procedures for music publishing, promotion and marketing, to reach a wider audience. Similarly, while the design of the sleeve could be taken on by untrained members or friends of the group, the actual printing, folding and gluing was often left to the services of a professional print studio, such as the almost ubiquitous Delga Press in Bromley, South London.

Punk fanzines and the DIY ethos also had a significant impact on an emerging post-punk cassette culture that combined rudimentary graphic styles with cheap home taping, eliminating the need for professional recording, print and reproduction services. While cassette tape technology dated back to the mid-1960s, it was the launch of the Sony Walkman in July 1979 and the boom in cheap stereo players and recorders for home use that provided an opportunity to post-punk artists to bypass the traditional music industry altogether (together with the bootleggers and illegal tape traders who frequented market stalls across the country). At least until new technologies evolved for recording, reproducing and distributing music, the early pioneers of do-it-yourself punk were to

2.10 The Atoms (1979), 'Max Bygraves Killed My Mother', 7" single, United Kingdom: Rinka Records. Screen printed picture sleeve and inserts. Design by The Atoms/Keith Allen, collection of the author.

be forever hampered by access to, and ownership of, the means of production. Technological change was around the corner, bringing firstly access to cheap and fairly simple home-recording and duplication equipment (particularly the four-track cassette and tape-to-tape recorders) and subsequently digital technologies that took music distribution away from physical formats altogether.

Cut and paste

A practice that in many ways intersects both amateur and professional design practices, cut and paste – cutting out images and text or line elements and assembling them on flat art board using tape or glue – is almost ubiquitous in punk graphics. Perhaps the central tenet of DIY punk graphic design, the obvious simplicity and immediacy of the method – something familiar to most children in their early ventures into art – cut and paste has a kind of universal utilitarianism. For punk do-it-yourself amateurs, it afforded an easy way to add images – often cut from newspapers or magazines – to a composition and to arrange type and other visual elements in place ready for duplication or reproduction. It did take a little time for punk fanzine producers to adopt the practice, however. Early issues of *Sniffin' Glue* were almost entirely text-based, with others such as *Ripped & Torn*, *Sideburns* and *Bondage* largely following suit, beyond the inclusion of a single cover image culled from the music press or gig flyers. Some more artful practitioners took a much more sophisticated, image-based approach, notably Jon Savage with *London's Outrage* and Andy Palmer with *Andy Palmer's Observer*,[12] but the rough and ready cut-and-paste punk style did not become ubiquitous until punk's DIY creatives figured out ways to successfully reproduce their artwork in print, without it vanishing in a blur of Xerox toner.

Punk graphics often revealed the process of construction in the final product, enabling and encouraging others to take up the challenge to do it themselves. Cut-and-paste techniques retained marks and textures from original visual elements and didn't attempt to smooth the distinction between figure and ground, including the hard, angular borders of cut-out 'ransom note' letters, the roughly torn edges of photographs, mistakes, redactions, dirty marks, fingerprints and residue from the printing process. Such visual approaches implied directness, authenticity and an urgency of the message that superseded the desire for perfection.

Professional designers also utilised a more carefully considered and precise assembly process to create design roughs ready to pass to reprographics departments and specialist teams, or to take directly to camera, ready to make plates. In some ways, this might suggest a parallel between work by DIY amateur producers and the practices of skilled designers and artworkers in the pre-desktop publishing era. However, there are subtle, though important, differences. Each method involved cutting out visual elements – type, image, line work etc – and assembling it within a composition for reproduction. The work of professional designers and artworkers relied on craft skill and precision, with the final artwork transferred to film on one or more layers to create separate colour plates. Pre-press artworkers would use scalpels, scissors, glue, precisely engineered pens and marking tools, halftone sheets and an array of modern, technical devices to prepare high-quality photographic films ready for print. DIY punk graphics, for fanzines, flyers or independent record covers, tended more towards imprecision, where messiness, errors and dirt were all part of the punk aesthetic, with most artwork assembled on paper rather than film and usually reproduced in a single colour via the photocopier or a similar lo-tech print method. The printer may have required conversion of photographs and continuous tone work to halftones – the midtones converted into small black dots of different sizes to give the impression of a range of grey tones[13] – before running the job on press, but the DIY punk designer was not in control of (or often even aware of) that process.

Appropriation

The appropriation of visual material and the use of détournement as a subversive method was a widespread punk practice, in many ways mirroring what Hebdige described as punk's bricolage approach to dress and decoration. The first edition of the *Internationale Situationiste* journal in June 1958 provided a useful definition of the practice of détournement, though its widespread adoption by punk designers was not theorised to any great extent.

> Détournement: The integration of present or past artistic production into a superior construction of a milieu ... in a more primitive sense, détournement within the old cultural spheres is a method of propaganda, a method which testifies to the wearing out and loss of importance of those spheres.[14]

Much has been made of the supposed connection between the Situationist International and the first wave of UK punk. It is not the intention here to retread this territory in great depth, but the term détournement is useful as a summary of a method of agit-prop collage that utilises powerful media imagery to attack the core values of the status quo. Détournement also requires a strong visual signifier as a starting point – either a recognisable figure of authority or an image that represents a particular situation. The much broader notion of appropriation, when utilised by punk graphic designers within collage work, employs found images that simply reflect a social condition (television, suburbia, locality, sex, war, government, the police) or the cultural zeitgeist, with a less direct critical or political message. Punk-inspired designers made heavy use of found images, historical ephemera and contemporary news media to produce a satirical commentary on cultural traditions and practices, authority figures, political movements, religious icons and anything else that they found distasteful or objectionable.

> Punk appropriated concepts, styles, and strategies from the most diverse sources: the historical avant-gardes, student revolts, pop, guerrilla combat, fin-de-siècle ambiance, cartoon universes, and many more.[15]

Sometimes, this approach was clearly adopted to communicate a strong political or ideological message, while at others it was simply an amusing or ironic comment on the media and the emerging discourse of punk, or even the glorious serendipity of combining whatever images came to hand (Figure 2.11). Designer Rob O'Connor remembers being fascinated by some of the graphic approaches of punk groups visiting his college in Brighton in the summer of 1977.

> There was always music coming through and what was really interesting to me was seeing that the bands who played at the art college – The Damned, Buzzcocks, Banshees, Vibrators – were all bringing their own

2.11 Victim (1977), 'Strange Thing By Night', 7" single, Northern Ireland: Good Vibrations. Design by Terri Hooley, collection of the author.

graphics with them. I mean, nothing crazy, but things like the Buzzcocks posters that were all printed onto copies of the *Manchester Evening News*. And I just thought that it was so exciting to see something that genuinely was punk.[16]

A central strategy for Jamie Reid, the practice of détournement was based around the use of an iconic image, which could be appropriated as a symbol of authority, hierarchy or tradition. In the case of 'God Save The Queen', the second single by the Sex Pistols (1977), the use of an image of the head of state at a time of national celebration was highly provocative. By taking the official photographic portrait of Queen Elizabeth II that had been reproduced on everything from stamps to posters, mugs, t-shirts, badges, bunting and flags for the 1977 Silver Jubilee celebrations and adding another visual element to alter its context, the power of the original image could be subverted. The single sleeve featured the image with strips torn across the eyes and mouth, bearing the song title and name of the group, while further versions for press advertisements and publicity posters incorporated a safety pin through the Queen's lips, set against a union flag background. Reid spent a great deal of time working on variations of the image, with the safety pin version for press advertisements and posters becoming the most widely recognised (Figure 2.12).

> I must have done literally hundreds of different images around that particular photo of the Queen's face. Which was an official Cecil Beaton portrait that I got from the *Daily Express*. I did two days of photographic sessions with Carol Moss until I came up with the safety pin.[17]

Rick Poynor argues that the sleeve is an early example of postmodernist deconstruction in graphic design,[18] while Reid's graphic work has been critically acclaimed by art historians and cultural institutions including the Victoria and Albert Museum, and the National Portrait Gallery in London and the Museum of Modern Art in New York.

Much of the graphic language of punk drew on found material and either the use of collage or a contrast between image and text. The design for the Sex Pistols' fourth single 'Holidays in The Sun' (1977) features an adaptation of a holiday brochure produced by the Belgian Travel Service. Jamie Reid took the comic strip story of a family enjoying their holiday, rearranged the sequence in an irregular grid and simply replaced the words in the speech balloons with the lyrics of the song – ending with a frame of a smiling young couple, with the man repeating the song's opening lyrical refrain, 'A cheap holiday in other people's misery'. The visual language of the package holiday brochure is quite generic – the reader does not need to know that the original refers to holidays in Belgium, for instance – and Reid also adapted visual devices such as the smiling sun and the decorative type styles and colour palette of the original. Glitterbest management and Virgin Records were presented with an injunction by the owners of the plagiarised tourist brochure and the sleeve was withdrawn, with Reid being required to destroy the artwork in the presence of the company's solicitor. The single was subsequently issued in a plain white sleeve and quickly dropped out of the charts, with the original picture cover becoming a collectors' item. A similar fate beset Reid's artwork for the Sex Pistols' single 'The Great Rock'n'roll Swindle' released two years later: the sleeve featured a mock Sex Pistols credit card copied directly from the American Express card design. Once again, Virgin were forced to withdraw the sleeve, though not before around eight thousand copies had been sold.

After the Sex Pistols split in early 1978, production continued for the film *The Great Rock'n'roll Swindle*, with group members Sid Vicious, Paul

2.12 Jamie Reid, Sex Pistols *God Save The Queen* poster 1977. Image Jamie Reid © Sex Pistols Residuals. Courtesy John Marchant Gallery.

Cook and Steve Jones still involved in the soundtrack. Jamie Reid was part of the production team and his graphics during this period reflect a growing dissatisfaction with the music industry and deliberate antagonism towards the group's label, Virgin Records, and its owner Richard Branson. While many of the covers for later Sex Pistols records had high reproduction values – single sleeves were full colour and featured a series of stills from the film – Reid went back to basics with posters and press ads, using crude collage and distressed photocopy techniques. He even revisited the swastika – a symbol whose relationship to punk had been short-lived, usually misconstrued and ultimately discredited several years earlier – in a series of collages, including one swastika symbol made up of cannabis leaves beside the Virgin logo and the phrase 'Never trust a hippie' (one of many direct attacks on Branson). The final straw came with the release of the *Flogging a Dead Horse* singles compilation album in October 1979. For his initial design, Reid – along with his regular collaborator, photographer Trevor Key – simply took the covers of the two previous Sex Pistols albums, *Never Mind the Bollocks* and *The Great Rock'n'roll Swindle* and scrawled the new title on top of the original artwork. The design was rejected by Virgin, so Reid found a stock image of a model from a cheap agency and based the cover on that.

> It was just taking the piss out of my own artwork and out of the whole Sex Pistols phenomenon. I got paid £2,000 for five minutes work. When Virgin rejected it, Trevor Key and I found the most tacky photo we could find of a model from a tacky agency. We just used the most boring sort of rope Letraset ... Like the swastika sleeves and the Who/Monkees sleeve, it was a final fuck off to Virgin.[19]

During the early 1980s, the political agenda of the Conservative government had a massive impact on the UK and was widely perceived to be both authoritarian and discriminatory. Unemployment soared, while a major overhaul of the welfare and tax systems had a direct impact on young people and the poor. It was natural, therefore, that Prime Minister Margaret Thatcher should take on a central role as a negative figure of authority within oppositional politics and satire and within punk's language of protest. Conservative Secretary of State for Employment Norman Tebbit put forward a range of new, hard-line rules regarding access to unemployment benefits, with the aim of forcing young people into work – a move which also resulted in attacks from both the opposition and protest groups across the country. The 1982 Falklands War resulted in a rift between pro- and anti-war activists and these attitudes were also played out within the punk scene. Thatcher and her cabinet provided a common enemy for many punk groups and fans and their iconic status as the bêtes noires of the political underclass was utilised in countless song lyrics and record sleeves.

2.13 Crass (1984), 'You're Already Dead', 7" single, United Kingdom: Crass Records. Design by Gee Vaucher/Crass, collection of the author.

In much the same way that the Silver Jubilee of 1977 had provided the Sex Pistols with an iconic image to attack, many 1980s punks took Margaret Thatcher as a figurehead for their collective anger. Anarcho-punk scene leaders Crass made repeated lyrical references to Thatcher and the Conservative government, though they didn't spare any political parties or activist movements of left or right from their barbed critique. The sleeve to the 1984 Crass single 'You're Already Dead', designed by Gee Vaucher, featured images of Thatcher and Defence Secretary Michael Heseltine, with Thatcher's eyes and Heseltine's mouth crudely scratched out (Figure 2.13).

Parody and satire

Humour was another key weapon in the punk armoury.[20] Beneath all the rhetoric and 'shocking' behaviour, the early scene in the United Kingdom displayed a deep-seated, ironic intelligence, played out in interviews, lyrics, performance and the personas of leading figures such as Johnny Rotten, Hugh Cornwell, Captain Sensible and Rat Scabies. Once the media had seized upon the followers of this strange, new subculture as the bêtes noires of the conservative establishment, punk became a subject for comedians, cartoonists and cultural commentators to mock and abuse, though in practice such a strategy was doomed to failure. The scene was already deeply self-aware and parodic, with a keen sense of the absurdity of its own rebellion and an accompanying, self-effacing wit. Punk's embrace of parody, pastiche and irony was played out in lyrics, dress, interviews, artwork and music. These kinds of strategies were not unfamiliar to artists and designers, particularly those whose work engaged with political agitation and protest. The long tradition of satirical insurrection, from Dada to Duchamp, the Surrealists to the Situationist International, offered a rich resource for punk graphic designers and visual communicators to plunder.

In a similar vein to punk songwriters reflecting on the history, philosophy and future direction of the subculture, the use of meta-punk references within punk sleeve graphics was not unusual. During the early years of UK punk, they could imply that the group were a part of the emerging scene or could be used as parody to satirise the visual language of punk from both inside and outside the subculture. As the movement progressed and became more widely recognised, later punk sleeves incorporated visual references to earlier punk icons as either a form of homage or as a negative comment on the selling out of punk's original ideology and the ways in which those who had originally attacked the establishment had become a part of the establishment themselves.

In one notable example, Gee Vaucher created a satirical image which combined punk icons and authority figures for the Crass single 'Bloody Revolutions' in 1980. The image, an exquisitely detailed gouache illustration, is based on a publicity photograph of the Sex Pistols from 1977, with the individual's heads substituted by those of the Queen, Pope John Paul II, the statue of justice and Margaret Thatcher. The record sleeve folds out to reveal a poster of the original image, which sets the figures in the context of a decaying street scene (Figure 2.14).[21] This complex image works on several levels. Primarily, it satirises the Sex Pistols as recuperated figures of authority and the state, passing an ironic comment on their failure – and that of the punk establishment – to live up to a revolutionary ideal. However, the heads of the figures also represent a détournement of those icons, a more formal and direct critique within the context of a punk rock record. Crass strongly criticised the failure of the punk movement in

2.14 Crass (1980), 'Bloody Revolutions', 7" single, United Kingdom: Crass Records. Fold-out poster. Gouache painting by Gee Vaucher, collection of the artist.

general to engage with a political direction, satirising The Clash, the Sex Pistols and other punk heroes in their lyrics, and this attitude was reflected in their artwork.

One particularly striking and original sleeve was designed by a group of teenagers from Torquay, Das Schnitz, who released one EP, *4AM*, on the Ellie Jay label in 1979. The group couldn't afford to produce a sleeve for their record, so they decided on an unusual strategy which – unknowingly to them – takes Jamie Reid's concept for the last Sex Pistols album one stage further. The group got hold of record sleeves for a range of contemporary chart releases – including releases by Chaka Khan, Darts, Chic, The Shadows and Funkadelic – and wrote their own titles on the covers with marker pens, together with comments related to the wording on the original sleeve (Figure 2.15). Das Schnitz guitarist Nadi Jahangiri remembers it was a spur of the minute decision.

> From what I remember, incredibly there was a stall at a local market that just sold picture sleeves in bulk from singles of the day. I can't think if he sold anything else but that's where we got the sleeves. It was purely a financial decision as there was not enough money to get our own sleeves printed. We then defaced them one Saturday afternoon at the drummer's house … Chaka Khan's record label wrote to us threatening to sue us if we carried on selling the single in her sleeve, but nothing came of it.[22]

2.15 Das Schnitz (1979), *4AM*, 7″ vinyl EP, United Kingdom: Ellie Jay. Design by Nadi Jahangiri /Das Schnitz, collection of the author.

Many punk-related graphic designers employed parody, irony and what might be termed a form of self-referential intertextuality in their work. While the notion of détournement suggests a politically charged, subversive intent, much punk graphic design appropriation was simply playful and witty, utilising visual material from advertising, the media and found photography to provide cultural context and a sense of common understanding through which to bond with its audience. The image wasn't chosen to denote a specific person or place, it was the environment that they were situated within, a shared cultural history. Other artists and designers chose to comment ironically on their own status and the nature of the commercial music business. A playful inversion of graphic information and the visual deconstruction of the usually invisible aspects of record cover design also forms the central element on the XTC album *Go2*, designed by legendary music graphics studio Hipgnosis. Using clever copywriting, the text on the cover states; 'This is a Record Cover. This writing is the Design upon the record cover. The Design is to help Sell the record'.[23] The text continues in a similar vein, informing the reader that they are being lured into buying a product.

> what we are really suggesting is that you are FOOLISH to buy or not buy an album merely as a consequence of the design on its cover. This is a con because if you agree then you'll probably like this writing – which is the cover design – and hence the album inside.[24]

The postmodern consumer dilemma exposed.

Collage and photomontage

Extending from the appropriation of single images, many amateur designers chose collage as a relatively simple graphic method for the creation of artwork that was intended to offer a critical, or sometimes humorous, commentary. Whereas détournement usually centred on a single appropriated image, collage was often more ambiguous, offering a broader thematic context – consumerism, authority figures, popular music, television and popular culture – to vent against. Collage also featured heavily in the developing visual language of punk fanzines. It was relatively easy to cut or tear out photographs from newspapers and to arrange them on the page to say something vaguely critical about British (or US) culture, the media, history or politics. Handily, many photographs were already printed as halftone images, making them much easier to reproduce with a photocopier while subtly revealing their source (the news media) at the same time. The resulting critique could often be less barbed and more unfocused than many of the leading examples of punk détournement, but collage could be an effective tool for projecting a more general sense of agitation or dissatisfaction.

> Cut and paste as either collage or montage, combined with overarching strategies of visual appropriation, thrived as a punk practice for obvious reasons. It fell neatly in line with the punk DIY ethos of downplaying or obliterating expertise (music in the first instance, painterly traditions in the second) and celebrating auto-didacticism. In terms of practicality, the source materials were free and plentiful, and tools of use rarely extended beyond a scalpel or scissors and pot of glue.[25]

The art of collage normally involves combining two-dimensional visual material from a variety of sources to create a new whole that reveals its construction and does not result in a single, unified image. Strictly speaking, most punk collage employed found photographs, often sourced from books, magazines and the news media, but few other graphic or illustrative elements. As such, it could be said to overlap with montage, where a single coherent whole is constructed from several separate images to create a dramatic effect, and with photomontage, which has its roots in lens-based practice. While Jamie Reid's work included numerous examples of détournement and collage, utilising a variety of visual and graphic source material, Linder Sterling was perhaps the leading pioneer in what might be termed punk montage as an intricate, photorealistic practice. Sterling drew inspiration from Dada collagists John Heartfield and Hannah Höch, creating complex visual assemblages that combined pornographic images with painstakingly cut-out interior design spaces, household objects and domestic appliances from homewares catalogues and women's magazines (Figure 2.16). An exhibition of Heartfield's work at the Institute of Contemporary Arts, London, in the summer of 1977 has been cited as providing inspiration by several punk artists and designers including Jonh Ingham and Jon Savage, whose *London's Burning* and *London's Outrage* fanzines adopted a more complex visual approach than many of their punk counterparts. Art historian Dawn Ades had published the first edition of her acclaimed book on the subject, *Photomontage*, in 1976, reflecting an interest in collage, montage and photomontage spanning both art colleges and the wider public.[26] Along with Herbert Spencer's classic book on the history of early modernist graphic design and typography, *Pioneers of Modern Typography*,[27] in drawing together examples of work by George Grosz, John Heartfield, Hannah Höch, Raoul Hausmann and El Lissitzky, among others, Ades' book had a significant impact on a generation of upcoming, punk-era designers, particularly those at art school in the mid-1970s.

Though lacking the graphic skill and sensibility of Reid or Sterling, early examples of punk collage and montage in record sleeve design include the *Youthanasia* EP by The Pigs (1977), 'Put You in the Picture' by PVC2 (1977), 'System' by Front (1978) and 'Defiant Pose', the second single by The Cortinas. Of these, the Pigs sleeve is by far the most basic, combining eight crudely cut out hexagonal images of faces, some taken from recent horror films and contemporary news stories, along with a photograph of two policemen, a close-up image of a tower block and a union flag all arranged on a black background (Figure 2.17). Band name and song titles are overlaid with irregularly cut white backgrounds. Designed by Tim Clifford and Roy Savage, the visual message – if one exists – is hard to discern. The PVC2 sleeve is more sophisticated. Printed in black and white, the arrangement features a degree of visual harmony, with darker sections top left and bottom right and a hierarchy of elements including a screaming face, a woman's torso and a wounded man's head, set against torn-out text with hand-rendered lettering.[28] The Front single was released by former Sex Pistols producer Dave Goodman's label, The Label, and featured a more complex design still. Tightly cropped cuttings from newspapers, archive photographs, cartoons and comics are overlaid with red, green and yellow typographic elements and silhouettes

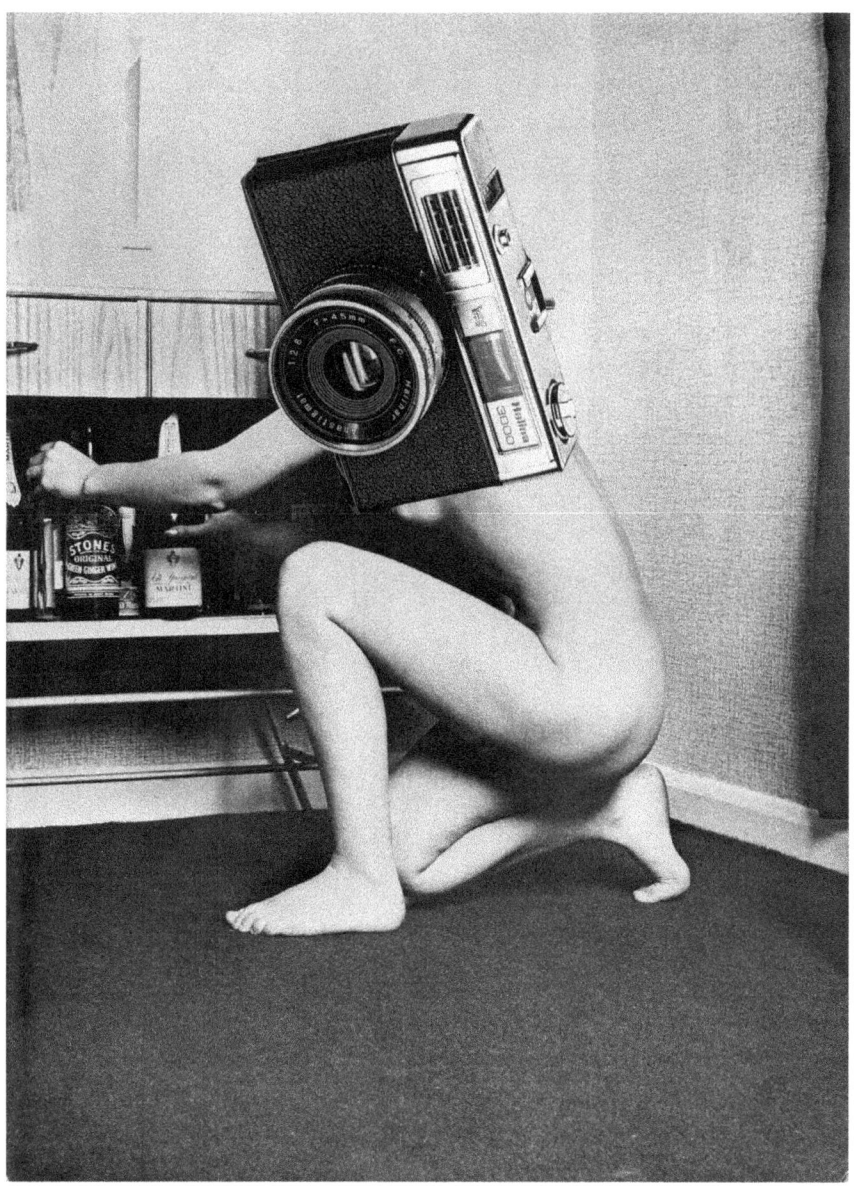

2.16 Linder, Pretty Girls, 1977. Photomontage. Courtesy of the artist and Stuart Shave/Modern Art.

of fighter jets. There is a clear sense of visual harmony in the design, which is simply credited to Not Bad. Several steps further up the punk montage ladder of sophistication, the Cortinas single cover belies the professional team behind its creation through its relatively complex, though still punk-inflected and aesthetically raw, visual construction (Figure 2.18).

2.17 The Pigs (1977), *Youthanasia*, 7" vinyl EP, United Kingdom: New Bristol Records. Design by Tim Clifford and Roy Savage, collection of the author.

The cover was designed by TCP, a short-lived alternative moniker adopted by high-profile design group Hipgnosis, the initials standing for (Storm) Thorgerson, (Peter) Christopherson, and (Aubrey) Powell.

Gee Vaucher also utilised collage and montage techniques at times, though much of her work was created by hand, offering a degree of photorealism through her meticulously crafted drawing technique. Vaucher inspired a generation of what would become known retrospectively as anarcho-punk artists to mimic her style, though nearly all employed rough montage techniques using images cut from newspapers, books and magazines and lacked any sense of the finesse and expertise of the original artist. This graphic language was especially dominant in punk fanzine culture in the early 1980s as anarcho-punk and hardcore scenes started to proliferate and a consensus of lyrical and visual messaging

2.18 The Cortinas (1977), 'Defiant Pose', 7" single, United Kingdom: Step Forward Records. Design by TCP © Mark Perry. Collection of the author.

about war, the police, militarism, the state, global politics and animal rights prevailed.[29] Meanwhile, a new movement shaped by younger punk groups and fans coming of age in the late 1970s heralded a resurgence of interest in the subculture at the turn of the decade, though by now punk fashions and visual styles were becoming far more tightly constrained and factionalised. Younger designers – often members of bands or their close friends – were employed to create record covers, flyers and other graphic ephemera, often drawing upon earlier punk graphic conventions and the convenience and immediacy of hand drawing, collage and Letraset typography.

By the early 1980s, punk collage styles were widely embedded in the subculture as a visual convention for punk flyers, fanzines and record covers. Sleeves for The Exploited's 'Exploited Barmy Army' (1980) and

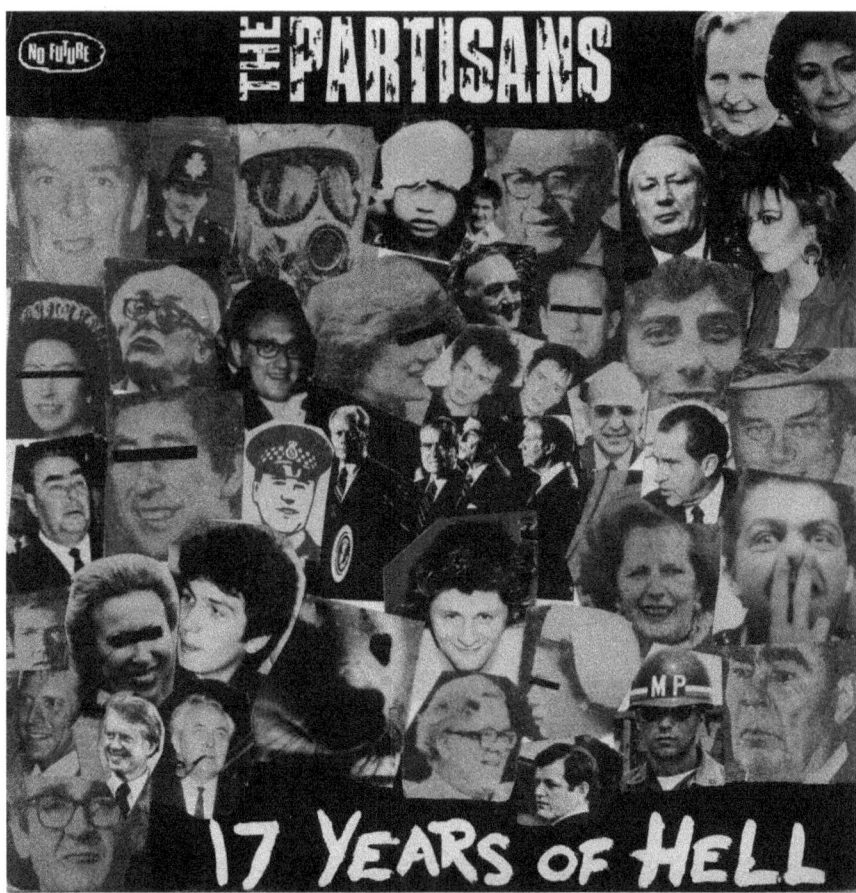

2.19 The Partisans (1982), '17 Years of Hell', 7" single, United Kingdom: No Future. Collection of the author.

The Partisans' '17 Years of Hell' (1982) feature collaged photographs of well-known figures from the media and popular culture, interspersed with photos of the band or their fans. The Partisans sleeve features politicians including Margaret Thatcher, Harold Wilson, Ted Heath, Michael Foot, Edwina Curry, US Presidents Richard Nixon, Jimmy Carter and Ronald Reagan and former Soviet President Leonid Brezhnev, together with members of the Royal Family (Princess Anne, the Princess of Wales, Prince Charles, Prince Philip and the Queen), and celebrities such as US television soap character J. R. Ewing, Telly Savalas, Sid Vicious, Johnny Rotten and Barry Manilow (Figure 2.19). These are mixed with further anonymous faces, a baby seal, images of policemen and snapshots of the group themselves. The eyes of each member of the Royal Family have been obscured with a black line – a direct visual reference to Reid's 'God Save The Queen'

2.20 Poster promoting the compilation album *New Wave*, released by Vertigo Records, 1977. Photography by Peter Kodick, from the collection of Andrew Krivine.

sleeve. Apart from this and the inclusion of Johnny Rotten and Sid Vicious, a more subtle meta-punk reference is communicated through the inclusion of a photograph of London Councillor Bernard Brook Partridge, who had appeared on television in 1977 to denounce the punk movement with the infamous words 'the Sex Pistols would be vastly improved by sudden death, they are the antithesis of humankind. I would like to see someone dig a huge hole and bury the lot of them in it'.[30]

Signs of distress

The punk design brief embodied visual strategies to project a sense of distortion, disruption and decay. Punk was an unholy alliance between the dirty, rough and ready, cheap and instant. Common visual tropes included collage, détournement, parody, pastiche, torn edges, limited colour palettes,[31] a self-conscious model of DIY and the use of instant, hands-on tools and techniques for origination and reproduction (the photocopier, rubber stamps, stencils and direct printing techniques). At the same time, punk graphic designers embraced the ephemeral, employing simple tools and mark-making techniques that indicated distortion, decay, rawness and urgency. Visual styles in early punk graphics embodied a timeworn aesthetic through graphic techniques ranging from simple DIY mark-making to carefully constructed images that project a sense of decay while at the same time disguising their complex origins.

The debut single by The Clash, 'White Riot' (1977), features an unusual group photograph, with the three key members of the band shot from behind, their hands placed high against a wall in a pose reminiscent of a police search or arrest.[32] The photograph was taken by *Melody Maker* journalist Caroline Coon in the band's rehearsal space, Rehearsal Rehearsals, in Camden, North London. While the stance of the group members is a key consideration, the graphic treatment of the photograph should not be overlooked. The image was reproduced in high contrast, heavily distressed monochrome, printed in black against a bright green background for the promotional poster and in green for the single cover. Both feature the name of the group overlaid in heavily distressed custom type (printed in red on the poster and magenta on the record cover) at an angle to the bottom right corner, knocked out to a white base.[33] The group members' clothing is hand painted with polemical slogans, some relating to song lyrics: 1977, Sten Guns in Knightsbridge, White Riot and Heavy Duty Discipline.

The cover of the band's self-titled debut album, *The Clash* (1977), also centres on a photograph of the group, though it also features a range of visual metaphors to communicate rough and ready, instant graphics. The front cover is based on a photograph by Kate Simon depicting the three main group members, Paul Simonon, Joe Strummer and Mick Jones in an alleyway adjacent to their rehearsal studio. Wearing suitably punk stage clothing, the musicians look directly at the camera without smiling. The connotations of the image are clear: punks are embattled urban survivors, their territory the rundown city street. The photograph is reproduced in stark, high contrast black and white, with all the midtones stripped out through a deliberately heavy halftone image treatment. The customised typography for the band name, mirroring the 'White Riot' sleeve is overlaid in a bright orange/pink spot colour, with the background knocked out to base white card through a photographic process in the pre-press studio. All the visual elements are offset against a dark green background on the left and right sides, with a graphic representation of torn edges at an angle to the vertical.

The back cover, meanwhile, features a photograph of police running in the street, taken by Rocco Macauley during the Notting Hill Carnival riots in the summer of 1976, with a similar impression of torn edges set at an angle to the horizontal. The photograph is again rendered in extremely high contrast, with typewritten song titles and album credits overlaid in pink, again knocked out quite roughly against the green background, together with some airbrushed pink and orange splashes of colour beneath the black print layer. While the album cover offers several graphic references to the visual language of punk fanzines and the DIY revolution, this is a sophisticated graphic composition that sets out to play down the technical skill of the designer and the range of options available in print production. The raw simplicity of the colour palette also belies the fact that, even working within budget and material constraints the in-house designers at CBS, Janusz Guttner and senior art director Rosłav Szaybo, could have produced a high-quality, photographic cover that reflected standard rock music conventions of the time: other contemporary designs by Szaybo and Guttner included albums by Sailor, Johnny Mathis, The New Seekers and children's television litter pickers The Wombles.

Press advertisements further compounded the complex relationship between professional design and the DIY punk fanzine aesthetic. Since newspaper print production was dominated by the trade unions, adverts were almost always created by registered pre-press artwork studios. As such, they were one step removed even from the creative teams at the record labels. A full-page press advert for *The Clash* published in November 1977 featured rough, black and white images of the front and back cover along with handwritten titles: 'The album of '77', 'the one they are afraid of!' and 'How can you face '78 without it?' (Figure 2.21). A more complex, two-colour advert for the third single by The Stranglers, 'Something Better Change', centred on stylised ransom note typography and typeset phrases mimicking newspaper headlines alongside hand-drawn shading and handwritten details: 'available from Sat 23 July' and 'in pic sleeve!' (Figure 2.22).

2.21 Press advert for The Clash, *The Clash*, *New Musical Express*, 19 November 1977. Collection of the author.

2.22 Press advert for The Stranglers, 'Something Better Change', *New Musical Express*, 23 July 1977. Collection of the author.

Art history

The tension between those early punk participants who had experienced an art school education and those whose interest in the scene stemmed from the context of contemporary rock and pop was played out in the lyrics and graphics of some of the pioneering groups. Several art school graduates and dropouts within the early punk movement cited art historical references in their work. Adam and the Ants – whose singer, Stuart Goddard had attended Hornsey School of Art – sang about the Futurists in the song 'Animals & Men', first recorded in July 1978.

> Marinetti, Boccioni, Carra, Balla, Palasechi!
> Futurist manifesto![34]

Meanwhile, an Irish new wave group from Dún Laoghaire, The Boomtown Rats, had relocated to London and were making significant inroads into the British charts. The group made a knowing reference to Marcel Duchamp's *L.H.O.O.Q.*, as well as commenting on widely criticised links between punk and Nazi imagery in the lyrics to their third hit single, 'She's So Modern' (1978).

> Jean confided to me
> She's Mona Lisa's biggest fan
> She drew a moustache on her face
> She's always seen her as a man[35]

The single reached number twelve in the national charts and the group even performed the song live on *Top of The Pops* three times between April and May 1978. The group's second album, *A Tonic for The Troops*, hit the Top Ten in June 1978, but the rather obscure lyrical reference was most probably lost on many listeners. Similarly, the adoption of a John Heartfield political photomontage for the cover of the German language Siouxsie and the Banshees single 'Mittageisen' (1979) could easily have been misconstrued by an unknowing audience as simply a further link between punk visual style and Nazi iconography.

In another direct art historical 'lift', the debut single by Generation X, 'Your Generation' (1977), featured a sleeve designed by Barney Bubbles that mimicked typographic experiments produced by El Lissitzky, Henryk Berlewi and the Russian Constructivists in the 1920s. Bubbles was no stranger to raiding the art historical image box. His sleeve for the second album by The Damned, *Music for Pleasure* (1977), was an abstract graphic illustration of the group in the visual style of Wassily Kandinsky. Rick Poynor argues that the cover 'is not exactly a parody – more a tribute that gleefully embraces its source material'.[36] The album was originally intended to be a crossover between punk and the group's original love of psychedelia and was produced by Pink Floyd drummer Nick Mason, but the resulting confused musical direction was subject to widespread criticism. Other sleeves produced by Bubbles for the Stiff and Radar labels for Elvis Costello, Nick Lowe, Ian Dury and The Rumour also utilised graceful, curved arcs, ellipses and lines combined with strong, flat colours and playfully constructed images, perhaps saying more about the signature style of the designer than the individual artists and groups. Meanwhile, his famous 'blockhead' square logotype for Ian Dury and The Blockheads bore a striking similarity to the typographic identity of the Left Book Club, a left-wing publishing group that was active in the United Kingdom between 1936 and 1948.

This mining of earlier typographic styles continued in the work of Peter Saville at Factory Records, while others including Neville Brody, Malcolm Garrett, Vaughan Oliver and Chris Bigg also caught the zeitgeist. Garrett had studied typography at Reading but left after one year to join the graphic design programme at Manchester Polytechnic, taking with him a copy of Herbert Spencer's *Pioneers of Modern Typography*,[37] featuring work by Herbert Bayer, Jan Tschichold, El Lissitzky and Alexander Rodchenko. The book's influence on a generation of young British designers at the end of the 1970s was subsequently acknowledged by Rick Poynor in his summary of appropriation as a design method.[38] For his part, Saville paid homage to Tschichold's two bodies of work that ranged from an early embrace of asymmetry and sans serif modernism to centred styles and serif typefaces later in his career.[39]

Other punk sleeve designers also drew on art and design references from the early twentieth century. Jill Mumford made links to the work of Surrealist artist and photographer Man Ray in her later sleeves for The Skids, though her work could be seen as more of an homage than a direct appropriation. Her sleeves for the 1980 sequence of singles by the group, 'Circus Games', 'Goodbye Civilian' and 'Woman in Winter' featured abstract images based on carefully airbrushed, curved lines and forms, with the accompanying description 'from a Man Ray Aerograph'. It should be noted, however, that these examples were operating within a wider and more sophisticated musical and visual arena than earlier punk output. Manchester's Factory Records, Joy Division and New Order were central to the evolution of a post-punk identity and Peter Saville's record cover and poster designs helped to define a new era.[40] The surrounding discourse in the music press attempted to raise the intellectual bar away from 'outdated' and inarticulate punk themes and into an aspirational new decade. The Skids had also by this time attempted to move away from their earlier pop punk identity towards a more articulate (and verbose) engagement with the developing post-punk and New Romantic scenes.

By the early 1980s, the employment of knowing art historical references was becoming something of a cliché. In 1983, Jon Savage wrote a polemical article in *The Face*, arguing that the by now rather lazy act of copying earlier art conventions had exhausted its original intentions.

> Perhaps the most irritating manifestation of the Culture Club is the way that the whole of 20th Century Art and – more recently – any amount of ethnic material have been used with increasing desperation to tart up product that has increasingly less meaning.[41]

Designer, industry, technology

Punk graphic design, then, featured several common themes that were put into practice by both amateur, would-be-designers and experienced music industry design professionals seeking to tap into the emerging visual styles of the subculture. The other half of the equation related to the technology available to designers for artwork construction, manipulation and – importantly – print reproduction. Simplicity, immediacy and an abrasive, raw energy were more than conceptual approaches drawn from the designer's imagination, or from a sense of art historical nostalgia or homage. They fitted punk's musical, sartorial and philosophical ethos, while neatly reflecting the economic, material and technological constraints within which many punk graphic designers were working.

The notion of a direct association between work by prominent punk designers such as Jamie Reid and the emergence of a *new* visual language of parody or agit-prop does merit critical scrutiny. Indeed, many of the techniques adopted by Reid were already widely accepted as the natural graphic languages of anger and protest. The *samizdat* tradition of subversive, lo-tech graphic material disseminated through personal networks, originally a feature of the Russian underground where the term denoted the clandestine copying and distribution of government-suppressed literature or other media, led to the evolution of a particular visual style. The natural limitations of simple tools and materials, as well as the quick production of graphic work by untrained designers, led to a repetition of graphic conventions: single or two-colour artwork, hand folding and binding techniques and hand-rendered, stencilled or typewritten text. These basic graphic elements were also key to avant-garde art movements during the early part of the twentieth century and became closely associated with the visual communication of subversion or political protest. Reid's awareness of the work of the Situationist International and the late hippie underground in Europe and the USA may have led him towards more informed versions of agit-prop graphic material, but many other punk designers made no such historical allusions – the look was simple, dirty and aggressive, and it meant 'punk'.

Notes

1. Bestley and Burgess, 'Fan artefacts and doing it themselves'.
2. Kevin Lycett (2000), email interview with the author, 4 February.
3. The front cover also lists the names of the songs on the EP, introduced by a self-referential text that describes the cover as 'the sleeve for a Gang of Four recording of …'.
4. Bob Last (2024), telephone interview with the author, 9 February.
5. Designed by Paul Renner in 1927.
6. Following the critical success of their debut EP, Gang of Four signed to EMI and continued the conceptual theme on the cover of their debut album, *Entertainment!*, art directed by band members Andy Gill and Jon King, this time featuring a comic strip-style illustration of an exchange between a stereotypical 'cowboy' and 'indian'.
7. Television Personalities (1978), *Where's Bill Grundy Now?*, vinyl EP, United Kingdom: Kings Road.
8. Russ Bestley (2018), 'Design it yourself? Punk's division of labour', *Punk & Post-Punk* 7:1, pp. 7–24.
9. Chris Treweek and Jonathan Zeitlyn, with the Islington Bus Co. (1983), *The Alternative Printing Handbook*, Harmondsworth: Penguin, pp. 82–83.
10. Treweek and Zeitlyn, *The Alternative Printing Handbook*, p. 72.
11. Fletcher, *The Best of Jamming!*, p. 21.
12. Worley, *Zerox Machine*, pp. 47–48.
13. During the halftone process, lighter areas of the photograph are converted to small black dots on a white background, known as highlight dots, while darker areas are reproduced through small white dots on a black background, termed shadow dots.
14. Iwona Blazwick (ed.) (1989), *An Endless Adventure … An Endless Passion … An Endless Banquet: A Situationist Scrapbook*, London: ICA Publications, p. 22.
15. Skov, *Punk Art History*, pp. 145–146.
16. Rob O'Connor (2023), email interview with the author, 18 October.
17. Reid and Savage, *Up They Rise*, p. 65. The original photograph was not, in fact, by Cecil Beaton – it was Peter Grugeon's officially commissioned Silver Jubilee portrait of the Queen. Carol Moss was a photography technician at the London College of Printing.
18. Rick Poynor (2003), *No More Rules: Graphic Design and Postmodernism*, London: Laurence King, p. 39
19. Reid and Savage, *Up They Rise*, p. 104.
20. Russ Bestley (2018), 'Holiday in Cambodia: Punk's acerbic comedy', in Krista Bonello Rutter Giappone, Fred Francis and Iain Mackenzie (eds), *Comedy and Critical Thought: Laughter as Resistance*, London: Rowman & Littlefield International, pp. 165–183.
21. Vaucher, *Crass Art and Other Pre Post-Modernist Monsters*, p. 44. See also Binns, *Gee Vaucher: Beyond Punk*, pp. 108–109.
22. Nadi Jahangiri (2005), email interview with the author, 14 March.
23. Russ Bestley (2013), 'Art attacks and killing jokes: The graphic language of punk humour', *Punk & Post-Punk* 2:3, pp. 231–267.
24. XTC (1978), *Go2*, vinyl album, United Kingdom: Virgin Records.
25. Ian Trowell (2020), 'Counter-realities and conflicted place: Gee Vaucher's *The Feeding of the Five Thousand* in the punk art tradition', *Punk & Post-Punk* 9:3, pp. 402–403.
26. Dawn Ades (1976), *Photomontage*, London: Thames & Hudson.
27. Herbert Spencer (1969), *Pioneers of Modern Typography*, London: Lund Humphries Publishers.

28 PVC2 emerged from professional glam rock band Slik and featured soon-to-be rock superstar Midge Ure, with the single released by Zoom, a Scottish independent label later affiliated to Arista Records.
29 Russ Bestley and Rebecca Binns (2018), 'The evolution of an anarcho-punk narrative (1978–84)', in Subcultures Network (eds), *Ripped, Torn and Cut*, pp. 129–149.
30 *Punk Rock* (1977), dir. Roger Casstles and Derek Towers, episode of *Brass Tacks* (3 August, BBC Television).
31 Limited colour palettes were often determined by budgets, technology and resources, particularly in relation to punk fanzines and independent or low-key single sleeves. However, a limited use of colour could sometimes reflect a design choice, where a designer wanted to project a sense of authenticity and/or draw conscious parallels with the DIY scene.
32 Matthew Worley suggests a subtle reference to Joe Gibbs and The Professionals' *State of Emergency* reggae album from 1976. Worley, *No Future*, p. 11.
33 Designed by Sebastian Conran, this was the closest the group ever came to a standardised logo. The same distressed type was used on the following single, 'London's Burning', and the debut album, *The Clash*, but was then replaced with a series of different designs including several variations of an upper-case stencil typeface that proved popular with fans and merchandisers for its ease of reproduction.
34 Adam and the Ants (1978), 'Animals & Men', *Dirk Wears White Sox*, vinyl album, United Kingdom: Do It.
35 The Boomtown Rats (1978), 'She's So Modern', *A Tonic for The Troops*, vinyl album, United Kingdom: Ensign.
36 Poynor, *No More Rules*, p. 73.
37 Spencer, *Pioneers of Modern Typography*.
38 Poynor, *No More Rules*, p. 73.
39 King, *Designed by Peter Saville*, p. 12.
40 King, *Designed by Peter Saville*.
41 Savage, 'The age of plunder', p. 48.

3

Design it yourself: the punk diaspora

Punk scenes in the United Kingdom were neither uniform nor static and were subject to rapid and dramatic change over time, particularly as local scenes sprang up across the country. Indeed, punk's evolutionary diaspora was as much geographical as it was temporal and aesthetic. While cultural theorists had traditionally limited subcultures to a tightly delineated set of entrepreneurs, artists, locations and innovators, and within a narrow time frame, later commentators have acknowledged the ways in which they migrate, adapt and change. Dick Hebdige's concern with the notion of authenticity and the innovators of the punk movement, drawing on subcultural theories developed at the Centre for Contemporary Cultural Studies in Birmingham, was later brought into sharp critical focus by Gary Clarke:

> Hebdige concerns himself only with the innovative punks, the original 'authentic' and 'genuine' punks concentrated in the London area. This is characteristic of most of the Centre's subcultural theory – it explains why certain youths develop a particular style say, in the East End, but youth subcultures elsewhere are usually dismissed as part of the incorporation and containment of the subversive implications of that style. We are never given reasons why youths 'in the sticks' are inclined to adopt a particular style. Hebdige's analysis begins with a heatwave in Oxford Street and ends in a Kings Road boutique.[1]

Punk scenes evolved over time and place. Equally, punk graphic practices embraced both the amateur and the professional, do-it-yourself and the traditional music industry. Lauded artists who played big venues in large cities operated alongside unheralded, largely unknown teenagers in Britain's faraway towns, each creating their own interpretation of punk. Visual conventions also varied over time – while certain themes and processes continued to resonate, new styles emerged to reflect new punk subgenres. In many ways, the subculture operated in waves, both temporal and geographical, and punk in London in 1976 was quite a different entity to punk in Sunderland, Brighton, Bristol or Swansea in the early 1980s.

Punk and post-punk

By the late 1970s, UK punk had morphed into a range of scenes, all competing for attention and driven as much by commercial interests as by the groups themselves. The early punk umbrella had contained a wide variety of styles and approaches, though most had not been named or marketed as such. As the incandescent flash of the initial punk explosion was becoming tarnished in the media, early participants were moving on to seek out new styles (with many developing successful careers within the established music industry), and a new generation of punks moved in to take up the reins. Some of the resulting shifts were aesthetic and stylistic, some commercially driven, while others were ideological or political – feminism and gender politics took a more central role than previously, alongside a more considered and critical approach towards race and class disparities. Punk morphed into new wave, hardcore, street punk, Two Tone, anarcho-punk and goth, and continued to fragment and shatter as time went on. The relationship between the music graphics profession and these diverse scenes also varied enormously, with major label investment during punk's initial peak period eventually tailing off and a transition towards low-key, do-it-yourself outfits and smaller, independent design studios servicing a variety of artists and labels. Ironically, while many of these stylistic elements, from radio-friendly pop sheen to abrasive, avant-garde experimentation, football terrace glam rock to overt political dogma, had been a part of punk all along, their separation into different punk subgenres only hastened the development of a range of visual and aesthetic templates that were to become further entrenched over time.

One key change centred on a stylistic expansion from what had by now become a core set of punk musical and visual conventions, leading to the development of what has retrospectively become known as 'post-punk'.[2] Unfortunately, one book by music journalist Simon Reynolds, *Rip it Up and Start Again: Post-Punk 1978–84*, seems to have set various stylistic boundaries in place, though they are largely based on Reynolds' personal tastes and preferences, rather than more objective criteria.[3] At its most basic level, post-punk was just another strand in the diversification of punk, mixing elements from earlier rock styles (variously including progressive rock, the electronic avant-garde, Krautrock, reggae, funk and dub) with a punk-infused sensibility. If there was such a thing as an *ethos* of post-punk, then it wasn't markedly much different to an ethos of punk, beside perhaps adopting more overt and personal expressions regarding the politics of identity than the monolithic Rock Against Racism and Rock Against Sexism campaigns of the past. Several key artists and groups that have been described as post-punk did make a clear break with earlier punk, both musically and visually, but their overlap with the early punk scene demonstrates the problem with definitions, particularly the temporality implied by the term 'post' (some writers have even attributed a post-punk definition to artists whose work was created some years before the initial punk explosion). The debut album by Wire, *Pink Flag*, was released in November 1977 on the Harvest label, an imprint more usually associated with the likes of Pink Floyd, Soft Machine and the Electric Light Orchestra. With an abstract cover image of a flagpole set against a plain blue sky,[4] the album's twenty-one tracks reflected brevity, speed and simplicity as founding principles. Over the following two years, Wire shifted styles to embrace synthesisers and longer, more ambient compositions built around space and repetition, further reinforcing the comments by some of their critics that they were a continuation of an earlier era of progressive rock, rather than a break with the past.

Another group tagged by critics in the music press with prog rock sensibilities, Magazine, released their debut single 'Shot By Both Sides' in January 1978,[5] with the album *Real Life* following five months later.[6] Formed by original Buzzcocks singer Howard Devoto, Magazine were unapologetic in their desire to move beyond the narrow confines of punk rock as it began to become commercially and artistically codified. Siouxsie and the Banshees had also moved on from their early approach by the time they signed to Polydor Records and released their debut single, 'Hong Kong Garden', and album, *The Scream*, in the Autumn of 1978. The group's sound was angular, jarring and discordant, and the accompanying cover designs by Jill Mumford[7] further emphasised the unsettling nature of the music and lyrics.

After the Sex Pistols split at the end of a disastrous US tour in January 1978, singer Johnny Rotten reverted to his real name, John Lydon, and quickly set about forming a new group, Public Image Ltd., that moved away from the musical and visual style of his previous outfit. The debut single, 'Public Image', and album, *Public Image (First Issue)*, were a diversion from the punk rock template, but it was the follow-up album, *Metal Box*, released in November 1979, that really heralded a complete break with the past. Three twelve-inch EPs were housed in a round metal canister with the group's logo, *PIL*, embossed in the centre. Blending dub rhythms with an abrasive, slashing guitar and Lydon's leftfield, poetic lyrics, the album drew critical comparison with German Krautrock legends Can, while the packaging, designed by photographer Dennis Morris (who had shot portraits of the group members for the cover and inner sleeve of their debut album), was ground-breaking. *Metal Box* has since been heralded as a definitive post-punk statement, though Lydon's persona and his struggle to jettison the overbearing weight of his past placed him in an awkward situation, both within and apart from punk's continued evolution.

Other groups were following a parallel path, a continuation and extension of punk's creative disruption. While sections of the original punk scene ossified around a set of fixed aesthetic conventions, some artists continued to move forward. Still adhering to many of the original punk ideals – DIY, autonomy, novelty, experimentation, a rejection the performer-as-star-figure – many of these groups gigged on the by now established punk live circuit and were only retrospectively attributed the term post-punk. Spanning the invisible punk/post-punk divide, key groups included Wire, Ultravox, Siouxsie and the Banshees, Magazine, The Slits, The Pop Group, Public Image Ltd., Gang of Four, Joy Division, The Fall, Au Pairs, The Raincoats, The Mekons, Killing Joke, Cabaret Voltaire and Throbbing Gristle. Several US groups were also extremely influential on the developing UK scene, particularly Devo, Talking Heads, Suicide and Pere Ubu, together with various artists from the New York no wave scene championed by former Roxy Music keyboard player and Bowie collaborator Brian Eno. There was no common lyrical or musical theme tying these disparate groups together. Some adopted an 'anti-rockist' musical approach in a direct critique of the mainstream music industry (Wire, The Fall, The Slits, The Mekons), while others presented an overtly political position, particularly regarding racism, sexism and commercial exploitation (Gang of Four, The Pop Group, Au Pairs, The Raincoats).[8] Others were more interested in pushing musical or lyrical boundaries and sonic experimentation (Public Image Ltd., Joy Division, Cabaret Voltaire, Throbbing Gristle), but the common ground in wanting to move punk forward placed many of these groups in a separate space to the by now aesthetically embedded punk scene (Figure 3.1).

Any sense of uniformity or common purpose within the cadre of new bands that sprang up in response to the original punk explosion was surpassed by the increased confidence of its progenitors to develop their own autonomous agendas – a self-assurance which was also reflected in lyrical concerns, press interviews and public pronouncements as the market for the new wave grew exponentially through the late 1970s. This increased confidence was also partly due to the establishment of a successful independent music scene, championed by the music press (*Sounds*, *New Musical Express*, *Record Mirror* and *Melody Maker*) and DJs including John Peel at Radio One and Stuart Henry at Radio Luxembourg, together with the by now burgeoning punk and post-punk fanzines. While early independent record releases were potentially risky commercial undertakings, the establishment of a market and a receptive audience meant that later groups and labels could be reasonably confident of a return on their investment.

Those successful early punk groups that had secured major label deals were presented with both an opportunity and a dilemma – they could turn their back on the financial and commercial support offered by the

3.1 Various Artists (1979), *Earcom 3*, double 7" EP, United Kingdom: Fast Product. © Bob Last.

mainstream music industry to set up on their own or join one of the new smaller, independent operators, or they could stick with their contracts and work with their labels to play a strategic game. Since the independent scene was booming, bands could set up their own label imprint and identity that gave the impression of autonomy and control while at the same time benefitting from major label marketing and distribution (as was the case with, for instance, Bright, Pogo, DinDisc and Fiction Records, though many independent labels signed manufacturing and distribution deals with the majors). In many ways, this strategy pre-empted the impact of the 'indie' scene a decade later, where major labels including EMI, Polydor and Warner Bros. established their own 'independent' label subsidiaries and set up licensing and distribution deals with others.[9] The independent music scene, like punk and post-punk before it, became something of a symbolic gesture, reflecting a particular set of aesthetic principles but operating in a strictly commercial arena.

By contrast, the DIY post-punk scene was far more ideologically driven, with the notion of artistic control, honesty, autonomy and ethics front and centre in the goals of many participants. As the new independent scene evolved, groups could set up their own label and commission production of their own records, selling direct to customers at gigs or by mail order. They were, however, still at the mercy of a national distribution system, together with long-established procedures for music publishing, promotion and marketing to a wider audience. This did change incrementally over the following decade, with the success (and subsequent collapse) of the Cartel independent distribution network, but the rhetoric of empowerment linked to punk's do-it-yourself message was in many ways overstated. Some early UK punk groups, including The Desperate Bicycles, Scritti Politti and the Television Personalities, made notable attempts to reveal the practicalities of production to others, passing on acquired knowledge from their own experiences. More generally, the sense of enabling a subcultural takeover of the means of production was limited to areas such as fanzines or flyers, though even here anything beyond a very short print run required access to often elusive and expensive technical processes for print reproduction.

Whereas punk originally operated largely within the structures – and the restrictions – of the music industry, its subsequent post-punk evolution saw a massive growth in independent labels and DIY production. National music business listings included those releases that were distributed by the major networks or by key independents such as Rough Trade, but the plethora of self-produced, self-distributed records outside of this framework, along with a genuinely DIY cassette scene, often failed to register. Some fanzines and music papers did publish punk and alternative charts in the late 1970s, often based on rather subjective and flimsy data, but it was not until January 1980 that a recognised national independent chart was put in place. Following a suggestion by David Marlow at *ZigZag* magazine, in collaboration with Cherry Red label owner Iain McNay, the music trade paper *Record Business* began compiling a chart of those independent records (or, as they were later to become termed, 'indies' – a classification which was to become associated with a narrow musical style by the 1990s) which were not manufactured and distributed by the major label system. As Barry Lazell, a researcher at the paper given the task of compiling the weekly chart, recalls.

> Most importantly … indie is not a musical or artistic definition … To have indie status, a record – or the label on which it was released – had to be one which was independently distributed: produced, manufactured, marketed and put into the shops without recourse to the major record companies which have traditionally controlled virtually all aspects of the record industry.[10]

Launched on 19 January 1980, the Independent Chart was an immediate success, providing information to retailers and radio stations and giving a voice to the smaller labels in a competitive international market. Many punk and post-punk releases were to feature in the Independent Chart from the outset, and the chart was extended (from the top thirty singles and top fifteen albums to a top fifty and top twenty respectively) and published in *Sounds* from February 1980 onwards.

Extreme punk politics

As punk changed over time, more direct political subgenres began to come to the fore, often seizing the opportunities produced by the do-it-yourself and independent scenes to fashion a new punk along ideological lines. The rhetorical punk anarchism of the early punk pioneers was critiqued and refashioned by a new generation of groups in a scene that would belatedly become known as anarcho-punk.[11] A subgenre that developed partly as a reaction to increased political polarisation within punk as a whole and as a connection to earlier concerns of the underground movement of the 1960s, anarcho-punk employed explicit visual and verbal attacks on the power of the state and authority figures, together with strong anti-war, feminist or animal rights sentiments.[12] Anarcho-punk records tended to follow certain unspoken aesthetic rules, often directly influenced by the output of Crass, a collective based in a shared house near Epping Forest on the outskirts of London.

In the late 1970s, the members of this loose-knit group formed a punk band to relay their anarchist message following the networks established by Rock Against Racism and a wide base of support for CND, the Campaign for Nuclear Disarmament. Their media interruptions – incorporating records, books, films, events, concerts and posters – employed a distinctive visual style and paved the way for an entire subgenre of anarchist punk bands. The group's utopian visions of the future, coupled with an aggressive refusal to cooperate with the mainstream, saw them frequently in direct confrontation with authority. A successful marketing and promotion strategy, based on word-of-mouth communications and the underground networks born out of the early punk scene, saw the band's name stencilled on walls across the country. Using a strategy of (low) maximum price details on the sleeves, visual devices centred on a heavy black circle (initially derived from the band's central visual identity), the anarchist symbol and fold-out posters, the group's graphic output was designed to project strong political messages.

Crass influenced countless other young groups who shared their concerns about the threat of nuclear war and the exploitation inherent within the capitalist system, though they often expressed this in less convincing terms. Many of the Crass collective were from an older, and more educated, background than their followers, and their erudite philosophical statements were mirrored through (often inarticulate) copycat pieces by younger bands. Crass also supported underground networks – gigs were set up by local activists in small venues across the country, often outside of the regular music industry circuit and the group engaged directly with fanzine writers rather than the mainstream music press. Many of these events raised funds for a range of political causes, from CND to the Animal Liberation Front, as well as smaller local campaigns. Book and record stalls at venues provided access to the underground and anarchist media and gigs were sometimes scheduled for afternoons without a bar licence to give admittance a younger audience.

Anarcho-punk evolved as both a literal interpretation of the subversive potential of the original punk explosion and in opposition to what the punk movement had become. Anarcho-punk scenes fragmented further as the subgenre developed during the 1980s. While Crass continued to offer a largely pacifist critique of the British government's involvement in the Falklands War and the threat of global nuclear conflict, others such as Flux of Pink Indians and Conflict took on more extreme positions against animal testing and the meat industry. Conflict also encouraged a more proactive form of resistance through direct action, in complete contrast to the peaceful protest put forward by the Crass camp, and forged strong links with the Animal Liberation Front.

Some punk groups attracted a broad following which included hooligan, skinhead and right-wing elements, and punk's incoherent rage could be adopted by political activists for a variety of purposes. The rise in skinhead fashion in the late 1970s, together with a resurgence in support for political parties such as the National Front, led to increasing numbers of far-right skinheads attending punk gigs and causing trouble. These activities came to a head for Sham 69 in the early part of 1979 and the band were reluctantly forced to abandon playing live gigs altogether. Similar problems beset live performances by Menace, Angelic Upstarts, Cock Sparrer and the Cockney Rejects. None of these groups could be reasonably described as promoting an overtly right-wing agenda. Others, however, can be seen as more closely implicated in the development of an explicitly neo-fascist punk scene.[13]

In Leeds, the National Front had no less than three active branches in the late 1970s, with strong support in Bradford, Huddersfield, Halifax, Sheffield, Hull and York, as well as numerous smaller towns. One club in Leeds became adopted by punk groups and audiences – the F Club, in Chapeltown, began booking punk gigs and became a centre of attention for both far-right groups and the Anti-Nazi League. A far-right punk fanzine, *Punk Front*, was distributed by the Leeds NF, and local organisers felt that they were making strong headway in influencing the punk scene in the city. Subsequently, an organisation called Rock Against Communism

(RAC) was established as a direct response to the successes of the left-wing Rock Against Racism campaign. Although this did generate some publicity for the National Front, the national party was fast losing political support and splits in the leadership led to the formation of several breakaway groups. Following a disastrous showing in the May 1979 general election, the National Front split into three separate rival organisations: the National Front, the British Movement and the New National Front (led by hard-line nationalist John Tyndall), the latter soon to be renamed the British National Party.

The punk group most associated with extreme far-right politics was Skrewdriver, originally formed in Blackpool in 1977 and signed to the London-based Chiswick label. The group's early singles, 'You're So Dumb' and 'Anti-Social' (both released in 1977) were apolitical examples of what would later become known as street punk. They were not commercially successful and, following several image changes and an unsuccessful relocation to Manchester, the group split in 1979. Lead singer Ian Stuart Donaldson went on to form a new line-up of the group in the early 1980s, this time adopting an openly political stance in support of the National Front and operating under the Rock Against Communism banner. A split between Stuart's followers and the National Front in 1987 led to the formation of the Blood & Honour movement, named after a Skrewdriver song released in 1986 and intended to provide an outlet for far-right skinhead music and a network for live gigs and fundraising for neo-fascist political groups.[14] Early neo-fascist punk graphics employed ambiguous visual metaphors to evoke a mythical Aryan identity (Viking and Celtic symbols, runes), but these were eventually superseded by a more extreme form of visual communication. Explicit connotations of brotherhood, persecution, endurance, Norse mythology and the nation eventually gave way to direct calls to arms and pledges of allegiance with White Power and neo-Nazi terrorist groups.[15]

Hitsville UK

Punk's centre of gravity shifted from London in the period 1976–77 to the wider regions of the UK over the following five years. The bulk of first wave punk record releases were produced by groups based in and around London. Since London was the central hub for the music industry, many musicians had traditionally relocated to the city to seek their fortune over the previous two decades and the commercially successful punk scene largely followed suit, though Manchester was important as punk's second city (largely through the activity of a relatively small number of groups including Buzzcocks, The Drones, Magazine, Slaughter & the Dogs and The Fall). Other cities, including Liverpool, Leeds and Birmingham, were also very active early on, in part because of their importance to the national touring circuit for live gigs. Scotland and Northern Ireland produced successful groups including The Skids, The Rezillos, Stiff Little Fingers, The Undertones, Rudi and The Outcasts, while the long-standing historical connection between Irish popular music and the British scene continued with the impact of The Boomtown Rats and Radiators From Space in Dublin. By contrast, many later punk and post-punk record releases originated in the provincial regions of England, from smaller towns and cities in the North, West Midlands and the South West, along with a thriving Scottish post-punk scene centred around bands such as The Scars, Altered Images, Fire Engines, Josef K, The Associates, Aztec Camera and Orange Juice.[16]

Punk's migration did not follow the more traditional pattern from rural areas towards the major commercial centres (as had happened in the development of country music, jazz and blues in the USA, for instance), but rather acted inversely, as a largely inner-city urban style which shifted over time away from the city centres and out to the regions of the UK. At the same time, punk did not encompass a general shift towards either commercial acceptance (as with country music and rock'n'roll) or a growing status as a form of high art (as with jazz) – although certain styles such as new wave were to evolve as a more acceptable commercial interpretation of the genre. A significant strand of punk subculture engaged in a battle with the music industry to remain underground, avant-garde and resolutely uncommercial. As the industry invested in new wave, for instance, participants in other punk subgenres sought to distance themselves from what they saw as the commercialisation of the movement. The development of several increasingly aggressive, abrasive and deliberately awkward subgenres (hardcore, street punk and anarcho-punk, as well as the more radical elements of DIY and post-punk) might be seen as a reaction to punk's co-option into the mainstream and patterns can be observed in the way that waves of acceptance and opposition play out over time. These patterns can be seen to have been both political and aesthetic – from the lyrics and public statements of the groups involved to the musical and visual styles of their records.

The oral traditions of folk music, together with regional forms of music and speech or dialect, are explored by John Connell and Chris Gibson in *Sound Tracks: Popular Music, Identity and Place* (2003). By mapping the notion of 'authenticity' within a geographical and historical model, the authors draw parallels between ancient forms of local musical identity and contemporary, mass-produced commercial rock music. They go on to note that, over time, the notion of authenticity starts to blend in with what might be described as credibility

> where any form of popular music has provided some link with place and community (including the fans), displayed some sense of history, or claimed some heritage (in instruments, local performers or ethnicity) and evoked lived experience there have been claims to authenticity.[17]

One classic example which displays a wry sense of humour while documenting the real lives of local people is a 1977 single by US punk originators The Ramones, a group that had a huge formative influence on punk's musical, lyrical and visual aesthetic both in the United Kingdom and internationally. 'Rockaway Beach' takes the musical and lyrical codes of the (Californian) Beach Boys' 'Surfin' USA' and reapplies them to the East Side beaches of New York:

> Chewing out a rhythm on my bubble gum,
> The sun is out, and I want some,
> It's not hard, not far to reach,
> We can hitch a ride to Rockaway Beach[18]

There followed numerous examples of punk lyrics paying homage – paradoxical, ironic, critical or celebratory – to their locality and that of their fans, which in many cases meant their close friends and immediate circle, rather than any pretence to a wider audience. The Clash were celebrated for lyrics about their local environment in London (including 'London's Burning', 'Clash City Rockers', '(White Man) in Hammersmith Palais', 'The Guns of Brixton' and 'London Calling'). Many punk bands following in their wake chose to sing about what they knew, their immediate surroundings and the issues that affected their local community. The language used and local cultural reference points could then be very particular and specific, for instance the ironic, parochial boast in the first verse of the Anti-Nowhere League's 'So What' (1981). Introducing the song's key commentary, the lyrics describe the nearest seaside towns to the group's own hometown of Tunbridge Wells, Kent.

> I've been to Hastings
> I've been to Brighton
> I've been to Eastbourne too
> So what[19]

The gradual shift in punk's emphasis from London to the regions is reflected in the lyrical concerns of many punk records, as well as in references on record sleeves. Early examples of punk recordings reflecting a developing London scene included The Stranglers' 'London Lady' (1977), Television Personalities' 'Oxford Street W1' (1978) and Menace's 'GLC' (1978). Other examples of a direct association included band names such as London SS, Chelsea and London and later groups such as London PX, London Cowboys, Local Heroes SW9 and the Leyton Buzzards. While The Maniacs were celebrating the area around the Kings Road on their single 'Chelsea '77', The Vibrators' 'London Girls' featured a photograph of a young girl in front of a shop window, next to a small plaque declaring 'Kings Road, Borough of Chelsea, SW3'. This close association between punk and the capital city – and West London in particular – was set to continue and remains something of a clichéd lyrical or visual trope in the context of British punk.

As the punk diaspora spread more widely, examples of 'provincial' songwriting became more common, with lyrics by newer punk groups describing life in towns and cities across the UK. Examples include Stiff Little Fingers' (from Belfast) 'Suspect Device', 'Alternative Ulster', 'State of Emergency', 'Barbed Wire Love' (all reflecting the troubles in Northern Ireland) (1978–79); The Fall's (from Manchester) 'In My Area' and 'Leave the Capitol' (1978) and The Prefects' (from Birmingham) 'Bristol Road Leads to Dachau' and 'Barbarellas' (1978). The Panik (from Manchester) released the *It Won't Sell* EP on the Rainy City label in 1977, with the provocative label note, 'We're so bored with London', striking a blow for a local identity away from the capital. This anti-London sentiment reflected the media attention paid to London during the early development of the punk scene. Another notable example, 'We're from Bradford' by The Negatives, features a chorus chant of 'We're from Bradford, not from London / B-R-A-D-F-O-R-D!', while Sheffield group 2.3 took an even more provocative stance with their song '(I Don't Care About) London' that included the lyric 'London's burning they all shout / But I wouldn't even piss on it to put the fire out'.

Clay Fav, a group formed in the popular tourist destination of Windermere in the Lake District, released one single on their own label in 1979. The lead track 'Air Lakeland' declares, 'The street where I live is dead neat / Claife Ave in Windermere' before going on to complain about tourists flocking to the area each summer. However, in the end they ironically purport to accept this position as a natural state of affairs: 'It's all ok / It's all our fault / We chose to live in this beautiful spot'. Rural themes came even further to the fore in the early 1980s. Several West Country thrash punk groups even moved into humorous self-parody on later releases, as evidenced by tracks such as Disorder's 'Buy I Gurt Pint', Chaos UK's 'Farmyard Boogie' and Chaotic Dischord's 'Anarchy in Woolworths', 'And There Wuz Cows' and 'Get Off My Fuckin' Allotment'.

This shift to the regions went beyond mere derivative copies of the 'authentic' originators of punk in London. Even some of the early UK punk pioneers have revised their opinions of the later punk groups in retrospect, as Mark Perry suggests in a personal summary of the differences between the different periods of punk's development.

> I think there was almost too many professional musicians in punk to really make it like revolutionary in a street-fighting sense. ... The real punk bands came a couple of years later, the bands we all hated like The Exploited and all those nasty working-class people [laughs] that have convictions and have been in trouble with the police, and they were from out of London.[20]

There are also powerful links between locality and perceived notions of authenticity and originality. The apparent paradox in the relationship between 'original' punks and 'hangers on' was explored in detail by David Muggleton, who questions the distinctions made by Dick Hebdige regarding originality and authenticity in the late 1970s. Muggleton's work makes connections between disparate localities and chronologies in relation to the evolution of subcultures – particularly the ways in which subcultural styles might be further adapted by those taking them up over time. Through such analysis, the notion of an authentic group of 'original' punks is brought into question and the importance of later developments and interpretations is not overlooked.

Later punk groups often referred directly to their local towns, music scenes and venues in lyrics and song titles and occasionally in their sleeve graphics. Many single sleeves included thanks and credits to local friends and fans of the bands, with some groups going so far as to recognise their local scenes in song. One such example was the track 'Livi Punkz' by The Skroteez on their debut *Overspill* EP, a tribute to their local crowd in the Scottish new town of Livingston. The spelling of the word Punkz here follows a convention developed across many independent punk releases in the form of group credits: tributes would often be paid to the local 'punx' or 'crew' who followed the band. Sometimes local references were made in more negative terms – another track on the EP, 'New Town', includes the biting lyric, 'They should blow it up / Or else burn it all down!' and the single sleeve shows an aerial photograph of the group's hometown of Livingston, a post-war overspill estate to the south-west of the city of Edinburgh.

This also demonstrates an important point regarding locality and punk. While many groups recorded songs which were critical of the boredom of their immediate surroundings and the lack of opportunity in their hometowns, a sense of celebration of the local punk scene was often also evident in a kind of inverted civic pride. It is also interesting to note that some groups – notably The Boomtown Rats and Radiators From Space (both from the Dublin area) and Stiff Little Fingers (from Belfast) – faced strong criticism from their local punk scenes for 'deserting' the area and relocating to London to boost their careers, thus breaking two unspoken punk codes of conduct – turning their backs on their original supporters and pursuing commercial gain. Conversely, groups such as The Rezillos (from Edinburgh) and The Undertones (from Derry) cite the fact that they remained close to their hometown as having had a negative effect on their long-term musical careers. The difficulty in seeking recognition from a location away from the music industry 'centre' in London, together with their ideological position in remaining close to home, was further articulated by Rezillos singer Eugene Reynolds:

of course, coming from Scotland ensured that we did not get the type of hype that many London area bands got, and so were never (at the time) given the kind of media acceptance that the southerners managed to get. Our attitude was 'Fuck London! We're gonna make our scene where we are and not follow the bandwagon'.[21]

The Cult Maniax, from Torrington in Devon, gained some local notoriety in 1981 with the release of their *Frenzie* EP, featuring the track 'Black Horse', which documented the group members' series of disagreements with a local pub landlord. Other songs – such as 'Colchester Council' (1982) by Special Duties and 'Nottingham Problem' (1983) by Resistance 77 – targeted local government policy and the lack of venues for bands to play. The sleeve for the latter single features a photograph of the group standing in front of a major local venue, which is advertising a concert by a classical orchestra, while the reverse of the sleeve pays tribute to the 'Somercotes, Jacksdale, Alfreton & Ripley Punx', naming four small towns to the north-west of Nottingham. Interestingly, the group's antipathy towards their hometown was not all encompassing and local allegiances ran deep – a year later, Resistance 77 recorded the single 'You Reds' in tribute to their local football team. Football allegiances were also mirrored across the early 1980s punk landscape: the Cockney Rejects released the single 'I'm Forever Blowing Bubbles' (1980), a punk interpretation of the West Ham terrace chant, with a sleeve printed in the colours of the West Ham football team, and many other groups within the Oi! punk subgenre displayed a keen interest in the game. Local punk scenes also tended to be quite territorial and outsiders could be treated with some suspicion: in common with football supporters, punks from adjacent towns tended to display the greatest rivalry, while those visiting from further afield were often welcomed more warmly.

In stark contrast to these highly critical punk voices, the sleeve for the *Honour Before Glory* EP (1980) by the Nuclear Socketts clearly demonstrates a positive regional stance, declaring the group 'West Norfolk's finest' and acknowledging 'all the King's Lynn kids whose enthusiasm has made this single possible'. Examples such as these highlight something of a double-edged sword in relation to local identity: groups often reflected local scenes, sang about local issues, credited the local 'punx' on their sleeves and were photographed against local landmarks. However, their attitudes displayed an antipathy to the local council, authorities, landowners, pub landlords and decried the fact that life was boring in their town, displaying a conflict between pride in their local or regional identity and the punk spirit of antagonism and opposition.

In my area

The emphasis given to London in the lyrics and titles of early punk releases was also reflected in the design of record sleeves. The Clash

Design it yourself: the punk diaspora 117

3.2 The Rings (1977), 'I Wanna Be Free', 7" single, United Kingdom: Chiswick Records. Photography by Pete Kodick/Peter Gravelle. Courtesy Ted Carroll, collection of the author.

used photographs of confrontations between the police and crowds at the Notting Hill Carnival in 1976 on the reverse sleeve of their debut album *The Clash* (1977) and featured photographs of punk youths in London streets for the group's fourth single 'Clash City Rockers' (1978). The cover of the first Lurkers single, 'Shadow' (1977), included a photograph of the group standing outside the Red Cow in Hammersmith, a popular early punk venue, while 'I Wanna Be Free' (1977) by The Rings pictured the group in front of the Rock On record shop, the home of the Chiswick label (Figure 3.2). The Menace single 'GLC' (1978) featured a torn photograph of the civic offices of the Greater London Council. In a humorous and self-deprecating manner firmly in tune with the anti-star status of the early punk groups, the reverse sleeve of the debut single by Croydon group The

Banned, 'Little Girl' (1977), incorporated a close-up photograph of stone-cut lettering from the South London HM Coroner's office and a badge stating ironically 'Today Croydon, Tomorrow Bromley'.

Once punk had developed into a widely popular style, visual associations such as these became more frequent, again mirroring the lyrical trend to first focus on London and, later, regional locations. The sleeve of the third single by the Gang of Four, 'Outside the Trains Don't Run on Time' (1980), designed by group members Jon King and Andy Gill, features a reproduction of black and white photograph of Leeds Town Hall. A further cutting of the building's official description is reproduced on the centre record label, defiantly placing the band in a specific (northern England) location outside of London. Similarly, Stiff Little Fingers, a politically outspoken group from Northern Ireland, chose to use an image from the streets of Belfast on their second single, 'Alternative Ulster' (1978). The black and white photograph depicts a British soldier in full body armour crouching, rifle in hand, while a small boy leans over a wall behind him, laughing at the camera. A similarly dark-humoured use of images, though again centred on the capital, was displayed on the front and reverse sleeve of the second single by South London group The Straps. The front cover of the single, 'Brixton' (1982), includes a black and white photograph of an overturned vehicle and rioting black youths taken during the Brixton riots of April 1981, while the reverse features a photograph of the railway bridge over the main street, emblazoned with the motto 'Welcome to Brixton'. The cover of the third single by The Lurkers, 'Ain't Got a Clue' (1978), features a pencil illustration of the group in a rural setting, with trees, rolling fields and hills in the background and a road sign pointing towards Kingston, Ickenham and Fulham. This depiction of the group outside the urban environment, but with directions towards West London, reflects a link to the punk scene from their homes outside the city. By contrast, the front cover of Sunderland band Red Alert's debut EP, *In Britain* (1982), used a photograph of the group leaning against a wall in front of Big Ben in London, a generic reference to a stereotypical Britain rather than a direct connection to the group's hometown, and Anti-Social's *Made in England* EP (1982) simply uses graffiti on a wall to imply nationality, rather than locality.

The sense of locality expressed by individual groups was also reflected in the names and graphic approaches of punk-oriented record labels, particularly those created in direct response to the subculture. Clay Records, a label founded in 1980 by Mike Stone, a former employee at Beggars Banquet Records in London (itself an early punk-centred independent) who had just relocated to Stoke-on-Trent and opened a local record shop, was one such example. The town of Stoke has a long historical association with the ceramics industry. The Staffordshire potteries of Josiah Wedgwood, Joseph Spode and Thomas Minton made the area world famous for high-quality production, placing it at the forefront of the Industrial Revolution during the eighteenth century. The area subsequently became known as the Potteries, a term which lasted well into the twentieth century, even when local industries were in decline. The municipality of Stoke-on-Trent eventually brought together the boroughs of Hanley, Burslem, Longton and Stoke and the districts of Tunstall and Fenton in 1910. Stoke-on-Trent gained city status in 1925, though residents still refer to the area as the Potteries, recognising the historic distinctions between the six towns that make up the city.

Stone's identity for his new label, Clay Records, derives directly from these local associations. The centre labels of records released by Clay featured an illustration of three bottle kilns set in perspective (Figure 3.3). From the eighteenth century until the 1960s, these brick chimneys were a dominating architectural feature of the Staffordshire Potteries, when over two thousand such structures had towered above the local skyline. The use of this image on the label identity therefore gives a strong local connection, which would be instantly recognisable to anyone familiar with the area. As Clay Records became more established, following chart success with early hardcore record releases by local group Discharge and GBH from Birmingham, the label illustration was distilled further to create a simple graphic identity for the company.

This approach was not entirely new: other early independent punk labels had used their locality as a basis for a graphic identity. The Deptford Fun City label, based in South East London and home to Squeeze and ATV, was not only given an ironic name based on its location, but also used photographs of the local high street on record centre labels. The fact that the photographs were simply mundane snapshots, featuring dull shop fronts, advertising hoardings and to let signs only adds to the sense of ordinariness and boredom sarcastically implied in the label name. Similarly, Brighton label Attrix Records, established by local record shop owner Rick Blair, used a stylised hand-drawn silhouette of the local skyline, featuring the neoclassical domes and minarets of the Royal Pavilion as both the company logo and on centre labels. The cutting of silhouettes had been a seaside tradition on the West Pier from its opening in 1866 through to the early 1970s and their use on the Attrix identity and sleeve artwork also reflected a local craft history.

The Attrix label was to release three compilation albums documenting the local punk and new wave scene, entitled *Vaultage '78*, *Vaultage '79* and *Vaultage '80*, named after The Vault, a local band rehearsal and performance space. The front covers for *Vaultage '78* and *Vaultage '79* followed slight variations on the silhouette theme, incorporating elements of the buildings in the label identity, together with the town's central Clock Tower and Palace Pier, each set against a brightly coloured two-tone wash background. By contrast, the back covers featured a reversed silhouette of

3.3 Label design, Clay Records, Stoke 1980. Design by Mike Stone. Collection of the author.

the same skyline but fallen into ruin. The Vault, along with the Community Resource Centre within which it was based, was destroyed by a fire in early 1980, though the Attrix shop and label continued. With the third and final album in the series, *Vaultage '80*, the front cover image changed to depict the damaged West Pier, capped with spirals of barbed wire. The West Pier had closed in 1975 on the grounds of public safety and had been subject to persistent local government wrangling regarding its future ever since. In the ensuing years, it fell rapidly into decay and was fenced off to prevent access. The album artwork depicts the rooftops in the town as similarly distressed and ruined, reflecting a wider sense of decay and the decline of the West Pier as symbolic of the town itself and the disillusionment of local groups in response to the loss of their communal base. By contrast again, the back cover silhouette depicts a refurbished and perhaps gentrified town and West Pier, complete with fairground rides and a high-rise contemporary building near the Clock Tower.

Fragmentation

Punk groups and sleeve designers reflected local environments, regional identities and punk scenes away from the capital, in parallel to the evolution of a range of distinct subgenres as punk became established over time. As UK punk gained a favourable critical reception and developed a strong commercial market, the record industry was keen to cash in on the subculture, using a range of novel marketing techniques, many of which were drawn from innovations in the independent DIY avant-garde that thrived in the late 1970s. Punk's internal discourse highlighted the ways in which the subculture was fragmenting during the early 1980s, with 'punk about punk' record releases, lyrical and visual references and a puritanical backlash against the commodification and recuperation of what many saw as an authentic punk ideology. This, in turn, led to the establishment of further codes of practice in the formulation of music and lyrics and in the design of record sleeves and graphic identities produced by the groups themselves.

Punk's visual style, like the music, was often aggressive and contemporary, reflecting and commenting on its surroundings. It was also, especially regarding later developments, raw and untrained, employing a do-it-yourself graphic commentary that utilised crude visual conventions to drive the point home. Early UK punk often followed visual conventions and patterns of behaviour, drawn from classic examples such as the first album covers of The Ramones, The Clash and the Sex Pistols (each employing different graphic approaches in themselves), together with a media-inspired connection to London and the inner-city. Such codes and visual tropes were initially hard to break down, but subsequent developments of post-punk identity did go on to reflect a wider range of reflections on location, audience and cultural context. As punk became commercially recuperated, new punk identities sought to position themselves in relation to the punk establishment. These positions could take the form of embracing a myth of punk ideology or opposing its co-option within the mainstream music industry. Regional punk identities embodied both approaches – an often ironic or satirical reflection on the group's immediate environment, together with a reliance on support networks close to home and a sense of pride in local identity

Notes

1 Simon Frith and Andrew Goodwin (1990), *On Record*, London: Routledge, p. 86.
2 Gavin Butt, Kodwo Eshun and Mark Fisher (eds) (2016), *Post-Punk Then and Now*, London: Repeater Books.

3 Reynolds, *Rip it Up and Start Again*.
4 Designed by David Dragon.
5 Cover illustration by Linder Sterling, design by Malcolm Garrett/Abstruse Images.
6 Cover monoprint by Linder Sterling.
7 'Hong Kong Garden' featured the bandaged figure of Rose Lemoine, taken from the 1950s book *Dear Dead Days* by Charles Addams. The cover for *The Scream* featured a photograph of a swimmer underwater by Paul Wakefield.
8 David Wilkinson (2016), *Post-Punk, Politics and Pleasure in Britain*, London: Palgrave.
9 In the early 1980s, EMI resurrected its former Zonophone label to release records by leading groups in the new punk revival, including Angelic Upstarts, Cockney Rejects and Vice Squad.
10 Barry Lazell (1997), *Indie Hits: The Complete UK Independent Charts 1980–1989*, London: Cherry Red Books, p. ii.
11 Bestley and Binns, 'The evolution of an anarcho-punk narrative (1978–84)', pp. 129–149.
12 Russ Bestley (2016), 'Big A little a: The graphic language of anarchy', in Matthew Worley and Mike Dines (eds), *The Aesthetic of Our Anger: Anarcho-Punk, Politics, Music*, New York: Autonomedia, pp. 43–65.
13 Matthew Worley and Nigel Copsey (2017), 'White youth: The far right, punk and British youth culture, 1977–87', in N. Copsey and M. Worley (eds), *Tomorrow Belongs to Us: The British Far Right Since 1967*, London: Routledge, pp. 113–131.
14 Stuart was eventually killed in a car accident in September 1993, but the global impact of Blood & Honour and the music-related activities of far-right political groups such as Combat 18 were significant in the late 1980s and early 1990s.
15 Ana Raposo and Russ Bestley (2020), 'Designing fascism: The evolution of a neo-Nazi punk aesthetic', *Punk & Post-Punk* 9:3, pp. 467–498.
16 Douglas MacIntyre and Grant McPhee (2022), *Hungry Beat: The Scottish Independent Pop Underground Movement (1977–1984)*, London: White Rabbit.
17 John Connell and Chris Gibson (2003), *Sound Tracks: Popular Music, Identity and Place*, Abingdon: Routledge, p. 43.
18 Ramones, 'Rockaway Beach', *Leave Home*, vinyl album, USA: Sire.
19 Anti-Nowhere League, 'So What', 7" single, United Kingdom: WXYZ Records.
20 Robb, *Punk Rock: An Oral History*, p. 340.
21 Robb, *Punk Rock: An Oral History*, p. 492.

4
Your generation: punk designers and the art departments

This chapter introduces three loosely defined groups involved in the production of punk and post-punk graphics in the United Kingdom between 1976 and 1986. While the first section, Rank amateurs, acknowledges that punk's do-it-yourself mantra inspired significant numbers of individuals to create their own clothes, or to write, edit and design fanzines, badges, flyers and other graphic material, the focus of this chapter is on professional services relating to branding, identity and packaging for those artists and groups that managed to record and distribute their music in the form of records or cassettes. In the first phase of punk, this was largely through the mainstream music industry and the major labels, while increasing numbers of later punk and post-punk bands took a more autonomous route, setting up their own labels or collaborating with one of the new independents such as Rough Trade, Small Wonder or Beggars Banquet.[1] Several independent labels, including Stiff and Chiswick, secured manufacturing and distribution deals with the majors and their commercial reach meant that design teams benefited from access to increased budgets and higher quality production.

Some groups signed to major labels managed to bring their own designer along with them – Jamie Reid with the Sex Pistols and Malcolm Garrett with Buzzcocks, for instance. Several independent labels created a sympathetic visual style across their catalogue through the dedicated work of label owners – Bob Last at Fast Product, for example – or by directly employing an in-house creative team, such as design group 23 Envelope, comprising creative director Vaughan Oliver and photographer Nigel Grierson, at 4AD Records. Many other punk groups were forced to work with in-house design teams, with varying degrees of control over their representation to the wider world. In effect, two generations of designers spanned the divide between the new and the old – the younger, punk-inspired or punk-aligned avant-garde and the established design professionals, some of whom had been working in the popular music industry since the 1960s.

Rank amateurs

A significant part of the emerging punk aesthetic was driven by enthusiastic followers and amateur producers, from clothing and dress styles to fanzines, perhaps the ultimate vehicle for fans to get directly involved in the new scene. While there was obviously a two-way relationship between the visual style of the punk fanzines and the 'official' branding of leading groups and artists (in particular, the Sex Pistols, The Damned and The Clash), the fanzine makers were heavily reliant on a combination of enthusiasm, (limited) access to technology and the confidence or willingness to have a go at doing it themselves. In many cases, these new editors and producers had little or no art or design education, relying on their imagination and the cooperation of their peers to pull together a finished magazine.[2] The visual style of punk fanzines such as *Sniffin' Glue*, *Ripped & Torn*, *Panache*, *Jamming!*, *Chainsaw*, *Bondage*, *Strangled*, *Vague*, *Safety in Numbers*, *London's Outrage*, *48 Thrills*, *London's Burning*, *In The City*, *Gun Rubber*, *Kill Your Pet Puppy*, *Adventures in Reality* and *Toxic Grafity* needs to be recognised as important in the story of an evolving punk aesthetic (Figure 4.1).[3] The creative design work, as well as the writing, of fanzine producers such as Mark Perry, Tony Moon, Charlie Chainsaw, Mick Mercer, Tony Fletcher, Mike Diboll, Tom Vague, Tony Drayton, Ken Brown, Alan Rider and many others both offered inspiration and held up a mirror to the emerging punk graphic styles in the music industry, from record covers to marketing and advertising materials.

The new punk designers

The history of punk graphics in the United Kingdom starts – but doesn't end – with Jamie Reid. While the Sex Pistols led the way – musically and aesthetically – particularly in their wider impact in the media and their influence on a generation of peers, Reid's graphics for the group captured the spirit of the new wave perfectly. Much has been written about the Sex Pistols and Reid's work, which has itself entered the canon of art history to the extent that it tends to dominate discussions of the visual identity of the punk subculture. To a degree, that was always the case – many punk designers felt pressured to steer clear of what was becoming even by 1977 a set of stylistic conventions that dominated the media depiction of the new movement. We have already discussed Reid's work at length in previous chapters, so here we turn to another group of design practitioners who

4.1 *Chainsaw* fanzine no.2, September/October 1977. Design by Charlie Chainsaw.

entered the fray around the same time as the punk explosion. Many were inspired by the subculture to follow a creative path, while others shifted their established practices to join the new movement.

Several designers gained their punk graphic design reputations through close collaboration with up-and-coming groups or labels, including Barney Bubbles (Colin Fulcher) (Stiff and Radar), Chris Morton (Stiff), Malcolm Garrett (Buzzcocks and Magazine), Peter Saville (Factory), Gee Vaucher (Crass), Vaughan Oliver (4AD) and Mike Coles (Malicious Damage). A loan from Dr. Feelgood singer Lee Brilleaux helped to set up the new, independent Stiff Records (founded by Brinsley Schwarz manager Dave Robinson and former Dr. Feelgood manager Jake Riviera), which was to become closely associated with punk after signing The Damned and issuing their debut single, 'New Rose', in October 1976, and album *Damned Damned Damned* in February 1977. Stiff employed graphic designer (and former Hawkwind lighting man) Barney Bubbles and Chris Morton (aka c-more-tone) to develop their visual identity, helping to establish a fresh, contemporary and witty brand image that was to prove influential across the wider punk and new wave subculture.[4] Bubbles was more experienced within the graphic design profession, having worked as a senior designer for the Conran Group in the 1960s and subsequently designed album sleeves for Hawkwind, the Sutherland Brothers, Kevin Coyne, the Edgar Broughton Band and many others. However, his connection to the music and his attitude towards the corporate music industry helped set him apart from many of the established designers at the major label studios, finding favour with the new generation of punk-inspired designers.

Morton had been involved from the start, even before Bubbles joined the Stiff team; he had drawn the label's original typographic identity and created the template for labels and branded record bags that was to endure for the life of the business. After meeting Riviera at a gig at The Roundhouse in Chalk Farm, North London, in 1976, Morton recalls a conversation where 'he said he remembered meeting me and seeing as I did record cover stuff – which I hadn't technically actually done yet – [and] would I like to do some roughs and ideas for a new record label he was setting up?'[5] This encounter led directly to Morton designing the identity for Stiff Records, which was to become a significant contributor to the budding punk and new wave scene as well as an inspiration for the explosion of independent record labels that was to follow over the next decade (Figure 4.2). Sadly, Paul Gorman's otherwise superb history of the work of Barney Bubbles plays down Morton's contribution at Stiff, misspelling the designer's name and implying his 'relatively unsophisticated' approach was quickly superseded by Bubbles' far superior design ideas. Gorman also cites a former associate of Bubbles, David Wills, who recounts a story of a conversation with the designer in Westbourne Grove in 1977.

4.2 Stiff Records identity, 1977. Design by Chris Morton. Original artwork, courtesy Chris Morton.

While they talked about 'a religion of shape' arising from the Russian Constructivists, Wills claims a FedEx delivery truck drove by and Bubbles' pointed to it, saying 'Look! See what I mean? It's everywhere!'[6] Sadly for Wills' and Gorman's catchy story, however, the iconic FedEx arrowhead logo was in fact designed seventeen years later, by Lindon Leader at Landor Associates in 1994.

Stiff was an overnight success and Morton was thrown in at the deep end, working alongside Bubbles, who had been commissioned to work with the label once it began signing artists and moving into the production of records. The pair created an innovative and playful identity for the label just as it was achieving critical acclaim and commercial impact with artists such as The Damned, Ian Dury, Nick Lowe and Wreckless Eric. Learning on the job, Morton's work relied on craft skills and expertise in illustration, particularly in his use of Rapidograph pens and painstakingly hand-drawn line art and typography. As the label grew, he was able to access higher budgets and more sophisticated equipment, though he still sensed a separation between the old guard music graphics professionals and the younger generation of punk-inspired designers.

> There was a perceived attitude problem with established graphic designers, particularly those in the major record company art/publicity departments, snobbishly looking down on our adjudged lack of artworking ability and professionalism. Although I always suspected our deliberate lack of obediently following their time-honoured design theory protocols was really the problem – perhaps in the same way that the older generation of musicians feared and insulted the 'new wave' ...[7]

When Riviera left Stiff to form Radar Records with former United Artists A&R manager Andrew Lauder in late 1977, Bubbles worked across both labels, creating a strong visual identity for Ian Dury and The Blockheads at Stiff while also continuing to work with former Stiff charges Elvis Costello and the Attractions, Nick Lowe and the Yachts at Radar. Chris Morton remained at Stiff, taking on the role of art director and leading a team of new, innovative young designers.

> After the first stuff, Barney and I did most of the early design work. He was very helpful to me and a magical mentor, but then he went off with Jake to work for Radar full time. Everyone designing stuff for Stiff had been working freelance. I was asked by Dave Robinson to set up an art department and offered the full-time art director job when Jake left, so I was responsible for doing the design work for everyone on the roster – except for Ian Dury. I initially had an assistant, but that became three or four as the workload grew, including a young graduate fresh out of London College of Printing, Neville Brody.[8]

Morton also developed a unique visual style of his own, based on line drawings and traced photos and text that were subsequently photomechanically enhanced at the pre-press stage. Working from prints, or through halftone rescaling beforehand, Morton would construct a collage of disparately sized photographic images which he would then trace, adding texture, dots and tones by hand. The results were idiosyncratic and highly original (Figures 4.3 and 4.4).

Like Barney Bubbles, Peter 'Sleazy' Christopherson had enjoyed a longer professional career as a photographer, filmmaker and designer prior to the punk explosion and his subsequent involvement with industrial music pioneers Throbbing Gristle alongside Genesis P. Orridge, Cosey Fanni Tutti and Chris Carter. He was a partner with Storm Thorgerson and Aubrey Powell in the design group Hipgnosis, working on promotional graphics for major league rock bands including Pink Floyd, Led Zeppelin, 10CC and UFO, and was commissioned by Malcolm McLaren to take the first promotional photographs of the Sex Pistols soon after John Lydon joined the group. As a founder member of Throbbing Gristle, Christopherson helped the art/performance collective establish a uniquely leftfield, and sometimes disturbing, visual identity that combined what appeared to be innocuous images with often oblique references to sex, death and human depravity. Throbbing Gristle were hugely influential within a strand of post-punk combining sound collage and electronic

Punk designers and the art departments 129

4.3 Theatre of Hate (1980), 'Original Sin', 7" single, United Kingdom: SS Records. Original artwork, courtesy Chris Morton.

music, and their approach to graphic and visual identity set the tone for the industrial music genre going into the 1980s and beyond. Christopherson's visual work with Throbbing Gristle, and subsequent groups Psychic TV and Coil, places the designer alongside a new generation of creative practitioners though, like Barney Bubbles, Vaughan Oliver and Terry Jones, his experience links to the professional design establishment far more closely than many of his punk-related peers.

Malcolm Garrett met Manchester punk group Buzzcocks early in 1977 through a mutual friend, Linder Sterling, who was a graphic design student in the year above him at Manchester Polytechnic. By this time, Buzzcocks had already released the pioneering *Spiral Scratch* EP on their own New Hormones record label, with a monochrome picture sleeve designed by the group's manager, Richard Boon (Figure 4.5). The record cover featured a polaroid photograph of the group on the front cover and neatly typeset song titles with details of recording and overdubs on the reverse, arranged in a negative cross formation in a subtle tribute to Kazimir Malevich's suprematist typographic experiments of the 1920s (Figure 4.6). Garrett was studying graphic design at the time and, when he was asked by Boon to create a visual identity for the band, decided to adopt a unique approach that was quite different to the punk style that what was becoming rather

4.4 Theatre of Hate Westworld promotional poster, 1982. Courtesy Chris Morton.

4.5 Buzzcocks (1977), *Spiral Scratch*, 7" vinyl EP, United Kingdom: New Hormones. Front cover. Design by Richard Boon. Collection of the author.

generic in the wake of Jamie Reid's work for the Sex Pistols. His first commission was a poster that could be adapted for upcoming gigs, together with the classic Buzzcocks logo. The logo was created through a simple combination of hand drawing and Letraset type. The group name was first set out in Letraset Compacta Italic, then enlarged on the process camera before cutting and extending each character by hand, paying particular attention to the two Zs in the centre (Figure 4.7).[9]

Garrett attempted to reflect the ironic obtuseness of Buzzcocks' music and lyrics in his approach to their record sleeves and posters, to capture something of their sardonic wit in visual form: 'I felt that this approach reflected the group's lyrics, which were on the one hand quite domestic, but also bittersweet, slightly dehumanised (there is no 'he' or 'she' in a Buzzcocks lyric) and somewhat aggressive all at the same time'.[10] Other

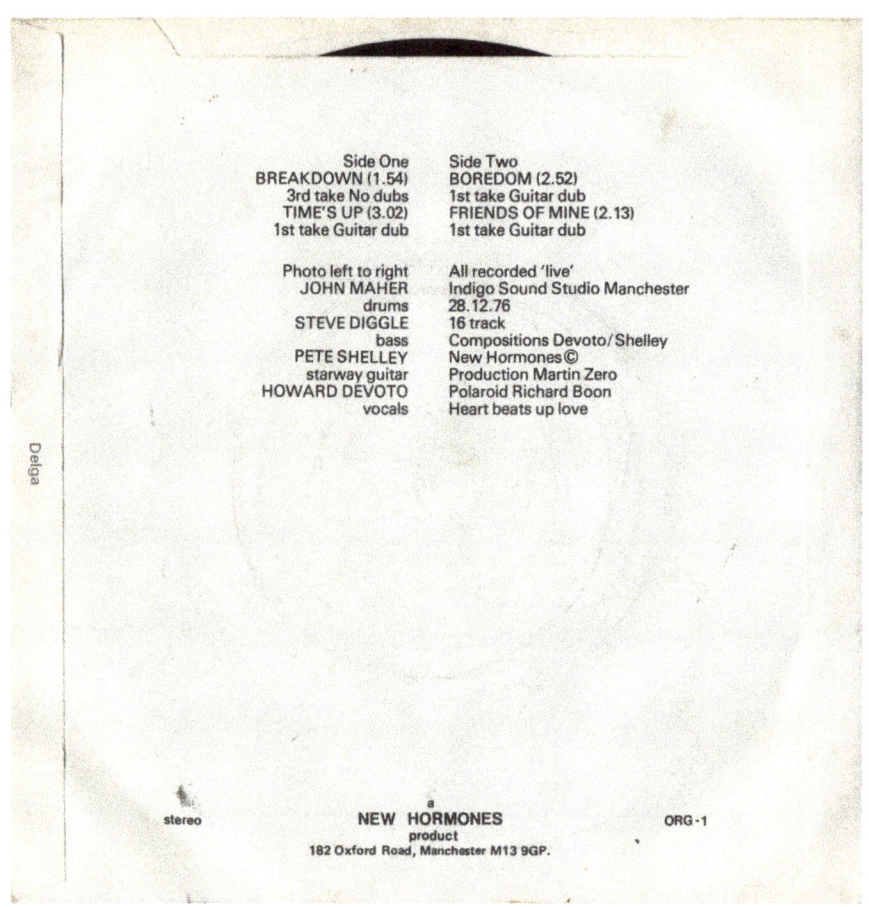

4.6 Buzzcocks (1977), *Spiral Scratch*, 7" vinyl EP, United Kingdom: New Hormones. Back cover. Design by Richard Boon. Collection of the author.

strategies included playfully highlighting the production process: for the 1978 single 'I Don't Mind', the United Artists logo and catalogue number were massively enlarged to dominate the sleeve instead of the usual band name and song titles (Figure 4.8). Garrett had visited the pressing plant at United Artists and noted how records were tracked simply by their catalogue number, with no reference to artist, songs or musical style and he chose to reflect this aspect of process and production in the design. However, the record label subsequently decided to reverse Garrett's artwork, moving the large logo to the back cover and song titles to the front.[11] Both songs on the single were taken from the debut album (contradicting punk's widespread value-for-money rhetoric), a label strategy that both the band and Garrett disagreed with. Garrett's deliberately obtuse promotional poster and press ad for the single boldly stated, 'marketing ploy: the

BUZZCOCKS

4.7 Buzzcocks logo. Design by Malcolm Garrett, courtesy Malcolm Garrett/Assorted Images.

4.8 Buzzcocks (1978), 'I Don't Mind', 7" single, United Kingdom: United Artists. Back cover. Design by Malcolm Garrett/Assembled Images, courtesy Malcolm Garrett/Assorted Images.

single from the album … this single out now, new single out soon'. Garrett saw himself and the new generation of punk-specific graphic designers as fundamentally distinct from the professional design studios that dominated the music industry and included Bubbles in his summary of that perceived divide – as part of the 'new'.

> I definitely felt at odds with, if not exactly at war with, the in-house designers and felt that their attempts to produce work for The Stranglers or 999 or whomever was simply not authentic in the way that mine or Barney's or Jamie's was. It isn't really to do with age or generation, just about attitude and involvement.[12]

Another graphic design student at Manchester Polytechnic, Peter Saville, seized a similar opportunity when he approached local television presenter Tony Wilson and offered to design a poster for The Factory, a new club night that Wilson was launching at The Russell Club, in the run-down, inner-city suburb of Moss Side in May 1978.[13] Saville had become fascinated by some of the work reproduced in Herbert Spencer's classic book on modernist design and typography, *Pioneers of Modern Typography*, first published in 1969 and subsequently reprinted in the autumn of 1977, which was widely taken up by graphic design courses across the UK as a key text on the origins and values of the profession.[14] While he was drawn to the work of Herbert Bayer, Saville's adopted visual style harked back to Jan Tschichold's typographic experimentation, adopting what Emily King describes as 'the whole body of [Tschichold's] work as a singular expression of typographic cool, the opposite to the frantic tussle of contemporary punk typography'.[15]

The Factory club was a success, leading to the launch of Factory Records, founded by Wilson, Saville and Wilson's business associate Alan Erasmus in the autumn of 1978. The first release on the label, a double seven-inch vinyl EP entitled *A Factory Sample*, featuring unsigned local bands Joy Division and The Durutti Column alongside poet John Dowie and Sheffield electronic post-punk pioneers Cabaret Voltaire, was released in January 1979. Wilson also presented Granada Television's culture, music and events programme, *So It Goes*, which featured many new and upcoming punk and new wave artists including the Sex Pistols, Buzzcocks, Elvis Costello, Ian Dury, The Stranglers, The Jam, X-Ray Spex, XTC, Siouxsie and the Banshees and Penetration. Such high-profile media links and an implicit connection to the evolving new music scene ensured a positive reception for Factory, with the label's leading group, Joy Division and Saville's iconic artwork taking centre stage.

The third leading figure in what would become something of a British graphic design and typography revival over the coming years, Neville Brody, was a year younger than Garrett and Saville. He had attended Hornsey College of Art – which had been a key site in the late 1960s counterculture, before taking up a place to study graphic design at London College of Printing. However, the young designer discovered the college was far more conservative than he had hoped, offering both a challenge and an opportunity.

> The way typography was taught at LCP destroyed the idea of type design for me back then. I was really interested in challenging the traditional ways of teaching graphic design. We were being taught that briefs have rigidly pre-defined outcomes – looking at what *should* happen, rather than what *might* happen through a creative process.[16]

Brody had been inspired by punk – he had been introduced to the scene through a fellow student at Hornsey, Mike Barson (who would later go on to form ska group Madness), and had been close friends with The Clash guitarist Keith Levene when growing up in North London. As far as he was concerned, creative approaches to design needed to acknowledge conventions while not falling into stylistic repetition. He also embraced the opportunities afforded by technologies at the college, particularly Letraset type and the use of the photocopier as a tool for origination rather than purely for reproduction. Alongside this flexibility in the use of technology and materials, Brody was keen to adopt a punk-infused creative approach to disrupt accepted graphic conventions.

> If something exists for practical reasons and those reasons were still relevant, then you needed to maintain that. But if something is there for reasons of tradition, or comfort, then those things are up for grabs.[17]

Such attitudes were not welcomed by some of the teaching staff at the college, with Brody's final degree award not without controversy. Other possibilities came through his position as a student, however. Taking the opportunity to leverage access to potential employers through his dissertation research, he interviewed Alex McDowell at Rocking Russian and was offered a job there on graduation. The job was to be relatively short-lived, however. Brody recalls that Rocking Russian was 'a great place to work but a terrible place to get paid' and he left to join Chris Morton at Stiff.

> I used to get to Stiff late every day, do a couple of record sleeves then bury myself in the darkroom with the PMT camera, doing freelance work for Cabaret Voltaire and Fetish Records. A year into the job I got fired by Dave Robinson who said, 'It's not because you're late every day, it's because you don't apologise for it'.[18]

In Scotland, Bob Last had been fascinated by art from childhood, finding inspiration in a late-night television screening of Jean-Luc Godard's *Alphaville*, together with Russian Constructivism and the work of film director Dziga Vertov. An exhibition at Edinburgh College of Art, *Strategy: Get Arts*, in 1970 introduced him to the work of Joseph Beuys and would have a lasting effect. Last's parents expected him to follow their path into the sciences, though he wanted to pursue a more creative direction. Reaching something of a compromise, he took up a place to study architecture, though he stepped out after a year to focus on a personal venture, Fast Product. Inspired by two exhibitions at the Fruitmarket gallery early in 1976 featuring work by Richard Hamilton, Victor Burgin and Hans Haacke, Fast Product started out as a self-consciously postmodernist conceptual art project rather than a record label. At the time, Last was listening to Miles Davis, Frank Zappa, Hatfield and the North and other complex, avant-garde rock music, though he became aware of punk as it began to impact beyond London by the end of the year.

A copy of Buzzcocks' *Spiral Scratch* EP, given to Last by his girlfriend at the time, was a key influence in his move into the scene. Picking up on the punk do-it-yourself ethos and embracing opportunities through his part-time work as a roadie for The Rezillos, he came across a local scene in Leeds[19] that seemed to reflect in microcosm many of the ideas he had been thinking about with Fast Product: Walter Benjamin, Bertolt Brecht, artificial creation, marketing and consumption and the notion of what Last describes as 'not just revealing the process but revelling in the process'.[20] The playfulness and inversion of expectations that was embodied in the musical and lyrical approach of The Mekons appealed to him and he offered to release their debut single, 'Never Been in a Riot', on the Fast Product label. The sleeve for *Spiral Scratch* had been printed by Delga Press in Kent, so Last telephoned them and was given instructions on how to prepare and specify artwork, including how to make separations on different sheets of tracing paper and add registration marks so that they could be combined in the final print. The logic of production resonated with his background in architecture, where 'creativity interacts with process'.[21]

Fast Product followed 'Never Been in a Riot' with further releases by Sheffield group 2.3, Gang of Four, The Human League, Scars and a second single by The Mekons, together with three compilation EPs, before Last made a conscious decision to close the label at its height after just a year, in what he calls a 'defined intervention'.[22] Last saw Fast Product as a launchpad for bands to move on to bigger labels and to extend their reach and influence, though he notes 'the inherent tension between the two worlds of radical left perception and the freedom that radical creativity requires'.[23] Last developed an approach to collage that was centred on process (Figure 4.9) and went on to produce two fanzine-style printed magazines, *The Quality of Life* and *Sexex*, that captured his graphic experimentation beyond the record artwork. He maintains that his design approach was more closely associated with collecting, mediating and editing than a purely creative model of artistic practice.

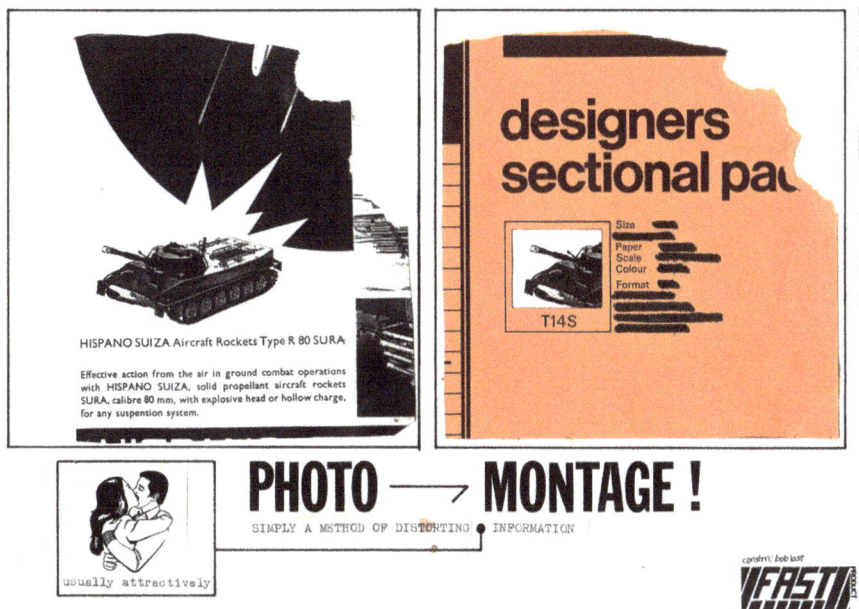

4.9 Bob Last, *Photo-Montage!*, 1977. © Bob Last.

> It is important to understand that my approach embodied the notion that I was editing. I didn't imagine myself as a graphic auteur. I was editing what I found and that was fundamental to the process.[24]

Although *The Quality of Life* and *Sexex* appeared to adopt the form of a fanzine, they had no actual literary content or reference to any music, as might be expected of the medium – 'they were if you will art editions in disguise'.[25] Last added pieces of orange peel to the first publication, ensuring each copy would be unique as it dried and rotted over time.

Another designer who was to become synonymous with a unique strand of post-punk graphic styles in the early 1980s, Gee Vaucher, was an experienced commercial illustrator, having studied art and design at South-East Essex Technical College and School of Art between 1961 and 1965. In 1967 she set up an open house in Epping Forest, Essex, with fellow art graduate Penny Rimbaud (Jeremy Ratter) and both were involved in the late 1960s counterculture. Vaucher travelled to New York in 1977, where she worked as a freelance illustrator for mainstream magazines, including *New York Magazine* and the *New York Times*, before returning to the UK to rejoin Rimbaud, who by this time had established a radically outspoken punk group, Crass.[26] Vaucher's visual work for Crass and for the label that they established, Crass Records, was highly charged and strongly political, reflecting the aesthetic and ideology of the group themselves. Crass would become hugely influential on a new punk subgenre, retrospectively known as anarcho-punk, and Vaucher's design aesthetic, employing a photomontage sensibility, though in practice largely hand-drawn by the artist herself, helped to establish a visual style for the movement. Virtually all the new designers who attempted to follow in Vaucher's footsteps lacked the technical skill and subtle appreciation of art history and philosophy that was embedded in her work, but at least some rudimentary graphic principles did translate – including stark, black and white designs featuring stencil typography and images depicting senior politicians, anti-war themes, animal exploitation, or gender relations.

Vaughan Oliver studied graphic design at Newcastle upon Tyne Polytechnic, subsequently working as a packaging designer for commercial design agencies Benchmark and Michael Peters and Partners. Moving on to music packaging, he teamed up with photographer Nigel Grierson to form 23 Envelope in 1983 and began what was to become a long-term collaboration with the esoteric, independent label 4AD. Oliver became renowned among his fellow designers for his radically experimental approach and his embrace of the design and printing process, particularly the merits of the PMT camera (photomechanical transfer – a large machine used in pre-press studios for scaling monochrome images and producing film copies ready to manufacture printing plates, otherwise known as a process camera). The PMT camera had proved ground-breaking for other professional designers, offering more control over the preparation of films ready for paste-up, but Oliver was better known for embracing the ghosts in the machine as much as its capacity for quality. He also employed seemingly innocuous analogue tools for print production in the predigital era that could be used, abused and manipulated to create a new visual aesthetic. His work was, in many ways, painterly, embracing collage, photomontage, overlaid transparencies, texture, photomechanical disruption and distortion.[27] Oliver's work process and impact was documented in a heavily illustrated biography by design historian Rick Poynor in 2000. In addition, a selection of material from his studio archive, now housed at the University of the Creative Arts in Epsom, was reproduced in two volumes by Unit Editions in 2018, then partly republished following his death in 2019.

Rob O'Connor recalls discovering dramatic visual effects with the PMT camera, though he acknowledges that Oliver had got there first and chose to leave the technique to his competitor.

> I'd realised that you can get some interesting effects by using old developer because it is textural and doesn't quite make it to black. It's this weird analogue sci-fi world. And if you if you peel the [photographic] sheets away and then put them back together, out of register, you get lovely double images. But once I'd seen what Vaughan was doing with it, I just thought, No, that's his. That's his realm. Let him do it![28]

4.10 Cocteau Twins (1982), *Lullabies*, 12" vinyl EP, United Kingdom: 4AD. Design by 23 Envelope, collection of the author.

Oliver could also be quite radical in his choice of colour palettes, embracing silver and gold metallic inks along with a range of hues that were seldom seen in other album sleeve designs of the post-punk era. Like some of the music that the images were intended to reflect or evoke, the approach was inspired by a sense of post-punk experimentation, where standard approaches and traditional rule books were jettisoned by a new generation of creative artists and designers (Figure 4.10).

Mike Coles, by contrast, had only briefly studied art and design prior to becoming involved in the industry. Coles attended art school in northeast England in the late 1960s but found the atmosphere stifling and left during his first year, spending some time drifting in Europe and working in various low-key occupations before relocating to London in 1976.

4.11 Killing Joke (1979), *Turn To Red*, 10" vinyl EP, United Kingdom: Malicious Damage. Design by Mike Coles/Malicious Damage, courtesy Mike Coles.

He managed to secure a job as a freelance paste-up artist at a studio that, in his words, was 'one of the last of the old-fashioned, traditional art studios left in London – hot metal type, Cow Gum, Letraset and a tea lady'.[29] A chance meeting with a group of musicians looking to set up a new record label gave him the opportunity to apply his design vision to a collective identity, Malicious Damage. The commercial success of the main band on the label, Killing Joke, afforded the designer a creative outlet, though he still had to work on commercial briefs for other clients to pay the bills.

Coles' early work for Killing Joke combined collage with drawing and his own photography and was as much a product of the mechanical processes he employed as his handiwork, as with the cover for the band's debut EP, *Turn To Red*, released in October 1979 (Figure 4.11). He made

4.12 Killing Joke (1980), *Killing Joke*, vinyl album, United Kingdom: Malicious Damage. Design by Mike Coles/Malicious Damage, courtesy Mike Coles.

extensive use of the photocopier, recopying repeatedly to increase the grain and tone of image and type, along with the PMT camera. For the cover of the debut Killing Joke album, Coles chose a photograph by renowned British war photographer Don McCullin showing Irish youths running away from British troops in Derry. The original photograph had been published in the *Sunday Times Magazine* on 16 December 1971 and (unusually) the band's management company, EG, asked the photographer for licensing rights to use the image. McCullin said yes, as long as he wasn't associated with the music. As the designer recalls, 'I think he thought it was some snotty bunch of punks who'd disappear in a few weeks'.[30]

Adding white gouache to render the Killing Joke band name, Coles distressed the photograph to create a stark, black and white, almost silhouetted graphic version of the original. Using a photocopier and PMT camera, he then carefully selected elements from different treatments, reassembling the final image to create the paste-up artwork ready for print. The album was issued with a gatefold cover, with the image running full bleed across the entire frame (Figure 4.12). For the inner cover spread, Coles employed another McCullin photograph from the same series, adding visual elements including a crucifix, a hand nailed to a cross and a Christ-like figure rising from the flames of a burning bonfire. Coles stepped away from working with the group in the late 1980s but returned in 1990 to create the front cover artwork for the album *Extremities, Dirt and Various Repressed Emotions* based on a photograph of actor Conrad Veidt from the 1920 German silent horror film *The Cabinet of Dr. Caligari* (Figure 4.13).

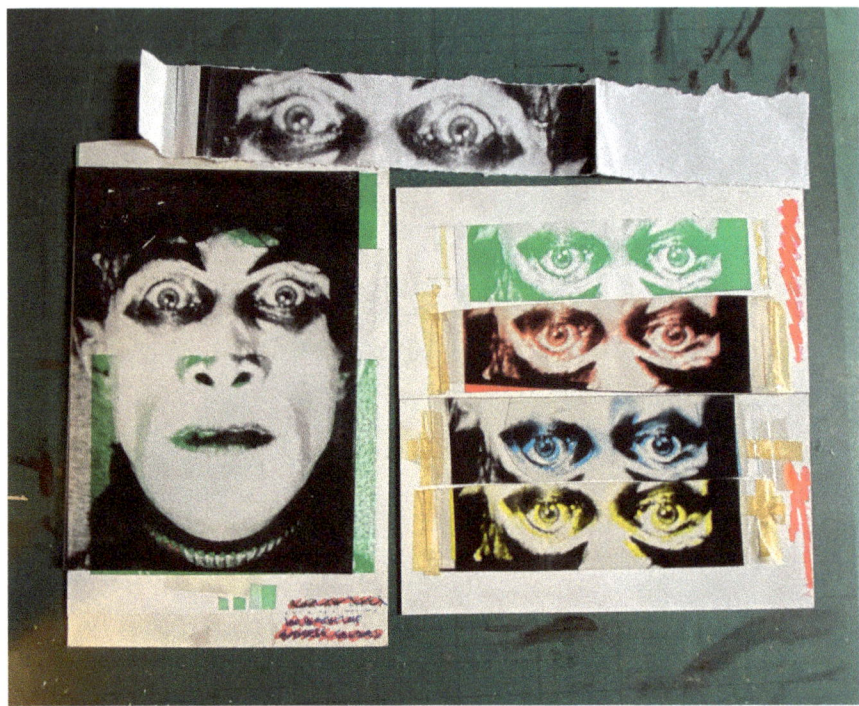

4.13 Killing Joke (1990), *Extremities, Dirt and Various Repressed Emotions*, vinyl album, Germany: Aggressive Rockproduktionen. Original artwork, courtesy Mike Coles.

Like Vaucher and other successful punk and post-punk graphic designers, the level of autonomy that the scene provided was key to Coles' approach:

> In my early studio days, I wasn't allowed within a typographical mile of a creative brief as I had no training or qualifications, but the artist in me was all the time struggling to get out. Hence the eagerness to get involved with the Malicious Damage set-up.[31]

The new punk generation of designers was, then, diverse. Some had studied design at art college and moved into the music graphics profession as a natural step in the development of a career, while others made the leap from amateur to professional due to the commercial success of the artists and labels they created work for. As punk fragmented and the post-punk DIY scene blossomed in the late 1970s and early 1980s, some of the newcomers stepped into design roles in the established major label art departments, while others remained firmly embedded with independent labels that were by now competing on the bigger stage. It was a two-way street: some of the successful designers and art directors who had started their careers within the major labels were able to step out and set up their own independent studios, taking on freelance work across the industry.

The creative studios

Within the graphic design groups at the major record labels, the need to tap into an evolving market while at the same time offering a sense of uniqueness and originality to artists on the roster was also very familiar. Former Polydor Records designer Rob O'Connor notes that each of the major labels employed a senior creative director in the 1970s, though the system was to change later.

> That's the way the old school was in the record company, though there was always someone who was creatively in control. For instance, it was Rosław Szaybo at CBS, Mike Ross at A&M and John Pasche at Chrysalis. All the major companies had these creative directors until such time as they wanted maximum savings and they got rid of them.[32]

Much like the muddy history of punk's musical evolution, the visual languages that came to be associated with punk had many antecedents and parallels. In some instances, the two came together – rock photographer Michael Beal's June 1976 sleeve for the second single by the Canvey Island rhythm and blues outfit Eddie and the Hot Rods (a cover of Sam the Sham and the Pharaohs' 1965 hit 'Wooly Bully') featured a striking graphic image that he would rework in colorised form for the group's debut album as slightly reinvented punks, *Teenage Depression*, later the same year. Eddie and the Hot Rods were at that time part of a wider pub rock scene that embraced hard-hitting rock music and a down-to-earth approach to live performance that was highly influential on the nascent UK punk scene. The music industry in the United Kingdom was also changing rapidly by the mid-1970s. The pub rock scene that had emerged in part as a reaction to the perceived inaccessibility and elitism of the rock supergroups of the period overlapped significantly with the early punk scene, while the A&R departments at the major record labels were already scouting for the next big thing.

Not only did the music of some of the harder-edged pub rock groups (including Dr. Feelgood, Brinsley Schwarz and Ian Dury's first band Kilburn and the High Roads) cross over to punk but approaches to visual communication also followed suit. Pub rock scene-leaders Dr. Feelgood released their debut album for United Artists, *Down by the Jetty*, in January 1975, and the sleeve by A.D. Design featured a raw, black and white photograph of the band with the windswept, industrialised Thames Estuary behind them. In some ways the design harked back to the era of Chicago blues, from which the band sourced much of their musical inspiration, but at the same time it looked ahead to the urban grit of a punk aesthetic.

Dr. Feelgood subsequently topped the charts in the summer of 1976 with *Stupidity*, an album that captured the band at the height of their power in live performance. The cover designer for that album, Paul Henry, would be heavily involved in marketing new United Artists signings from the punk scene, The Stranglers, the following year. The similarities did not stop there – plans for The Stranglers' debut initially centred on a live album provisionally titled *Dead on Arrival*, recorded at the Nashville Rooms, London, at the end of 1976. The album was intended to follow in the footsteps of *Stupidity* while at the same time capturing the spirit of the new wave, but plans were scrapped in favour of a studio recording of the same material, released under the title *Rattus Norvegicus* in April 1977.

Like the music, Henry's sophisticated designs for the early Stranglers albums – often working with photographer Trevor Rogers – set the band apart from most of their contemporaries. By the time of the group's 1978 third album, *Black and White*, The Stranglers were the most commercially successful of the original British punk and new wave groups. The cover of that album, designed by Kevin Sparrow (who had created the original band logo) and photographed by Ruan O'Lochlainn, featured a stark black and white portrait of the group against a plain white background, setting the tone for a new, post-punk direction in keeping with the emerging visual styles of the times.

Some of the professional designers working with the new groups signed to major labels in the rush to seize the market potential of punk and new wave music had a distinctly unpunk background. Bill Smith created identities for The Jam and The Cure at Polydor, as well as dozens of other artists from disparate musical fields such as The Fatback Band, The Count Basie Big Band, Peggy Lee, The Hollies and Hank Williams. The debut Clash album cover was created by a pair of experienced professional designers in the CBS art department, Janusz Guttner and Rosław Szaybo. Guttner had worked for CBS since 1975, designing albums covers for artists as diverse as Johnny Mathis, John Williams and Sailor, while Szaybo had a portfolio of work dating back to the early 1960s, creating album covers for a wide range of artists from Tony Bennett to Soft Machine, Scott Walker, The Mormon Tabernacle Choir and a group that was to be heavily influential on The Clash, Mott The Hoople. Prior to working with The Adverts, Nicholas de Ville had enjoyed a successful career as an art director, producing record covers for Roxy Music, Sparks and King Crimson. George 'God' Snow's identity for the punk group 999 at United Artists was direct, colourful and hard-hitting, with the group's signature logo based on a simple cloakroom ticket, while he also created work for the Groundhogs, Rick Wakeman and many others at several major labels. Meanwhile, Paul Henry's work for The Stranglers at United Artists sat beside his cover designs for Jan and Dean, Bing Crosby and Shirley Bassey.

4.14 Siouxsie & The Banshees (1978), 'Hong Kong Garden', 7" single, United Kingdom: Polydor. Design by Jill Mumford, collection of the author.

Experienced art directors brought lessons from earlier work in creating identities for rock bands to the new scene, reframed for the emerging punk aesthetic. Jill Mumford worked as an art director at Polydor for around three years, before leaving to work as a freelancer for other labels including Virgin, Island and Trojan Records, creating graphics for punk and new wave groups including XTC, The Depressions and The Skids alongside an eclectic selection of artists, including rockabilly performer Charlie Feathers and reggae artists The Gladiators, Sly Dunbar and Prince Far I.[33] At Polydor, she created notable designs for Siouxsie and the Banshees (Figure 4.14) and Sham 69, together with more traditional family fare such as Bert Kaempfert and His Orchestra, James Last, Captain Beaky and His Band and The Band of Her Majesty's Royal Naval Home Command, Portsmouth.

Mumford had studied graphics at Hornsey School of Art and went on to become a commercial illustrator, commuting into London from Hertfordshire. Following a chance encounter on a train she was offered a position as art director at Polydor in 1975 on the strength of her sketchbooks by two of the senior art directors, Ian Murray and Paul Welch. It was quite unusual for a woman to be appointed to a senior creative position in the music industry at that time, though she didn't encounter too many obstacles. She had experienced some low-level misogynistic bullying at other jobs, but she found the punk scene more inclusive in its attitudes and was able to avoid some of the more regressive elements of the industry.

> I remember I got a job for the *TV Times* or the *Radio Times*, and when I arrived there was a plastic rat in my drawer, which wasn't very funny at the time. At Polydor, I never saw it as a problem, though on reflection I'm sure there were lots of misogynistic people there. With punk, it was never really an issue. The A&R guys were all swaggery, but I just stayed clear of them. It was more ageist – when I was thirty, that's when it really hit me that I was too old for this job and I left to work on scenic art for film and video games.[34]

Mumford left Polydor in 1978 to return to freelance work for other labels, as she found she was being offered more exciting work. She could choose which artists she wanted to work with, rather than being tied to a traditional art department and forced to undertake design work for the disparate range of artists attached to the label.

> I was very into reggae at that time, thanks to punk rock. I went with a friend to New York, specifically to try to get work there, and we took a trip to Jamaica. When I got back to England, I started doing some work for Virgin and met one of their managers, Jumbo [Vanrennen], who was signing lots of reggae bands at that time, and it naturally fell into place. I designed a lot of reggae album covers as well as creating artwork for some of the punk and new wave groups signed to Virgin.[35]

Another member of the Polydor team, Bill Smith, had been interested in music graphics since childhood, attending part-time classes at Rochester College of Art in the late 1960s before enrolling at Maidstone School of Art to pursue his dream. He remembers that Maidstone offered a curriculum 'very much based on the Bauhaus mentality',[36] allowing him to learn more about Dada, Expressionism and the early twentieth-century avant-garde. He went on to London College of Printing to undertake a degree in design.

> LCP was an amazing place. Bill Brandt's brother [Rolf Brandt] was one of the lecturers, the head of school was Tom Eckersley, the British poster designer.[37]

In 1972, at the end of his second year at LCP, Smith undertook a placement at a small marketing and design company in central London, discovering that he could learn as much through professional practice as he could by staying in college. He chose to leave education, developing his skills on the job and moving on to a position as art director for a book publisher, Octopus Books, before a colleague he worked closely with, illustrator Brian Grimwood, told him that Polydor were looking for an art director to join their team in the summer of 1976. Smith got the job and spent most of his first year taking on less prestigious work passed down by the creative director, Jo Mirowski, before an opportunity arose to create a visual identity for a new group signed to the label by A&R manager Chris Parry, The Jam. Smith chose to tile a wall in the photography studio, then spray the name of the band as backdrop for the group photograph on the cover of debut album *In the City*. For the back cover, Smith smashed the tiles to communicate a sense of anger, vandalism and decay.

> I wanted to get punk elements into the first sleeve for *In the City*, such as the graffiti logo and the feeling of a train station toilet with them 'crashed out' against the wall, and as if they left their mark on the back cover. I wanted to get a black and white feel to give it a news story look, with that strong graphic approach.[38]

Equally, Smith saw the need to reflect the specific style and approach of the group, rather than adopt a generic punk aesthetic to fit contemporary trends.

> With The Jam I was desperate to incorporate the ferocity and the raggedness of punk, but quite quickly I thought the group don't want to be seen as a punk band and I needed to reflect the kind of style that they wanted to create.[39]

Shot in stark black and white by Martyn Goddard, the raw aesthetic communicated urgency, rebellion and urban decay, in much the same way that Roberta Bayley's group portrait on the cover of the eponymous debut album by US punk pioneers The Ramones had done the previous year and holding something in common with the debut album by The Clash, released a month previously. Such strategies were far from new – while an evolving punk visual aesthetic was developing through 1976 and 1977, influential images and identities were often the product of professional graphic design studios and designers who had experience of marketing youthful rebellion through rock music going back nearly twenty years. The Rolling Stones, The Who, Led Zeppelin, Black Sabbath, Slade, Alice Cooper and countless others had been branded as authentic representatives of rock music's dark mission and the punk brief was not entirely unfamiliar in this respect.

Leaving Polydor in 1978, Smith set up his own studio, BSS, in the corridor of a fashion house in Great Marlborough Street, London, undertaking freelance work with a wide range of artists. While he still had to outsource the technical jobs at this stage, only taking those parts of the process in house after moving to a dedicated studio, he continued to work with The Jam through to their 1980 album *Sound Affects*, along with other new wave artists including Johnny Thunders, Toyah and new signings The Cure. He had already designed the sleeve for The Cure's debut single, 'Killing An Arab', originally issued by the London-based independent Small Wonder Records. Polydor A&R manager Chris Parry had signed the band but wanted their first release to be on a small punk-related independent, so he did a deal with Small Wonder owner Pete Stennett to put it out as a limited run while he set up a bespoke identity for Fiction Records, a new label operating under the Polydor banner. Smith designed the single cover anonymously, incorporating a band logo that had already been adopted by the group.

Smith also designed covers for the following two singles, 'Boys Don't Cry' and 'Jumping Someone Else's Train', while his design concept for The Cure's debut album, *Three Imaginary Boys*, centred on the notion of a still life portrait of three everyday domestic appliances (Figure 4.15). Collaborating once again with photographer Martyn Goddard, the cover features a 1960s refrigerator, Hoover vacuum cleaner and lampstand, shot against a shocking pink background. Smith had been inspired by Richard Hamilton, together with the visual aesthetic of *Ideal Home* magazine in the 1960s, while serendipitously the image bears a striking similarity to work being developed by US artist Jeff Koons at around the same time.[40] Smith also chose to avoid typography on the cover and inner bag, instead using a variety of photographs and illustrations to denote the tracks on the album. Despite a positive critical reception, the band members of The Cure were not happy with the album cover and insisted on being consulted regarding all artwork decisions for their following album release, *Seventeen Seconds*, in 1980. Following on from a ground-breaking single release, 'A Forest', signalling a change of musical direction to a more dreamlike, proto-gothic sound, Smith's art direction moved into more ethereal territory, collaborating with photographer Andrew Douglas on heavily blurred, out of focus landscape photography.

At around the same time Mumford and Smith were beginning to work with the new punk signings at Polydor, Rob O'Connor was studying graphic design at Brighton Art College and working on the social committee, helping to put gigs on at the college. He recalls the radical distinction between the graphic material being produced for some of the punk bands he was beginning to encounter was quite different from the approach to design he was being taught at college.

> But then at the same time I was going into my college course and thinking, you know, I've come to college to learn how to be a graphic designer and what's going on out there is like, anti-design. Initially, I wondered whether the tutors at college were interested or even aware of this developing punk scene? Or were they more old school?[41]

4.15 The Cure (1979), *Three Imaginary Boys*, vinyl album, United Kingdom: Fiction Records. Design and art direction Bill Smith, photography by Martyn Goddard. Courtesy Bill Smith.

O'Connor considered various career options before deciding to opt for music graphics. On graduating from Brighton, he spent a few months at a local graphic design and marketing company in Gordon Street before taking up a job offer at Polydor Records in the Autumn of 1978. Since Jill Mumford had moved on from her art director role, Rob O'Connor took her desk in the Polydor art department, under the management of creative director Jo Mirowski, and produced work for a variety of artists including John Otway, The Passions and Siouxsie and the Banshees (Figure 4.16). He recalls that the studio didn't operate a strict hierarchy, though the two newly recruited younger designers – O'Connor and Alwyn Clayden – deferred to the knowledge and experience of their older mentor.

4.16 Siouxsie & The Banshees (1979), *Join Hands*, vinyl album, United Kingdom: Polydor. Design by Rob O'Connor, collection of the author.

At Polydor, there were three of us in the art department. There was a guy called Alwyn Clayden, who had just started about two or three months before me; he was a real character and he had tons of work experience at Hipgnosis. Just one day a week or something, but it leaves its mark ... Our boss was Jo Mirowski. He was the art director, although he was actually pretty good to us in many ways. He was a good mentor – very experienced as a designer and art director but had also managed bands and promoted gigs. There wasn't much of a hierarchy, except Jo had a lot more experience ... And then there was a lovely lady called Wendy Gilliatt, who was sort of our PA or secretary. There wasn't much of a junior/senior kind of thing, it was just Jo and us.[42]

Jo Mirowski had created record sleeves for Sham 69 alongside designs for Bing Crosby, The Dubliners, Slade, James Last and dozens of others at Polydor, such was the job of an in-house designer. O'Connor saw an opportunity to work with some exciting new artists at Polydor, though he acknowledges that the demands on a design department working with a major label whose roster spanned easy listening, pop, country, novelty and an assortment of rock genres meant he had to adopt a similarly flexible approach to his senior mentor. Meanwhile, he had his eyes on some of the new arrivals brought in by the Polydor A&R team.

> There were some great artists arriving at Polydor at the time. Chris Parry was the most exciting A&R guy at the time, he had signed The Jam and the Banshees. He was just in the process of setting up Fiction. So, he was signing bands like The Cure, The Associates, The Passions. And it was good to see all that stuff coming through the door, because the old guard was people like The Rubettes and The Sweet who had basically had their day.[43]

O'Connor bridged the perceived divide between a new generation of punk-related designers attached to a band or independent producer and the traditional design teams behind the scenes at the major labels. He eventually spent two years at Polydor before leaving to go it alone with his own studio, Stylorouge. At that point, setting up an independent design studio specialising in music graphics was a relatively hazardous path, though like Morton and others who made the leap from professional music graphics studios to set up on their own, the risk was softened by retaining clients he had already been working with for some time.

Despite the rhetoric of the punk 'revolution', little changed at the major labels, at least until the economic travails and radical restructuring of the 1990s. The recorded music industry was founded on the core principles of innovation and novelty, at least in relation to identifying new artists that could be moulded and exploited to generate popular appeal. The commercially viable areas of punk and new wave were rapidly absorbed, just like the at-the-time radical music and youth scenes that preceded them. Some existing major label acts were also subjected to a process of 'punkification', with songwriting and production mirroring the new competition and designers adopting new wave visual styles to update their image to align them more closely with contemporary trends.[44] With a clear objective to stay one step ahead and to shape the cultural environment in the interest of the market, the A&R managers, producers and studios had long been able to recruit innovative young recording artists and creative visual designers, absorbing new ideas and practices in turn. While some of the new breed of punk-inspired graphic designers set themselves apart from the traditional art departments, preferring to align themselves with specific artists or labels, many of the more successful practitioners joined the ranks of the commercial studios as time went on.

Meanwhile, a clear separation was evolving between the amateur punk DIY fanzine producers faced with growing demand for their work and little knowledge or expertise in how to step up print production and the professional designers – both the punk pioneers and the experienced art directors and creatives – who, in turn, were working in a rapidly changing industry. New technologies were impacting the traditional demarcation of job roles in pre-press art departments, leading to the dramatic restructuring of the newspaper industry, the labour market and the print unions. These themes will be explored further in the following chapters, 'New sounds, new styles: design and technology' and 'A different kind of tension: industry and the individual'.

Notes

1. Ogg, Alex (2009), *Independence Days: The Story of UK Independent Record Labels*, London: Cherry Red Books.
2. Worley, Matthew (2020), '"If I had more time it could be better, but the new wave's about spontaneity, right?": Finding meaning in Britain's early punk fanzines (1976–77)', *Punk & Post-Punk*, 9:2, pp. 223–245.
3. Worley, *Zerox Machine*.
4. See Gorman, *Reasons to be Cheerful* and Balls, Richard (2014), *Be Stiff: The Stiff Records Story*, London: Soundcheck Books.
5. Bestley, '"Fuck Art, Let's Dance"', pp. 353–377.
6. Gorman, *Reasons to be Cheerful*, p. 69.
7. Bestley, '"Fuck Art, Let's Dance"', p. 370.
8. Bestley, '"Fuck Art, Let's Dance"', p. 363.
9. Brook, Tony & Shaughnessy, Adrian (eds) (2017), *Letraset: The DIY Typography Revolution*, London: Unit Editions, p. 9.
10. Bestley & Ogg, *The Art of Punk*, p. 104.
11. Brook & Shaughnessy, *Action Time Vision*. See also Bestley & Ogg, *The Art of Punk*.
12. Garrett, Malcolm (2020), online interview with the author, 30th April.
13. King, Emily (ed.) (2003), *Designed by Peter Saville*, London: Frieze.
14. Spencer, *Pioneers of Modern Typography*.
15. King, *Designed by Peter Saville*, p. 12.
16. Brody (2024), online interview, 5th March.
17. Brody (2024), online interview, 5th March.
18. Brody (2024), online interview, 5th March.
19. Butt, *No Machos or Pop Stars*.
20. Last (2024), telephone interview, 9th February.
21. Last (2024), telephone interview, 9th February.
22. Last (2024), telephone interview, 9th February.
23. Last (2024), telephone interview, 9th February.
24. Last (2024), telephone interview, 9th February.
25. Last (2024), telephone interview, 9th February.
26. Binns, *Gee Vaucher*.
27. See Poynor, Rick (2000), *Vaughan Oliver: Visceral Pleasures*, London: Booth-Clibborn Editions and Brook, Tony & Shaughnessy, Adrian (eds) (2018), *Vaughan Oliver: Archive*, London: Unit Editions.
28. O'Connor (2023), email interview, 18th October.
29. Coles, Mike (2016), interview with the author, 22nd August.
30. Coles, Mike (2024), email conversation with the author, 24th March.
31. Coles (2016), interview, 22nd August.
32. O'Connor (2023), email interview, 18th October.
33. Mumford, Jill (2024), online interview with the author, 7th February.
34. Mumford (2024), online interview, 7th February.

35 Mumford (2024), online interview, 7th February. Mumford created artwork for XTC, Siouxsie & The Banshees, The Jam, The Depressions, Sham 69, The Skids, John Otway and Rip Rig + Panic, together with a host of reggae artists including The Gladiators, Prince Far I, Gregory Isaacs, I-Roy and Big Youth.
36 Smith, Bill (2024), online interview with the author, 13th February.
37 Smith (2024), online interview, 13th February.
38 Bestley & Ogg, *The Art of Punk*, p. 84.
39 Smith (2024), online interview, 13th February.
40 Smith, *Cover Stories*.
41 O'Connor (2023), email interview, 18th October.
42 O'Connor (2023), email interview, 18th October.
43 O'Connor (2023), email interview, 18th October.
44 Some of these developments reflected a genuine interest in the new wave – Bill Nelson's Red Noise, John Cale, Doctors of Madness, Deaf School and even archetypal space rockers Hawkwind. Others were more of a commercial gambit on the part of the artists, managers and promoters. The blurred lines that had always existed between pub rock, new wave and 'power pop' also led to 'new wave style' marketing for groups such as The Motors, Dr Feelgood, The Rumour, Dave Edmunds, The Cars, Cheap Trick, Yellow Dog, The Monks and even a novelty 'punk' b-side by US gay disco icons Village People.

5

New sounds, new styles: design and technology

The first wave of punk gave rise to some hugely influential and long-lasting design output, but it also empowered thousands of amateur designers to create their own interpretation of a visual language that mirrored the excitement and ambition of the new scene – some of it highly innovative, some of it awkward and ugly, but collectively comprising what could be called a punk design aesthetic. The natural limitations of simple tools and materials, limited budgets and the quick production of graphic work by untrained designers, led to a repetition of graphic conventions: black and white or single-colour artwork with hand-rendered, Letraset or typewritten text. Some more adventurous amateur typographers might use stencils or other rudimentary tools such as John Bull printing kits. As discussed in Chapter 1, there are subtle nuances at play here that need to be carefully reflected. The graphic material produced by punk's amateur flank – fanzine writers, local gig promoters, even punk fans who created their own personalised responses to the subculture in scrapbooks or for homemade record sleeves[1] – both informed the wider punk aesthetic and reflected common visual conventions that were emerging as the new subculture made a nationwide impact.

Professional designers working within the record industry attempted to capture the zeitgeist and to embrace the do-it-yourself visual styles bubbling up from below, while at the same time the material they designed had a wide commercial impact and helped shape the styles that the amateur producers aspired to. The cyclical nature of this process means that unpacking the 'authentic' origin of punk visual styles is something of an impossibility, though it can be valuable to map common themes and methods that resonated across the spectrum of punk activity. That might include amateur attempts to mimic the styles of mainstream punk or the adoption of deliberately lo-tech, rough and ready approaches by professional designers that ran counter to conventional practices in the music graphics industry.

This chapter sets out to describe a range of processes chosen by punk and post-punk designers for the origination and print reproduction of record sleeves, posters and other visual material. The focus here goes beyond the usual art historical approach that matches (often assumed) influences and inspiration with outcomes, instead focusing on the steps taken *in between* – the practice and craft deployed in the realisation of a designed object. Some of the most effective punk graphics were those that were explicit in their origins and processes – the creation of design work that enabled others to *do-it-themselves* through an open and accessible, self-reflective practice. As a result, the *form* of the designed object, not just the content, offered guidance and encouragement to others to create their own punk contributions.

A distinction is made between the creation of original artwork and its duplication through mechanical print methods. The two are, of course, closely intertwined, but it is useful to consider the use of some technologies – the photocopier, for instance, or relief printing, stencils and rubber stamps – as tools that could be utilised for the creation and manipulation of images, text and textures at the artwork stage as well as for multiple print reproduction. This is particularly true for flyers or fanzines, which retained a deliberately lo-tech aesthetic and were usually only printed in short runs – machine-printed 'final' objects could be further adapted or personalised through stamping, colouring, stencilling, handwriting or drawing at the final assembly stage.

Methods of origination

The professional graphic designer or art director's activities were traditionally based on a process of specification, whereby other skilled professionals in what was termed art production (designer-visualisers, phototypesetters, metal type compositors, illustrators, photoengravers, photo-retouching artists and platemakers) would be given detailed instructions to achieve the desired end results.

> Because we were art directors, we would rough out the design, we'd hire the photographer, we'd hire the graphic artist to do the lettering, then at the end of the day we'd give the whole thing – the layout, the photograph, the lettering – to an artwork studio. At Polydor we used a company called Wade Wood who were quite close by on Edgware Road.[2]

However, outsourcing part of the production brought its own complications in relation to design credits for the final work.

> Wade Wood quite often got the design or typesetting credit and only occasionally we might get a name credit too. We had to intervene and insist that we got the design credit, since it was all based on our concept and art direction.[3]

Job distinctions were strictly delineated and fiercely protected and the system was hierarchical, gendered and class-driven. Visualisers would work freehand using magic markers to mock up the layout, while specialist artworkers would convert these scamps into camera-ready artwork. Many had trained as technical illustrators and were skilled with mapping pens, scalpels and the variety of precision hand tools required for the job. Typesetting for both text and display was usually outsourced, along with photography, to specialist providers.

> At that time, most of the design layout, font work, typography etc was done outside. We had our own print department and they would put together final artwork with outside agencies. We would art direct the photographer and plan out the design, then pass it on to a production team to do the technical work.[4]

This complex chain of command, and the implicit hierarchy of craftsmen at each stage, was common in the design and print industry at that time. The professional design process largely centred on specification and engagement with pre-press design agencies to produce print-ready artwork. Following a brief spell at Bolton Street Tech in Dublin, under the mentorship of Phil Walsh, Steve Averill was offered a junior position at Walsh's advertising agency, Arks Advertising.

> Each creative group generally consisted of three people. Our role was creative conception, which usually meant working with a copywriter, as most of the work was advert-based. You would then produce a mock-up that was presented to the client. If that was passed, you would then work with the art department and the in-house typographer. This process involved the production of a layout for positioning the type – the team would work out the placement of each line of type and this was then sent to a typesetting facility who would return a print proof which the art department added to the flat, camera-ready artwork. If a photograph was required for the advert you worked with the in-house photographer or a commissioned freelancer depending on the budget and timescale.[5]

Copy cameras such as the Little John allowed designers to work on flat artwork, often at full size (abbreviated in instructions as S/S), which could then be passed to the printer for photographing prior to making up plates. In this way, novice designers could create sleeve designs by hand, using cut-and-paste techniques along with text either hand-written, typewritten, stencilled or applied with Letraset dry transfer rub-down lettering. The repro department – or the employee responsible for creating print-ready artwork at smaller, independent printers – would then take on the more technical task of preparing camera-ready artwork ready for plate-making. In the professional arena, illustrations, band logos and line art would often be created at a larger scale than the final artwork, allowing the pre-press studio to reduce it on the PMT camera to sharpen lines and reduce minor defects.

The repro department and platemakers working for printers were important in the process of origination. They'd often take shitty paste-ups and work magic on them at the film stage, using dot screens, rubylith, photopaque with a lot of skill at pre-press. The typesetters and pre-press people (often formerly compositors) preserved the old market and the old order where specifying was as prevalent as doing for a designer.[6]

There is also a clear distinction between larger display type and body copy. For record covers, the band name and title were often the most important, and therefore largest, typographic elements. The long-standing tradition of the band logo still held sway in the mid-1970s and this often entailed a high degree of customisation, with many designers creating bespoke lettering purely for the purpose, rather than resorting to off-the-shelf typesetting. Some used Letraset display faces, at times adapting them further by hand to create a more unique outcome, while others created logos by hand. Record titles were often less sensitive and could utilise standard typefaces, though like the band logos they often tended towards more expressive styles. The problem was that, like Jamie Reid's ransom note typographic styles for the Sex Pistols, the successful utilisation of a particular typeface to represent one group or artist limited the opportunity to use the same style elsewhere.

Punk's do-it-yourself pioneers, however, usually had little knowledge of these professional practices and the creation of artwork for print often involved simply assembling the material on a flat surface, often at the intended size of the final object, before printing multiple copies with simple duplicators ranging from drum Gestetner Cyclograph stencil machines to photocopiers. This distinction is important in any analysis of punk graphic conventions. While the 'look' of some professionally produced punk material mimicked the lo-tech, amateur styles of the DIY fanzine makers and amateur groups or promoters, the actual process of production was quite different.

Common punk visual tropes included the use of collage, détournement, parody, pastiche and the use of fast, hands-on tools and techniques for reproduction (the photocopier, rubber stamps, stencils and direct printing techniques). Many of these methods drew upon a much longer tradition of agitprop art and design, though punk provided a new context that extended into mainstream culture resulting in, it might be argued, a more powerful impact. In part this was due to the wider social and cultural resonance of punk and the ways in which prominent designers such as Jamie Reid, Malcolm Garrett, Linder Sterling, Chris Morton, Barney Bubbles, Peter Saville and Gee Vaucher could employ mass-produced objects within popular culture – record covers, magazines, posters, flyers, t-shirts and badges – as vehicles for their work. These were not fine art objects to be appreciated by connoisseurs in galleries and exhibitions; they were examples of mass-produced printed ephemera that conveyed a sense of identity and subcultural capital.

Importantly, they also helped build community. As Stephen Duncombe and Matthew Worley have both argued,[7] the amateur production of fanzines enabled 'subterranean' communities to reach out to one another and to blur the distinctions between producer and consumer. In the process, distinctions were also drawn between the 'authentic' subcultural production of *Sniffin' Glue*, *Ripped & Torn*, *Chainsaw*, *Panache* and dozens more and attempts to cash in on the scene with fanzine-like commercial publications – such as the official Rock Against Racism magazine *Temporary Hoarding* or the *Anarchy in the UK* newspaper produced by Sex Pistols management company Glitterbest.

It is worth noting that recent developments in academic research have paid greater attention to the relationship between aesthetics, the form of designed objects and changes in print technology. The field of comics studies, for instance, has witnessed a growth in research relating to the physical qualities of comics and graphic novels and the impact of new print technologies and wider cultural trends in media on artistic production. Comics theorists such as Gareth Brookes and Paul Williams have extended this discussion into the realm of production, distribution and reception to demonstrate the ways in which comics are always 'in dialogue' with other cultural objects.[8] Punk and post-punk design and artistic production might be analysed in the same manner, though to date the field is relatively underexplored.

Letraset

The Letraset company expanded their product range during the 1970s to include architectural figures, texture patterns (Letratone) and borders, signs and symbols and a large range of type designs in several standard sizes.[9] Letraset display type, hand-rendered typography and the use of simple lettering stencils available from many high street newsagents were commonly used techniques for titles on the front of UK punk record sleeves of the period, particularly those produced by smaller labels and DIY enterprises.

> Typesetting was expensive in those days, so Letraset was the preferred option, as most studios had drawers full of it. Sometimes a friendly typographer would sneak something onto a job in return for a few beers, but it still had to be smuggled through the system. Often the rough and ready look was because I didn't have large point Letraset, couldn't afford PMTs and used photocopies to enlarge it.[10]

Letraset is of key importance in many punk and post-punk sleeve designs. The laborious nature of rub-down lettering techniques, combined with the expense of materials, meant that it was useful for limited copy only, often at a fairly large size, such as headlines and titles in magazines.[11]

This means it also lent itself well to record sleeve design, as copy is usually limited to titles (artist, tracks) and little additional information. Letraset (together with several derivative copies of the product) could be purchased widely from print supply retailers and art materials shops and the transfer system was relatively easy to master (at least in a rudimentary fashion) by most would-be designers. It was also widely used professionally for larger type (headlines, artist names or album titles), allowing designers a little more flexibility and a wider range of options beyond the standard typefaces available from compositing studios.[12] Irish designer Steve Averill recalls how he created the original logo and single sleeve for his band The Radiators From Space, early in 1977. He initially hand-drew a variety of angular, offset letterforms (Figure 5.1), before developing a grid for the final design, though the main type was still hand-rendered (Figure 5.2).

> The Radiators logo was created by firstly drawing a pencil grid to get the zig-zag effect. I drew the outline with a Rapidograph, then filled the centre with a brush and ink ... The line effect used on the cover and other early band pictures was done with a homemade screen created by placing a sheet of close-lined Letraset onto a sheet of clear cell and then using the Repromaster.[13]

Meanwhile, typography on the internal lyric sheet for the Radiators From Space album, *TV Tube Heart* (1977), utilised a combination of Letraset and externally commissioned typesetting. Large blocks of smaller body copy were produced with an IBM Selectric typewriter – an electrically powered machine that allowed the user to select from a variety of typefaces by changing the 'golfball' mechanism, a metal sphere with all the characters arranged around its surface. In practice, a designer would combine typographic approaches to suit the task at hand, before using a photographic process to combine all elements within a unified whole.

> The Radiators font was hand-drawn and the other main type was taken from an old type book and done letter by letter. Then in the camera I added lines from a Letraset sheet. A slow but very deliberate process.[14]

For many designers in smaller studios, typesetting for body copy would typically be managed with a manual typewriter, a golfball-style electric typewriter or through a Varitype system, which featured a wider range of typefaces but produced a lower quality output. Phototypesetting was slow and expensive, though it did often provide better results. Again, however, the designer needed to be fully aware of the range of typefaces available and the inherent technical constraints.

> Once phototypesetting became the norm, we pretty much used them all the time until the arrival of the Mac, when composition began to be done onscreen. Though as with Letraset and the typesetter's fonts, the available choices were limited and you had to make sure that the company producing the film had the same version of the font. Even using a different cut of a font like Helvetica would cause problems initially.[15]

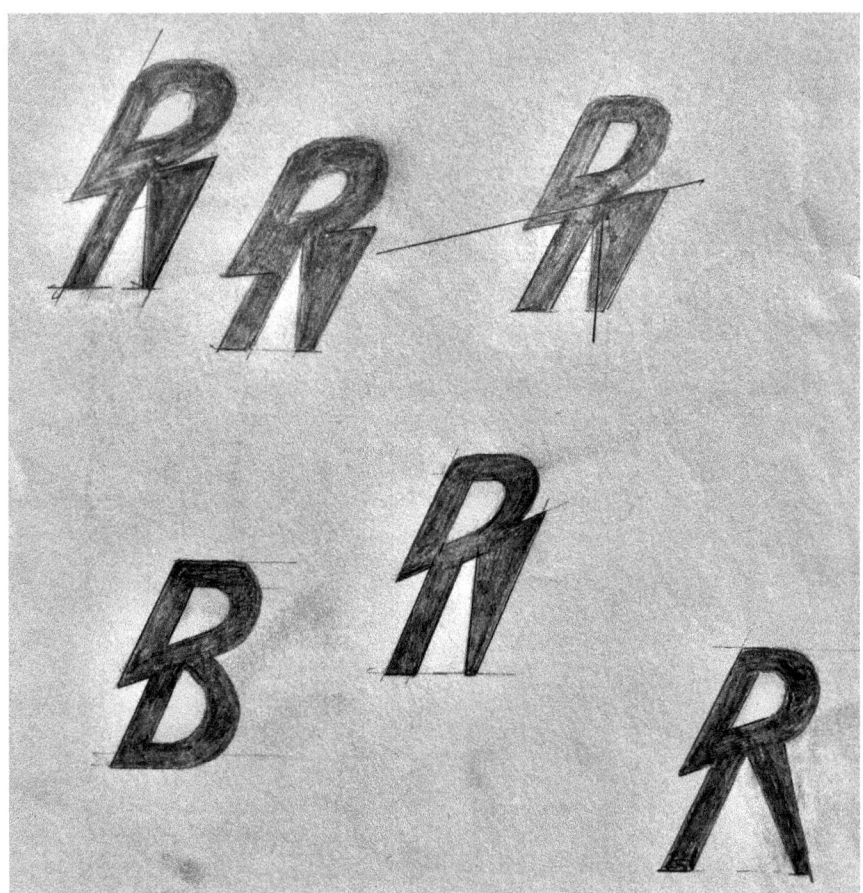

5.1 Steve Averill, pencil roughs for Radiators From Space logo, 1977. Courtesy Steve Averill.

Punk's Letraset typographers also took inspiration from the rule breaking, disruptive initiatives of the image makers and collage artists. Text did not necessarily need to adhere to a baseline, nor did it need to be rigidly systematic in the choice of typeface (as ransom note type styles had proved). Designers could employ a variety of Letraset typefaces in the same body of text, or they could use alternative characters as substitutes. Such experiments were sometimes driven by necessity – Letraset was expensive and the sheets contained limited numbers of each letter, reflecting anticipated demand. In other words, there were more vowels – e, a, i, o, u – and frequently used consonants – c, d, t, s, r – with a comparatively reduced number of less popular characters in the English language – x, z. When a designer ran out of a particular character, they could either buy another sheet of Letraset, try to copy the letter on film or photocopy and paste it

5.2 Radiators From Space (1977), 'Television Screen', 7" single, United Kingdom: Chiswick. Design by Steve Averill/Art On My Sleeve. Courtesy Ted Carroll, collection of the author.

down or cobble together some parts of others to approximate the same character. So, the letter p was sometimes inverted to create d, u could become a very rough n, v could be doubled up to create w. Numerals, punctuation and other typographic decorations could also be used creatively, the final effect ranging from a rough and ready approximation of the typewritten word to a playful, decorative and highly considered form of experimental typography, as in the track titles on the back cover of the debut Killing Joke album in 1980, designed by Mike Coles (Figure 5.3).

Another problem was that many examples of larger custom display typefaces in the Letraset catalogue were quite unsuitable for punk. The time delay between a new lettering style becoming popular and its marketisation as a commercial Letraset product meant that many expressive

5.3 Killing Joke (1980), *Killing Joke*, vinyl album, United Kingdom: Malicious Damage. Track titles. Design by Mike Coles/Malicious Damage, courtesy Mike Coles.

styles appeared out of date as soon as they entered the range. The late 1970s Letraset catalogue, for instance, included numerous decorative faces that seemed to have come from the previous era. Letraset faces such as Stripes,[16] Manuscript Caps,[17] Lazybones,[18] Candice[19] and Sinaloa[20] certainly seemed more Stevie Nicks than Poly Styrene. Shatter[21] (Figure 5.4) at least fitted the punk theme a little more closely, though it was not widely used on record sleeves.

Sometimes, Letraset type styles were chosen for more political reasons. The explicitly political agenda of the neo-Fascist punk in the early 1980s led to the development of visual and graphic conventions that helped define the emerging scene, in particular the use of Gothic and blackletter forms to suggest historical associations with Germany and Nazism.[22]

5.4 Letraset Shatter dry transfer lettering. Designed by Vic Carless (1973).

5.5 Letraset Walbaum Fraktur dry transfer lettering. Originally designed by Justus Erich Walbaum c.1800, Letraset design by Berthold (c.1960).

However, these typographic styles were also commonplace across the wider punk scene: The Damned employed a variety of hand-rendered Gothic styles for their posters, record covers and labels, while Chris Morton had played with the form at Stiff Records.[23] Punk designers seeking to use Gothic and blackletter styles faced a limited range of options. Within the Letraset range, Walbaum Fraktur[24] (Figure 5.5) was derived directly from traditional Gothic styles, though its relative inaccessibility in comparison with the widely available (and copied) Old English[25] (Figure 5.6) saw the latter more commonly adopted as a substitute. Other connotations may have been less desirable, including the widespread use of Old English type styles on traditional crafts, homemade jams and marmalade labels at village fêtes. Other amateur typographers chose to hand render their own interpretation of Gothic text for fanzines, flyers and record covers, with less than convincing results.

Do-it-yourself, independent post-punk was also set to become a clearly defined punk subgenre, with production and manufacturing concerns taking precedence over the actual style or content of the music. DIY groups took control of the whole process of recording and production of their records, usually along with the design and reproduction of sleeve artwork. Independence thus became an overtly ideological position as well as a self-initiated cottage industry for production and manufacture.

5.6 Letraset Old English dry transfer lettering. Originally designed by William Caslon c.1760, Letraset design by Monotype (c.1960).

> The DIY Letrasetting and collage came from a strongly held stance – no way were you going to let a designer near your artwork. You knew what you wanted to say and you were going to say it. No designer was going to come and pretty it all up and mess with what you were saying, making it just a pose.[26]

Simplicity was usually a pre-requisite for punk record sleeve designs, often created in black and white on one original layout. Second colours – usually a single spot colour selected from the Pantone range – would require separate artwork which when printed would integrate directly with the first. Image registration (aligning different coloured layers of artwork) was a particular concern and many multiple-coloured sleeve designs go no further than the use of a black and white image set against simple coloured background shapes or grids. The skilled designer could make use of overlays to extend the range of visible colours in the final design, but this took detailed knowledge of the process and an understanding of potential ink and tone combinations. Full-colour CMYK reproduction was much rarer among the punk DIY pioneers and was largely reserved for bigger budget releases on the major labels, with the established art directors, design and pre-press studios and printers all in place to support. Techniques of type and image composition were also usually very simple, with type either overlaid on a flat colour background (often in the simplest form of either black type on a white background or reversed white out of black), or as Letraset or stencil applied directly over a halftone image. In the simplest cases, the type was laid out on white strips of paper and stuck down over the background image on the camera-ready artwork.

Hand-cut letter stencils and hand-rendered text also featured heavily on many punk graphics, to the extent that typographic treatments based on the stencil became a popular visual style rather than a simple necessity. The problem with using physical stencils was one of availability: while cutting an original stencil required a certain degree of care and attention to detail, a very limited range of lettering stencils were widely available on the High Street – typically the plastic sets produced by the Helix company for school and college use.[27] The rounded figures of these letterforms afford them a quaint, homemade aesthetic and associations with schoolwork or arts and crafts are hard to avoid. As such, the use of these devices was limited and most punk stencil type reflected a harder-edged, more angular style.

For those designers and typographers who didn't want to go to the effort of creating their own stencil letterforms, Letraset Stencil Bold,[28] an almost military-looking face with rounded serifs, was widely available in upper case only and in a limited range of sizes (commonly 36pt and 60pt), while a generic version was also widely available from other high street stationery shops such as WH Smith and Woolworths. The employment of stencil lettering such as Stencil Bold or Glaser Stencil Bold[29] (a Letraset alternative to the former, being sans serif and comprising less condensed and harsher, more angular figures) also helped to fulfil a secondary purpose. Along with stencilled logos and high contrast images, they could be copied and reproduced by fans, particularly on clothing. The early 1980s saw a developing trend among punk fans in spray painting the backs of leather jackets with band names and logos, and the use of simple, easily replicated typographic styles and graphic figures certainly helped to facilitate this. The militaristic appearance of various stencil forms was also of importance to the reading of the intended message: many punk groups had flirted with uniforms, army surplus clothing and military chic.

Other Letraset products offered a simple method for creating illustrations and tone work. Letraset architectural symbols spanned a range of line art illustrations of trees and foliage, people, buildings, motor vehicles, household fittings and furniture, in plan view and elevation. In combination with the more sci-fi and futuristic Letraset typefaces, the clip art nature of some of these figures worked well for ironic use, notably in the emerging post-punk and electronic music scenes. Letratone and Instantex sheets allowed the designer or illustrator to cut out and apply areas of halftone tints or textures at the artwork stage.[30] Pantone colour overlay was also available in continuous tone flat or graduated colour sheets. While pre-press artwork for simple two- or three-colour sleeves would be supplied as black and white separations, with the individual colours specified in writing by the designer, the use of colour overlays could assist the designer in the visualisation of design jobs at the pre-press stage, both for print specification and as presentation roughs to show the client.

Artwork modification

A significant aspect of the translation of the artwork to film separations and hence to printed proof was in communicating to the individuals involved exactly how to assemble the various parts supplied by the designer. These instructions were usually written and drawn onto tracing paper overlays to the artwork, which were registered and held in place with pins or tape. The designer's role was to plan, predict and specify required outcomes, rather than to originate them in their entirety at the drawing board stage. While some skilled designers could make use of the flexibility offered by such pre-press tools as the PMT camera, most design studios were more limited in terms of the technology available. Such facilities were often reserved for major artwork departments rather than being readily available to designers as a tool for the creation of artwork.

> I then had to do all the boring stuff, as well as the nice stuff, after I went freelance. It was like punk – learn three chords and go. I worked from home and had to drive in to London, pick up PMTs [typesetting] and do the paste-up in the back of my car, then deliver it to Virgin. I got really good at doing paste-up in the car or borrowing a desk at the place I bought the PMTs from.[31]

One key distinction between the professional designer and amateur and DIY producers was in their detailed knowledge of the range of pre-press artworking and specification techniques available. Record cover design was technologically driven, with artwork reflecting the availability of materials together with the skills and training of the designer. In the professional music graphics sector, the distinction between specification and origination usually occurred at the artworking stage. The designer would produce what were commonly known as *positionals* – draft layouts with indicative notes for the placement of type and visual elements. They would then rely on specialists in the art production department to take their planned design to what was termed camera-ready artwork, a necessary step to create plates and move to print. Printer Tim Milne recalls that the general lack of dialogue or engagement between designers and printers could sometimes lead to problems.

> There was a huge divide between the middle-class designers who had been to university and the working-class printers. They were highly suspicious of each other. So, a scenario where the printer advised the designer would be quite rare – ordinarily they would just print it and it would look awful and the printer would say 'well, you did the artwork, you're supposed to be a designer'. There was no cooperation, just a mutual distrust. The printers viewed the designers as airy-fairy aesthetes and the designers thought the printers were a bunch of crooks.[32]

Many punk-inspired designers wanted more control, to move away from the established rulebook, to incorporate lo-tech or experimental processes and to engage more effectively in the adjustment of their work at the pre-press stage. Malcolm Garrett recalled using a photocopier to create a grainy monochrome treatment of Linder Sterling's colour photomontage for the Buzzcocks single 'Orgasm Addict' (Figures 5.7). However, when he took the artwork to the printer he was told that photocopies should not be used for image origination and the composition should have been created using high-resolution film.

> I remember having artworks sent back to me that the printer would not print. They would say 'We can't print this, it's not to a professional standard'. I pasted up a photocopy and they wouldn't accept that a photocopy was good enough artwork. So, somebody else came into the picture. I would have to draw something, send it off to a company. I can't remember the name of the company, but there were a couple around Tottenham Court Road, there was one off Rathbone Place. They wouldn't make a PMT, it would be a chemical transfer, a photographic version of my photocopy, which I would then paste up to send to the printer.[33]

The photocopier was a relatively new tool at that stage, largely used for straight duplication of original documents and seldom in creative practice. Many punk-inspired designers admired the visual quality (or lack of quality) of photocopied material, which gave it a slight sense of distortion or decay. Some designers sought out machines that provided the blackest black, the strongest contrast and the sharpest image quality. Others revelled in the aesthetics of cheap reproduction, in the grey midtones and the deliberate connotation of cheapness and disposability. At the same time, there was something of a professional unwritten rule that pre-press artworkers would not intervene in the designer's work.

> There was a strict dividing line between 'authorship' and 'reproduction'. A lot of that rested in the way the artwork was done. Everybody understood that the designer did the artwork and the printer did the reproduction. The repro house team was not there to fix mistakes, just to work with the marks made by the designer.[34]

This was not always the case, however. Neville Brody recalls some pre-press departments misunderstood his more radical ideas.

> I did covers where everything was at an angle and when it came back from the printer they had straightened it all up, as they thought it was a mistake.[35]

Technological developments also played a key role in the way record covers were designed. Barney Bubbles and Chris Morton were renowned for their use of the range of pre-press facilities available to the commercial designer, including recent developments in PMT camera technology and a strong familiarity with design specification for print. Following the trend towards photolithographic printing and phototypesetting which had been ongoing since the early 1960s, designers in the late 1970s

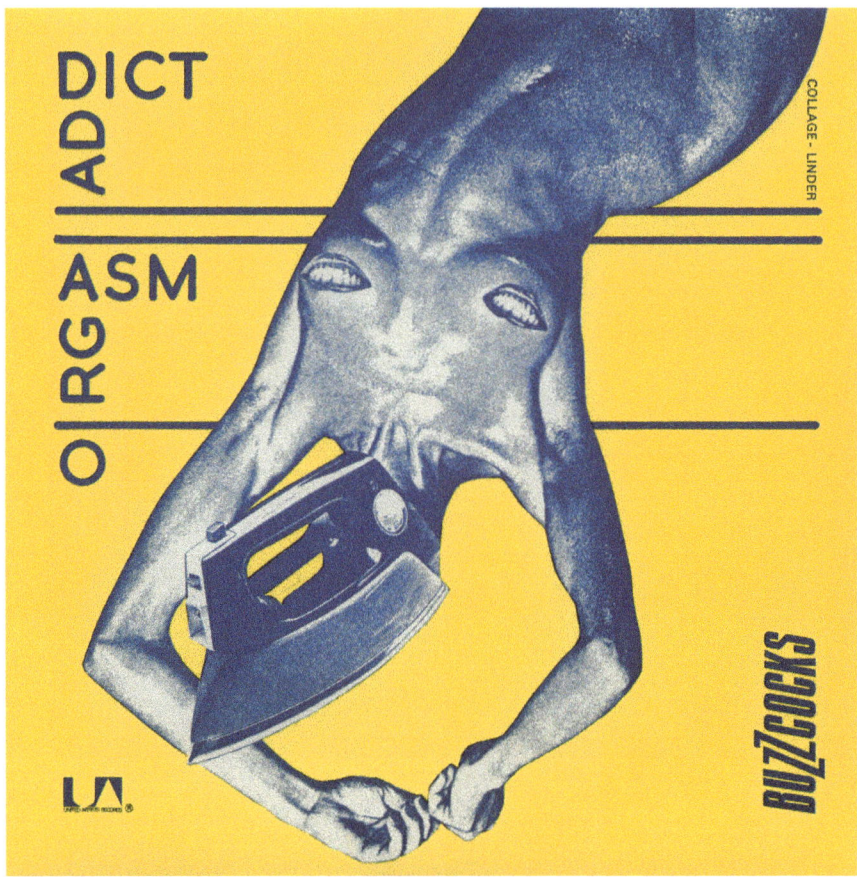

5.7 Buzzcocks (1977), 'Orgasm Addict', 7" single, United Kingdom: United Artists. Front cover. Design by Malcolm Garrett/Arbitrary Images, photomontage by Linder. Courtesy Malcolm Garrett/Assorted Images.

were able to work with pre-press operators to produce complex overlays which allowed a direct manipulation of text and image, line and tone. Professional designers could layer films to produce sophisticated designs incorporating interwoven blocks of flat colour and bold halftone images – often using found objects and stencils to create complex solid shapes and outlines. This freedom enabled record cover designers a great deal more control over the construction of artwork than before. Rather than detailing instructions for typesetting and picture reproduction, the designer could create camera-ready artwork for the printer to make printing plates, with the type, illustrations and halftones all in place. Using the PMT camera the designer could enlarge or reduce type, reverse it to white on black, vary the contrast of images and make creative adjustments to the layout before sending direct to print.

> The PMT machine was the holy grail for designers. Apart from the fact you could rescale type and images, a lot of the time the mistakes that happened were as interesting as if everything had gone right. The worst thing about it was that nothing lasted – you had to do something with that PMT relatively quickly, making sure it was correctly set.[36]

As photocopier technology improved, the new generation of designers began to use it more creatively in the origination and modification of artwork. Prior to this technological breakthrough, designers used a Grant projector to calculate the required magnification or reduction of an original piece of artwork. The user would place an object on a platform beneath an adjustable lens, then view the scaled image on a screen. Once the desired size was achieved through moving the platform, a piece of tracing paper could be placed on the screen and the outline marked to give an indication of required scale.[37] This information could then be used to instruct the PMT camera operator.[38]

> My whole attitude to things changed with photocopiers becoming really good quality, particularly the black and white ones. When they're scanning, you could move the paper and all that business. We had a lot of fun with that. And we were doing that for years after it stopped being fashionable just for the sheer hell of it. And the Grant enlarger, you know, and we had a PMT camera. I was in the dark room all the time and after I finished my work for the day I'd go in there and do some more stuff myself at night. I had a lot of fun with that. You used to have to screen your own imagery by using a series of halftone screens between image and the glass, which seems terribly archaic now.[39]

The effect of these technological changes was felt across the range of punk sleeve design and also enabled amateur designers to create simple designs without having to negotiate all the complex systems of (professional) specification – though this also led to something of a distinction between work produced by designers who had the knowledge to make use of these techniques and could therefore use them advantageously in their work and those who didn't. Knowledge wasn't the only factor: process cameras were expensive pieces of kit, both to purchase, maintain and run, limiting availability to larger pre-press studios and commercial printers. Some designers venturing out to set up their own studios after working in professional studios went so far as to invest in the technology upfront. After leaving Stiff, Chris Morton established a home studio, centred on a second-hand Agfa-Gevaert process camera in its own tiny darkroom.

> Undoubtedly my most important tool was/is a Repromaster Process Camera, which was the first thing I got when I left and went freelance. After that would come Letratone and the French rub-down equivalent, Mecanorma, which had a wider range of textures and arty graphic marks.[40]

Rob O'Connor also invested in a PMT camera when he set up Stylorouge, along with a Grant projector and a decent photocopier.

> So yeah, that was the first thing I did when I set up a new company. I wanted to make sure that I had access to a Grant enlarger and a PMT machine and a photocopier. So, they told me about the cost, the Grant enlarger dudes. It wasn't hydraulic it wasn't electric, it's literally a bellows camera – and it makes you sweat! But eventually, of course, it was replaced by the photocopier with its enlargement and reduction facilities. Up until then it was all about tracing paper and pen believe it or not. I mean very time consuming, hugely labour intensive when you're designing, but I loved that.[41]

The new technology separated the professionals from the amateurs, the commissioned from the vernacular. After he was commissioned by Jake Riviera to create a visual identity for the newly launched Stiff Records, Chris Morton created early posters by hand, using needlepoint Rapidograph pens – a technique he had developed at art college and in design commissions for Pete Frame at *ZigZag* and freelance work for *Men Only* magazine. As he gained experience, he discovered a range of industry standard prepress methods that were far more efficient.

> When I discovered the professional world of typesetting – which was quite a zap and another eye-opener – I hand-drew the artwork for the Stiff typeface I'd designed so we could specify sizes and get it photographically typeset and delivered back, which was a godsend compared to the amount of Letrasetting we were doing.[42]

Morton hand rendered an entire Stiff custom alphabet that could be converted to a typeface for use in all his design work for the label (Figure 5.8). The lettering was drawn in upper case at a standard four-inch height, then sent to phototypesetting at a supplier that had bought a family of fonts from the designer previously, just before he started full-time at Stiff. As a result, Morton and his team could order custom-set type at any size, with an exclusivity agreement on its use.

> It was proper posh phototypesetting – words, headlines, sentences, whole paragraphs all at any point size – I found it quite magical![43]

DIY methods of reproduction

At the same time, some of the punk amateurs, particularly in the fanzine market, were finding that they were victims of their own success. Early experiments with often illicitly accessed photocopiers and the manual collation of pages proved effective in establishing an identity and garnering interest from prospective readers, but most fanzine editors were discovering that the labour involved predicated a very limited print run. As demand increased and they established links with distributors and retailers, who in turn requested a larger and more consistent supply, some of the more successful fanzine producers began to work with professional print services. This shift did result in some compromises and what could

5.8 Stiff Records lettering, original artwork 1977. Courtesy Chris Morton.

potentially be seen as a watering down of the raw energy of the original punk DIY aesthetic.

> By then, the whole DIY punk graphics thing had been and gone. The moment a fanzine maker has to go to a commercial lithoprinter to produce a longer print run, that particular bit of magic goes up in smoke as they will be making damn sure that the artwork is right.[44]

It does also, however, illustrate the awkward balance that had to be struck between punk 'authenticity', the economics and technology of print production and the unfixed and uncertain elements of visual style. While the *look* of punk was starting to become recognised and accepted as a set of broad visual conventions, the *process* by which those objects were created and manufactured was often obscured, sometimes deliberately so. Simply put, a graphic composition could be made to look raw, rough and ready, but the work that led to its creation might tell a different story.

The first run of Mark Perry's *Sniffin' Glue* fanzine (around fifty copies) was photocopied by his girlfriend, Louise, in the office where she worked, with Ted Carroll's Rock On record shop in Portobello advancing the money to pay for subsequent photocopied print runs via a professional service provider. *Sniffin' Glue* grew in popularity, with Rock On also helping with distribution, and it was subsequently stocked at other record shops including Compendium in Camden and Bizarre in Paddington. By issue six in January 1977, circulation of *Sniffin' Glue* had gone into the thousands, so Perry and his team switched to commercial lithographic printing (a significantly cheaper technology for longer print runs than the photocopier). *SG* photographer Harry T. Murlowski made the business arrangements with the assistance of Stewart Joseph at Rough Trade, and Perry and his team were given space in a back room at the Rough Trade shop in West London to put the fanzine together.[45]

Hot on the heels of *Sniffin' Glue*, dozens more fanzine writers launched their own small-scale publications. Some of the best known – Tony Drayton's *Ripped & Torn*[46] (later *Kill Your Pet Puppy*, with Alistair Livingston), Mick Mercer's *Panache*, Tony Fletcher's *Jamming!*,[47] Charlie Chainsaw's *Chainsaw*, Frank Drake and Peter Gilbert's *In The City* – ran for several years and multiple issues, while others including Tony Moon's *Sideburns* (which quickly morphed into the long-running *Strangled*), Jon Savage's *London's Outrage* and Shane MacGowan's *Bondage* were to subsequently prove important contributions to the developing punk scene, even though they didn't last beyond 1977. Outside London, fanzines such as *Shy Talk* (Manchester), *Vague* (Salisbury),[48] *Gun Rubber* (Sheffield), *Adventures in Reality* (Coventry),[49] *Granite City* (Aberdeen), *Kingdom Come* (Fife), *Kid's Stuff* (Chessington), *Alternative Ulster* (Belfast) and *Safety in Numbers* (Portsmouth) reflected the development of scenes well beyond punk's stereotypical epicentre.[50]

Even though many of the more successful fanzines shifted production from the kitchen table and surreptitious use of a photocopier to longer print runs via cheap lithoprinters, their visual style held on to a form of graphic immediacy. In late 1977, *Sniffin' Glue* retained much of the raw simplicity of its original do-it-yourself design aesthetic, despite carrying advertisements for major label punk releases and moving to commercial printers and distributors. The final issue in September 1977 ran to twenty thousand copies and featured a free flexidisc of Perry's band Alternative TV. Like much other punk graphic material, it looked DIY but involved professional service providers behind the scenes.[51] Tony Drayton recalls working with several printers as the demand for *Ripped & Torn* began to grow. The flat artwork for the fanzine had been created using simple tools and techniques – cover titles were hand-rendered in thick felt-tip pen, with no discernible stylistic consistency, though Drayton adopted a masthead based on Letraset Old English later in 1977. A mixture of carefully handwritten and typewritten text on the features pages was roughly set in one- and two-column grids.

> The first ten copies I photocopied at my work, then the first properly printed copies of *Ripped & Torn*, were done locally at a printer in Glasgow I found in the Yellow Pages. I had to get them properly printed as Rough Trade and Compendium bookshop had ordered two hundred copies each. For the

next issue, I sent the pages to some printer somewhere and received the printed pages back by Red Star – I think Rough Trade may have guided me there. The next printer for *Ripped & Torn* was one in Cambridge who also printed *Sniffin' Glue*. They recommended him and Harry Murlowski drove us there and back with the finished copies.[52]

Local print shops and community centres provided opportunities for fanzine producers further afield. Alan Rider recalls accessing a variety of local print services for *Adventures in Reality*, based in Coventry.

At first, I used a copy shop called Parbury's in Coventry who did cheap Xerox copies. All the local fanzines used them. Later I progressed to offset litho and used the local polytechnic, youth training scheme, or community print shops. I also printed some inserts myself using a Gestetner duplicator and even screen-printed a paper bag one of the issues came in myself using borrowed facilities at the local art school.[53]

Ripped & Torn eventually evolved into a new title, *Kill Your Pet Puppy*. Launched in 1979, soon after the election of Margaret Thatcher's Conservative government, *Kill Your Pet Puppy* was a more political venture, reflecting the squatting scene in London and the emergence of the anarcho-punk scene. Regular contributor Alistair Livingston recalls working with a range of print providers.

I remember with *KYPP6* the first five hundred (or less) we went to a community print shop on the Holloway Road and did it on a Gestetner type machine. Fanzines printed by Better Badges usually had a Better Badges half page advert in them, so you can tell which ones were printed there. Better Badges also did distribution, selling the zines alongside the badges at gigs ... we printed a hundred copies of *KYPP6* at the Islington Bus Company, which was a community printers/community centre.[54]

Some smaller businesses and service providers did see the potential of affordable print technology for more creative ends, however. Among these, former Pink Fairies roadie Joly MacFie's Better Badges enterprise was to take a lead in supporting the emerging punk independents. Starting out as a manufacturer of pin badges, the business was run from the former premises of the *International Times*, for whom MacFie had served as music editor. Better Badges acted as a commercial enterprise (designing and manufacturing badges reflecting up-and-coming bands) and a service point for newcomers (bands could design their own badges and MacFie would manufacture them in short runs at fairly low cost) and the business might be better seen as a punk-era extension of the radical print shops that had served the needs of the counterculture during the late 1960s and early 1970s. MacFie had acquired a process camera through a hire purchase agreement in 1977, primarily to rescale images and to create halftones for better quality reproduction. At that point in time, most photocopiers could not resize artwork, let alone produce halftone or gradated images, and

PMT cameras were usually only available in the pre-press departments at large commercial printers. Badge printing was conducted on a tabletop Roneo Vickers machine.

Better Badges became more involved in the punk fanzine arena once the business invested in printing equipment specifically aimed at that purpose. In late 1978, MacFie bought out a failing print shop's kit, including three lithographic print machines. This was far more equipment than he needed, so he turned to printing fanzines for clients.

> I bought a process camera in 1977 and then started printing on a tabletop Roneo Vickers. In late 1978, I bought out a failing print shop's kit. This got me a Multilith 1250 and two Rotaprint machines – one A4 and one A3. Far more than I needed for badge production, so I turned to printing zines.[55]

Tony Drayton recalls his arrangement with MacFie for *Ripped & Torn* covered both printing and distribution.

> Joly proposed a business plan where he would take on the expenses of printing and I would buy copies off him at, I think, 10p per copy to sell at 25p. He would also sell the fanzine himself through his mail order and at gigs, the money he made doing this would be his.[56]

MacFie also seized the opportunity to experiment. He used the print production of Tony Fletcher's *Jamming!* fanzine to practice with different print techniques including multiple colours. The consideration of manufacturing processes extended right through the range of materials used, including two grades of paper. The better grade, Mellotex, was used for badges and fanzine covers, with lower grade paper for interior pages.[57] The development of new printing technologies allowed him to print relatively economically.

> Platemaking got a lot cheaper, even down to paper plates that would crap out after a hundred copies. Kodak and Agfa were driving it with cheaper materials for PMT. You could make metal offset plates for approximately 75p. I priced it out and came up with a rate of 2p per double-sided sheet for 'zines, but if we dropped in a BB ad I'd drop it to 1p. And we took pretty much all comers. You paid for what you took and we'd distro the rest. I always saw my role as empowering the voice of the fans vs the industry. With style.[58]

MacFie eventually expanded the fanzine part of the business to run three presses and print runs of up to several thousand copies for titles such as *Jamming!*, *Chainsaw* and *Rising Free*. By this time, Better Badges employed three in-house printers, including Nick Godwin from the group Zounds, extending their reach into the emerging post-punk scenes through personal connections. Later editions of *Ripped & Torn* had utilised two-colour processes, overprinting black text on a single-colour background image, initially just for the cover and later adding single-colour text pages in red, green or blue ink, interspersed with the standard black pages.[59] *Kill Your*

Pet Puppy went one stage further, utilising the available print technologies to create full-colour covers and internal pages (Figures 5.9 and 5.10).

> By the time of *KYPP* Joly had been experimenting with pouring different ink colours into his machine to create a multi-stripes pattern when printing flyers; and he encouraged me to use this for the first issue of *KYPP*. It was a bit of encouragement from both sides really, as we both wanted to see what it would look like and how far we could push it.[60]

Other radical print shops helped to facilitate the production of some of the more established punk fanzines. Some issues of *Vague* were printed by Aldgate Press, a worker's co-operative founded in 1981 as an offshoot of the Freedom Press, a radical print workshop originally set up by Charlotte Wilson, Nikolai Tchaikovsky, Francesco Saverio Merlino and Peter Kropotkin in 1886. Others including *Black Flag* were printed by Little @ Press, based in the former dockyard warehouses at Metropolitan Wharf, Wapping. Mike Diboll created several fanzines over a period of years. His first attempt, *No Real Reasons*, was, like many other small-scale punk fanzines, illicitly photocopied. The most successful, *Toxic Grafity*, centred on the anarcho-punk and squatting scenes in London.

> The first *TG* was done at a community print workshop in southeast London. The next two were lithoed at Better Badges, who also did badges and stickers ... the last one I did in the basement at 11 Nettleton Road, part of the Nettleton Road Housing Co-op where I was living, using a silk screen and colour duplicator gifted by Dial House. *TG*'s successor, *The Commonweal*, (only one issue) was lithoed at Little @ in Wapping.[61]

Generally, there were few tensions between the ideology of the punk fanzine producers and printers. Graphic designer and printer Andrew Howard, who worked at the Islington Bus Company, suggests a level of liberal-minded tolerance towards much of the material that the group was asked to print.

> We were used by a whole range of groups – sometimes using our duplicators and then later our photocopiers (we used Sharp copiers that produced really great blacks). We were cheaper than most places. I don't recall that we ever refused or censored anyone – we were a left-wing collective after all.[62]

However, such ease of collaboration was not always the case, as many of the print cooperatives operated strict codes of practice regarding what might be seen as ideologically opposed to members' strongly held beliefs.

> Most of the presses had policies about what they would not print, the constants being racist or sexist material, although they might include 'anti-socialist' (Paupers Press c.1976), 'not reactionary' or 'anti-working class' (Community Press 1979), 'party political' (Bath Printshop 1979) 'electioneering material' (Tyneside Free Press 1979), or content 'of a religious or right-wing nature' (Fly Press 1984).[63]

5.9 *Kill Your Pet Puppy* fanzine no.1, 1979. Inner page. Design by Tony Drayton/The Puppy Collective. Courtesy Tony Drayton.

5.10 *Kill Your Pet Puppy* fanzine no.3, 1980. Front cover. Design by Tony Drayton/The Puppy Collective. Courtesy Tony Drayton.

Tony Drayton came across some difficulties with shops and resellers of his *Ripped & Torn* fanzine, though not with the printers – though at the time his fanzines were printed by commercial printers rather than the more politically inclined radical print shops.[64]

> None of the printers ever refused anything I sent to them, I never thought about that happening when producing the fanzines. Rules were more set by shops who had the power to refuse to stock the fanzine. There was quite an issue when I put Raped on the cover of *Ripped & Torn 11* as Rough Trade had refused to sell the Raped EP due to the band's name (and the name of their EP).[65]

At this point, photocopiers were a relatively new tool for reproduction and were not widely viewed as a creative tool – they were more likely to be found in legal offices and libraries than design studios. As technology advanced, some monochrome photocopy machines could use single-colour toner cartridges, though again the intention was more technical than creative. Full-colour copiers were extremely rare. Letterstream in Shepherd Market, Mayfair, obtained a colour machine and offered a professional reproduction service.[66] After moving to larger premises near Regent Street, the company began to attract a small number of punk artists and designers, including Barry Jones (who designed flyers for the Roxy Club in Covent Garden) and Adam and the Ants collaborator Laurie Rae Chamberlain. Some early issues of Frank Drake and Peter Gilbert's *In The City* utilised colour photocopies for their cover, though the producers soon moved to a simpler, two-colour lithoprinted format that proved both cheaper and more effective. Joly MacFie also used Letterstream for colour Xerox work in the manufacture of badges and reflects that the visual effects produced by a combination of colour photocopy and lamination appear remarkable in retrospect.

> Colour Xerox is kind of remarkable now in that it is virtually unreproducible. The process of heat lamination that our factory – Universal in Bethnal Green – used, really emphasises the 'emboss' effect.[67]

All this serves to provide an overview of the relations – and distinctions – between do-it-yourself punk amateur production and established music graphics professional practices. Punk graphics span this traditional divide, with visual conventions drawn from the DIY underground to project a sense of authenticity and a new generation of professional designers willing to experiment and to break rules and standard conventions. Technological changes enabled at least part of this shift – process cameras became more widely accessible to designers for origination and composition of their work, affording more control from conception to final pre-press artwork. Photocopiers and other lo-tech tools that had previously been seen as unprofessional by printers improved in quality and in the range of tasks that could be undertaken, including enlargement and reduction. These changes in the social and technical practices of design blurred the boundaries between amateur and professional production. As with music, punk had enabled a partial break with the past and what would become later known as post-punk galvanised opportunities for new creative approaches in graphic design, along with a host of other creative arts practices, from fashion to film. Changing technologies and the culmination of an ongoing restructuring of the labour market, particularly in the printing industries, enabled more control along with creative freedom for a new generation of designers, though not without controversy, as will be seen in Chapter 6, 'A different kind of tension: industry and the individual'

Notes

1. Bestley and Burgess, 'Fan artefacts and doing it themselves'.
2. Mumford (2024), online interview, 7 February.
3. Smith (2024), online interview, 13 February.
4. Smith (2024), online interview, 13 February.
5. Russ Bestley (2020), 'Art On My Sleeve: An interview with Steve Averill, graphic designer', *Punk & Post-Punk* 9:3, pp. 550–551.
6. Paul McNeil (2023), in conversation with the author, 21 November.
7. Stephen Duncombe (2008), *Notes from Underground: Zines and the Politics of Alternative Culture*, Portland: Microcosm; Worley, *Zerox Machine*.
8. Paul Williams (2022), *The US Graphic Novel*, Edinburgh: Edinburgh University Press.
9. Brook and Shaughnessy, *Letraset*.
10. Mike Coles (2016), email correspondence with the author, 26 September.
11. Most Letraset typefaces were produced in a range of display sizes, from 24pt to 72pt. A more limited number of specific text faces were produced at smaller sizes, usually from 6pt or 8pt minimum size.
12. Malcolm Garrett is critical of the range of Letraset custom typefaces, termed Letragraphica, which were created for this market. Many Letragraphica styles appeared formulaic and out of date even at the time of their introduction to the catalogue, while the adoption of a custom face to reflect a particular artist or campaign tended to preclude its useful value to other designers.
13. Bestley, 'Art On My Sleeve', p. 554. Repromaster was a brand name for a PMT camera manufactured by Agfa-Gevaert.
14. Steve Averill (2023), online conversation with the author, 1 December.
15. Averill (2023), online conversation, 1 December.
16. Designed by Tony Wenman (1973).
17. Designed by Letraset (1972).
18. Designed by Letraset (1972).
19. Designed by Letraset (1976).
20. Designed by Rosemarie Tissie (1974).
21. Designed by Vic Carless (1973).
22. Raposo and Bestley, 'Designing fascism'. See also Ana Raposo and Roger Sabin (2017), 'New visual identities for British neofascist rock (1982–1987): White noise, "vikings" and the cult of Skrewdriver', in N. Copsey and M. Worley (eds), *Tomorrow Belongs to Us: The British Far Right Since 1967*, London: Routledge, pp. 132–149.
23. Bestley, '"Fuck Art, Let's Dance"'.
24. Originally designed by Justus Erich Walbaum *c.*1800, Letraset design by Berthold (*c.*1960).
25. Originally designed by William Caslon *c.*1760, Letraset design by Monotype (*c.*1960).

26 Kevin Lycett (2007), email correspondence with the author, 2 February.
27 Plastic lettering stencils, such as those produced by the Helix company in the UK, were manufactured in a limited range of sizes – commonly 10 mm (0.5"), 20 mm (0.75"), 30 mm (1.25") and 50 mm (2").
28 Original design *c.*1937, Letraset (*c.*1970).
29 Designed by Milton Glaser and George Leavitt *c.*1969, Letraset (1973).
30 Brook and Shaughnessy, *Letraset*.
31 Mumford (2024), online interview, 7 February.
32 Tim Milne (2024), online interview with the author, 30 April.
33 Garrett (2020), online interview 30 April.
34 Milne (2024), online interview, 30 April.
35 Brody (2024), online interview, 5 March.
36 Smith (2024), online interview, 13 February.
37 Lynn John (1988), *Preparing Design for Print*, Oxford: Phaidon.
38 For some exemplary examples reflecting the creative potential of the photocopier as a design tool, see Terry Jones and Catherine McDermott (1990), *Wink: Manual of Instant Design*, London: Architecture Design and Technology Press, and Mark Pawson (1989), *MaPk nAbCoH*, London: Mark Pawson.
39 O'Connor (2023), email interview, 18 October.
40 Bestley, '"Fuck Art, Let's Dance"', p. 363.
41 O'Connor (2023), email interview, 18 October.
42 Bestley, '"Fuck Art, Let's Dance"', p. 359.
43 Chris Morton (2024), in conversation with the author, 5 February.
44 Milne (2024), online interview, 30 April.
45 Perry, *Sniffin' Glue: The Essential Punk Accessory*, p. 30.
46 Drayton, *Ripped & Torn*.
47 Fletcher, *The Best of Jamming!*
48 Webb and Vague, *Vague Volume One*.
49 Rider, *Adventures in Reality*.
50 Worley, *Zerox Machine*.
51 Intriguingly, many of the advertisements placed within the pages of later editions of *Sniffin' Glue* don't look out of place, despite being produced in-house by design teams at some of the major record labels.
52 Tony Drayton (2016), email interview with the author, 18 December.
53 Alan Rider (2016), email interview with the author, 18 December.
54 Alistair Livingston (2016), email interview with the author, 4 December.
55 Joly MacFie (2016), email interview with the author, 4 December.
56 Drayton (2016), email interview, 18 December.
57 MacFie (2016), email interview, 4 December.
58 MacFie (2016), email interview, 4 December.
59 Drayton, *Ripped & Torn*.
60 Drayton (2016), email interview, 18 December.
61 Mike Diboll (2016), email interview with the author, 18 December.
62 Andrew Howard (2016), email interview with the author, 12 December.
63 Jessica Baines (2016), 'Democratising print? The field and practices of radical and community printshops in Britain 1968–98', PhD thesis, London School of Economics and Political Science, p. 101.
64 Drayton (2016), email interview, 18 December.
65 Drayton (2016), email interview, 18 December.
66 Letterstream, originally established in Shepherd Market, Mayfair and later based near Regent Street, had invested in a new A3 colour photocopier by 1976. According to MacFie, they had very forward-thinking management and Better Badges was able to produce some of their badge designs using their services.
67 MacFie (2016), email interview, 4 December.

6
A different kind of tension: industry and the individual

Not only was the rock music scene changing, but the design industry was also adapting to new technologies. The role of the designer, particularly in relation to the preparation of artwork for print production, changed radically between the mid-1960s and early 1980s. The relationship between the designer, printer and pre-press artworkers had traditionally been key to the design and construction of printed material. However, by the 1970s, rapid technological changes were dramatically impacting working practices and labour relations. A significant reduction in the chain of craft specialists between art director and printer was met with opposition from print unions and tradespeople whose livelihoods – and status within a deeply hierarchical employment model – were under threat.

> The machinery required to produce printed products was swiftly becoming more automated, making it increasingly attractive to employers. As a result, the period from the 1960s to the late 1980s saw the virtual extinction of hot-metal typesetting and letterpress printing in the global north. This period also witnessed the mainstream introduction of computerised typesetting and high-speed offset-lithographic printing. As a consequence, this three-decade period saw the almost complete disappearance of a swathe of printing crafts such as stereotyping, electrotyping, dot-etching, and engraving, hand-binding, hand-embossing, hand-composing, paper-ruling, Linotype and Monotype operation and pre-press camera operation.[1]

The crucial stage of the pre-press process involved the making of film separations for platemaking. This was the point where a prototype one-off was converted to a mass-produced artefact. Such pre-press operations were usually, though not always, owned by printers as a front end to their activities and were much more advanced technologically than artwork production houses, using a combination of photographic techniques and precise manual procedures. Technicians would use parallel motion light

6.1 Halftone image, inner cover of Siouxsie & The Banshees (1979), *Join Hands*, vinyl album, United Kingdom: Polydor. Design by Rob O'Connor, collection of the author.

box drawing boards to 'comp together' film negative separations of various types (halftone images, line work, halftone mechanical tint screens), which could then be produced as plates for the various colour separations on the printing press. The designer would supply pre-press departments with a variety of origination (line work and continuous tone work), usually with line work (type, line illustration, brush work and rules) already in situ and with only keyline indications of colour areas and images to be placed by the artwork department. Tone copy, which would include photographs or other artwork that involves the reproduction of shades of grey or colour, would be photographed separately using a halftone screen, which separates the continuous tone – the range of shades between black and white – into gradations of fine dots or lines of varying size, giving the optical impression of tonal continuity from light to dark (Figure 6.1). Areas of graphic tint and pattern could also be specified by the designer – a range of mechanical tints could be preselected and the area to be filled indicated by a keyline, with the platemaker then inserting the correct pattern at the pre-press stage using cut pieces of halftone film. Design and print technology was, however, changing rapidly, and some designers were embracing a greater degree of control to manage a group or label's entire visual identity, even though it impacted other parts of the pre-press chain.

Punk-related designers who wanted to retain a sense of control over all aspects of their work found themselves in an awkward position. The print unions, quite justifiably, wanted to retain their stranglehold, to protect the jobs of various specialists at each stage of the process through closed shop agreements and a requirement that artwork had to be stamped by a union official prior to acceptance for print production. Designers of press adverts and other marketing material were expected to join one of the affiliated trade unions, such as the Society of Lithographic Artists, Designers, Engravers and Process Workers (SLADE), and to work within an established hierarchy of specialist service providers. While most punk designers were not engaged in direct confrontation with the unions and established industry practices, a battle for control between the print unions and the owners of several national newspapers was to have significant ramifications throughout the industry in the early 1980s.

Complete control

The disconnect between the struggle for autonomy by punk designers and the cold reality of a print industry establishment was most pronounced in the production of adverts and marketing material for newspapers and magazines. Advertisements in the weekly music press – the *NME*, *Melody Maker*, *Sounds* and *Record Mirror* – were heavily controlled in relation to design practices and codes of professional conduct. While the print unions held a great deal of power in respect to all aspects of the industry, it was in Fleet Street, London, that they wielded the most authority. That control filtered down from the national press – the daily newspapers that were the beating heart of British news media – to the weekly music press, popular magazines and beyond. This led to something of a disjunct, with designers who were responsible for creating album covers not generally involved in designing press ads and marketing material for the same product. Design work for the press, along with much of the marketing and publicity material produced to support a new release on a major label, would be created by a specialist design agency such as Cream or Shoot That Tiger. The heavily union-controlled newspapers also required all submitted artwork to be registered and signed off with details of the affiliated union chapel before it could be taken forward to print (Figure 6.2). This was less of an issue for the art directors in the bigger creative studios at the major labels,

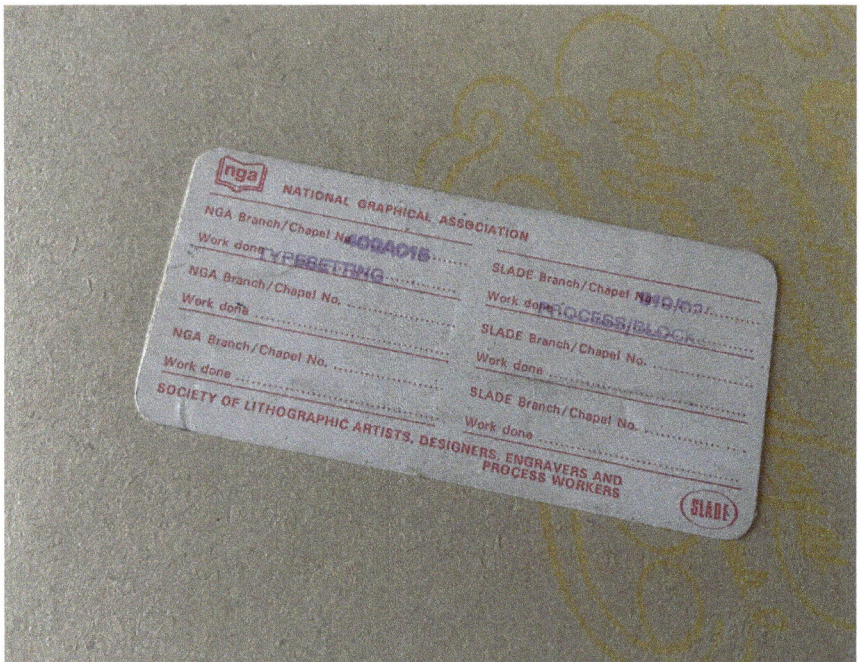

6.2 National Graphical Association (NGA) union stamp on rear of artwork. Courtesy Neil Horgan.

since much of the pre-press work was done by external agencies, which were in turn affiliated to the print unions, but it became more pronounced as independent designers began to take on the marketing and promotional work themselves.

> We weren't registered as NGA [National Graphical Association] members as individual designers or employees. Polydor wasn't NGA registered because it wasn't a print shop. So even if we had done artwork ourselves, we would have to send it to these guys in artwork or print studios and they could stamp it with the NGA stamps so the work could get printed … You would come up with the ideas, do the sketches, layouts and what have you and then you'd pass it over to an artwork company.[2]

While some music press adverts for early punk record releases mirrored the graphic style of the punk fanzines, they were almost always the product of a professional pre-press studio. The resulting work was often something of a pastiche of contemporary punk style, created by fully licensed and unionised designers and artworkers, rather than an example of 'authentic' grass-roots, do-it-yourself design.

Given the wide range of music paper and magazine formats, particularly regarding size specifications for adverts, teams of designers at dedicated pre-press studios were usually commissioned by the major record labels to produce print-ready artwork in a range of suitable formats. In effect, the autonomy that some punk graphic designers wanted to hold on to was undermined by systems that had been in operation for many years, though some did manage to retain at least a degree of control. Malcolm Garrett created the sleeve artwork for Buzzcocks' debut release on the United Artists label, 'Orgasm Addict', released in October 1977. Without Garrett's consent, the record label produced an accompanying promotional poster, though it clumsily misinterpreted many of the subtle typographic details in the original artwork.

For Garrett, the driving force behind the desire for new designers to have direct, hands-on involvement in all aspects of a band's identity was a kind of punk-inspired need for autonomy. Like the musicians who were seeking to pursue their own unique paths, graphic designers operating within the punk subculture saw a sense of authenticity in their own work that risked being undermined by the established practices of major label marketing teams.

> Because I wanted control, I wanted to take it as far as I could. You know, I learned very early on. I saw a poster for 'Orgasm Addict' on the streets of Manchester, and I thought 'Where the fuck did that come from?' I hadn't designed it. The record company had just done what they normally do.[3]

Garrett was frustrated that the record label had reworked his artwork without consultation or agreement and that they had made some glaring errors. While this seemed incongruous to a young designer new to the machinations of the music industry, it was a process that reflected common working practices at that time. As a result, Garrett took on a range of tasks normally ceded to junior designers or agencies, specifying the composition of a range of adverts to be passed to pre-press team before sending to print.

From the social contract to the Winter of Discontent

The mid- to late 1970s saw the collapse of the gold standard and the infamous Winter of Discontent of 1978–79, with levels of inflation spiralling out of control. Major changes to employment law also came into force, with the establishment of the Health & Safety at Work, Race Relations and Sex Discrimination Acts. Other advanced industrial nations, notably Germany and Japan, became prominent on the world economy, manufacturing more efficiently and producing what were seen as better quality and lower-priced products than the UK. Many traditional British industries declined rapidly: the UK car industry, for instance, suffered heavily in trying to compete with European and Far Eastern competitors and the growth of cheap imports. This was paralleled across heavy industries such as steel, coal, heavy machinery, freight and shipping, and within major national infrastructures and services such as British Rail, British Airways and the gas, electricity and water industries, ultimately paving the way for restructuring and privatisation a decade later.

The early 1970s had witnessed a disastrous period for industrial relations under Edward Heath's Conservative administration following its election in June 1970. After a short period of relative stability, the OPEC oil crisis of October 1973 caused economic turmoil, leading to Heath's declaration of a three-day week across the public sector, while at the same time tensions with the unions regarding proposed pay restraints led to strikes and the economy ran into recession. A hastily arranged general election in February 1974 resulted in a hung parliament, with the Labour Party under former Prime Minister Harold Wilson eventually forming a minority government. Faced with the difficulty of enacting legislation without a parliamentary majority, Wilson called another election in October 1974, which resulted in a three-seat majority for the incumbent administration. Negotiations between the Labour Party and the Trade Union Congress had already been taking place over the previous year, leading to a new social contract, which was extended in collaboration with the new government to include a voluntary incomes policy to combat inflation. Phase 2, agreed in May 1976, limited pay rises to between £2.50 and £4.00 per week,[4] temporarily forging an agreement between trade union senior leaders and the government, but at the same time catalysing shop stewards and left-wing activists in opposition.

In 1974 the Labour government repealed the 1971 Industrial Relations Act, which had been initiated by the Heath administration to try to better control industrial disputes. The government also responded to union demands with the 1974 Trade Union and Labour Relations Act (TULRA). The right not to be unfairly dismissed, which the 1971 Act had provided, was kept and strengthened. In addition, union officials were given more autonomy, with paid release from work to undertake training, though there were no parallel requirements put in place regarding statutory duties and responsibilities.

Long-standing problems with closed shop agreements in many areas of industry remained unresolved. Wilson resigned in March 1976, to be replaced by James Callaghan, by which time Labour's majority had been wiped out through a series of by-election defeats and defections and the party was forced to strike a confidence and supply agreement with the Liberal Party, significantly weakening their already tenuous capacity to drive constitutional change. The government's policy of national pay restraint continued to cause tensions with the unions, particularly as unemployment grew and inflation ran into double digits. Forced to seek a loan from the International Monetary Fund in June 1976, Chancellor Denis Healey was pushed into an impossible position. Against the wishes of many Labour Party activists and supporters, the government would be compelled to make urgent, swingeing spending cuts to restore confidence in the financial markets.

A heatwave through the summer months of 1976 – dubbed 'the long hot summer' – may have initially provided light relief for some from the typically damp British weather, but a severe drought in parts of the country forced local populations to ration water, with household supplies halted, standpipes in the streets and government directives to avoid waste. Temperatures were soaring in other ways, too. In August 1976 a strike by mostly women workers in the North London mail order film processing factory Grunwick Processing Laboratories led to secondary picketing by other trade unions and violent interventions by left-wing activists. The Notting Hill Carnival, on the bank holiday weekend of 28 August, erupted into a full-scale riot, an event immortalised in the lyrics of the debut single by The Clash, 'White Riot', the following year.

All this coincided with the initial punk explosion in the United Kingdom, providing a backdrop of economic decline and a heightened sense of frustration with the Labour administration. Punk was beginning to filter into public consciousness, initially through the music press, then by a series of sensationalist reports on television and in the national newspapers. The Damned hit the ground running with the first British punk rock single, 'New Rose' in October, swiftly followed by the debut release by the Sex Pistols, 'Anarchy in the U.K.' a month later, extending punk's reach beyond the live environment. Other singles by The Vibrators, Eddie and the Hot Rods, Nick Lowe and a smattering of punk parody releases (by The Water Pistols, Matt Black & The Doodlebugs and even one by ageing British comedian Charlie Drake)[5] caught the zeitgeist.

Events came to a head with a live television appearance by the Sex Pistols on the *Today* show, hosted by veteran TV journalist Bill Grundy, broadcast on 1 December 1976. The incident has gone down in punk history and does not merit extensive deconstruction here, but the group's foul-mouthed response to goading from Grundy resulted in a sensationalist backlash in the press the following day.[6] Punk was here to stay, offering concerned parents and self-styled moral authorities a contemporary form of degeneracy to rally against and rebellious teenagers a new set of heroes to follow. The subsequent Sex Pistols national tour, planned as a package revue along with The Clash, The Damned and The Heartbreakers, was heavily disrupted by protests, local council interventions and press hyperbole, resulting in just seven of the twenty planned gigs going ahead.

British punk's two big years – 1977 and 1978 – witnessed a boom in punk and new wave bands streaming into public view and screaming for attention. The Sex Pistols were famously sacked by two major record labels, EMI and A&M, before signing with Virgin, releasing one album and four brilliant singles, then imploding during their first US tour early in 1978. The Damned didn't last much longer, splitting after the release of their second album in the Autumn of 1977, then reforming with a revised line-up two years later. The Stranglers, The Clash, Buzzcocks and The Jam hit mainstream success, with major label record companies scrabbling to sign up their own stable of punk-related artists before the well ran dry. Dozens of other groups shone briefly (though not always brightly), with a plethora of punk, new wave and post-punk records released along with a degree of cynical marketing – from limited edition picture sleeves to coloured vinyl pressings – to tempt the cautious punk consumer.

> There was nothing like it. One minute I was listening to Neil Young at home and the next I was going to gigs with the Sex Pistols and The Heartbreakers. It was another world, but it was still rock'n'roll.[7]

Of course, every action has a reaction and the commercial exploitation of the new wave by the established music industry was countered – or mirrored, depending on your perspective – by the parallel growth in do-it-yourself punk output, from low-key fanzines to independent records. At the more ideological end of the spectrum, this presented a challenge to the establishment and an opportunity for punks to set their own rules and establish their own scenes. At the other end, it reflected a sense of entrepreneurship at best and bandwagon jumping and cashing in quick at worst. In either case, the ground was established for an independent record market that would endure for the next five decades.

A time of change

After the 1979 election, a tightening of fiscal policy by the new Conservative government was coupled with a clear aim to restructure the nationalised industries and to significantly overhaul employer–union relations. The impact of this was felt differently across the regions of the UK while it also had a more indirect effect on the developing punk-related economy. Key manufacturing regions were to be more directly affected by the shift towards a service economy in the early 1980s, while other areas benefited from the process. Sheffield lost its steel industry and the decline in coal mining (leading ultimately to the national miners' strike of 1984–85) had a drastic effect on small communities in Yorkshire, Lancashire, Nottinghamshire, South Wales and north-east England. Meanwhile, affluent areas of the central south and Greater London profited from the growth in new service-led industries and the investment economy created by the Thatcher government's privatisation policies. Between 1979 and 1986, the manufacturing sector lost 1.7 million jobs, while a similar number were created in the service industries between 1983 and 1987.[8] At the same time, between 1979 and 1987 the living standards of the poorest fifth of the population increased by 1 per cent while the wealthiest fifth gained 30 per cent.[9]

In 1981, the government began a radical programme of mass privatisation of key state-run industries, to cut 'uneconomic' production costs and to create a financial boom among those sections of British society who could afford to buy into such a scheme (including many Conservative voters). The sale of private shares in what were once publicly owned, nationalised utilities such as water, electricity, gas and the railways – many of which had originally been nationalised in the social and political reforms of the immediate post-war period of the late 1940s – took more than a decade to complete. However, the Thatcher government was restricted in its first term and national strikes by both the steelworkers and civil servants limited their ability to move towards full-scale privatisation.

Other policies involving the shift away from public provision towards individual 'responsibility' saw the mass selling-off of council housing stock and widespread moves to generate private enterprise and a market economy in schools, hospitals and local services. The fact that British manufacturing was undergoing a steady decline meant that predominantly working-class communities and individuals were directly affected more than the middle classes – many of whom could afford, in both economic and educational terms, to 'get on their bikes' and seek alternative means of employment. The turmoil caused by this shift in employment prospects did have a direct effect on British popular culture. Films and television dramas reflected a sense of despair at the loss of traditional social values and predicted a depressing end to the post-war economic boom and 'jobs for life'. In something of a return to a mid-1970s cultural mindset that Andy Beckett describes as a sense of declinism,[10] the unstable and unpredictable future envisaged at the turn of the decade resulted in a period of both cynical opportunism in business and a reflective sombreness in the arts. *Boys From the Blackstuff*, the first television series by Liverpool playwright Alan Bleasdale, was a critical triumph for BBC English Regions Drama, broadcast on BBC2 in October 1982 and winning a BAFTA award for best drama series of the year. Set in recession-hit Liverpool, it chronicled the attempts of five former British groundworkers to find work in a city hit hard by mounting unemployment and depression and managed to capture the public mood during a time of economic recession and anxiety about unemployment.

Alternative comedy was also making inroads into the mainstream in the early 1980s. The Comedy Store nightclub launched in London on 19 May 1979, taking inspiration from punk along with earlier comedians such as Lenny Bruce and contemporary television shows such as *Saturday Night Live* in the United States (which also had ties to punk subculture) and grew in influence over the following years.[11] November 1982 saw the debut series of *The Young Ones*, written by Ben Elton and starring Rik Mayall, Adrian Edmondson and Nigel Planer, again basing much of its content on the economic crisis and unemployment. Alternative comedy became very successful over the following year, with the commencement of the first series of BBC sitcom *Blackadder*, starring Rowan Atkinson, and the critically acclaimed *Comic Strip Presents* parodies on the newly launched Channel 4.

The sense of a great divide created between the 'haves' and the 'have nots' in the early 1980s were played out in popular drama, theatre, comedy, film and in music. Dramatic increases in the personal fortunes of some (such as investment bankers, share dealers and the upper middle classes) were mirrored by widespread unemployment and the destruction of communities based around traditional manufacturing centres. On 26 January 1982, UK unemployment figures topped three million for the first time since the 1930s, with regional blackspots such as Northern Ireland and parts of Scotland, Wales, the North and South West of England seeing between 15 and 20 per cent of workers registered for unemployment benefits. Television programmes reflected the sense of division, with documentaries on the unemployment crisis and plays based on the decline of traditional social structures. In this period of turmoil, dramatic shifts in the media and broadcasting technology also led to the creation of new newspaper and television media, including the launch of Channel 4 television in November 1982. Tensions reached their peak during the year-long miners' strike of 1984–85, with far-reaching consequences for both the trade unions and British industry.

The print unions

The print unions in Britain were particularly powerful in the 1970s, with closed shop agreements and so-called 'Spanish practices' restricting calls for technological modernisation and labour flexibility from employers. The industry was extremely hierarchical, with strict distinctions placed between different craft bodies and with the sons of senior craftsmen and union leaders following their fathers into bespoke apprenticeships. As Jessica Baines argues in her study of radical printshops and cooperatives in the United Kingdom during the 1970s and 1980s, many of whom had a difficult relationship with the unions despite their intersecting concerns regarding class and the support of workers, 'the print unions in particular had excluded women, were historically nepotistic and operated a rigid demarcation of job roles'.[12] The biggest print union, the National Graphical Association (NGA), was founded in 1964, when the Manchester-based Typographical Association merged with the London Typographical Society. In parallel to the evolution of the NGA, a major union representing semi-skilled and unskilled workers in the industry, the Society of Graphical and Allied Trades (SOGAT) incorporated several smaller associations including the semi-skilled National Society of Operative Printers and Assistants (NATSOPA) whose members included reader's assistants, clerical workers and cleaners.

A strategy paper in response to changes in the industry, dubbed the Programme for Action, was developed by the Joint Standing Committee (JSC), a group comprising union General Secretaries and chief executives from the newspaper publishers, chaired by SOGAT General Secretary Bill Keys. The paper was presented to the London Fleet Street print unions in February 1976, in an attempt to recognise the looming impact of new technology that had already been adopted in the United States and Europe and suggesting a common framework moving forward.[13] The NGA union leaders recommended acceptance, but by the following year industrial relations had soured even further and shop floor pressure against the Labour government's social contract led to a rejection of the programme, leaving individual newspaper owners and individual union chapels to negotiate changes on an ad hoc basis. At this time, the printing methods employed in the production of national newspapers in Britain had gone relatively unchanged since Linotype typesetting had replaced hand composition (Letterpress technology) in the 1890s.

The Linotype system was a large typesetting machine that required a skilled keyboard operator, or compositor, to operate it. The compositor would retype journalist's supplied copy, whereby a brass matrix of each character would be released along a chute to form a line of type in an assembly box. Once the type was set in this way and checked for spacing and justification, hot metal would be poured into the matrix to cast a line of type or 'slug', ready to be set in a galley for printing. Other typesetting machines manufactured by Monotype, Intertype and Ludlow followed a similar process to Linotype, though it remained the leading system in most high-profile print businesses. The angled Linotype keyboard had more than ninety keys arranged in a system known as ETAOIN/SHRDLU, quite different to the QWERTY system that would become ubiquitous in desktop computing, and which took over once the compositors were replaced by direct input systems in the shift from hot metal to cold metal or photocomposition – and later digital composition.[14] The mechanical nature of the Linotype machine was also quite different to the plastic keyboards and grey boxes of the new system, where the process was rendered invisible to the operator. This further alienated the craftsman from *his* craft – as Stein and Cockburn argue, the print professions were heavily male dominated, so the linguistic emphasis is justified.[15] The QWERTY system was also widely associated with unskilled and secretarial work in a gendered industry that centred on craft skills and long-standing, rigid hierarchies, emphasising the elevated position of the skilled compositor.

By the late 1960s, photocomposition had begun to replace hot metal in the United States and Europe and had made significant inroads in the British provincial press as well as the wider commercial print industry, including music graphics.[16] However, while smaller design and print studios had enough flexibility to adopt new technologies, the bigger industrial players were finding it harder to make changes that would impact directly on their workforce. The powerful print unions blocked the introduction of photocomposition in newspaper production centres right through to the mid-1970s, and even by 1985 most British national newspapers still relied on hot metal typesetting. The logical extension of phototypesetting was direct entry or 'single keystroking', whereby journalists could type directly into a visual display, thus removing the need for a keyboard operator, and the unions recognised that this would lead to a dramatic restructuring of the industry and the loss of many jobs.

> The arrival of computer technologies in the 1970s and 1980s meant that compositors were not merely deskilled but wholly undermined, eventually becoming entirely redundant in the printing process.[17]

The first national newspaper producer to attempt the switch was Reed International, owner of the *Daily Mirror*, *Sunday Mirror*, *Sunday People* and the *Sporting Life*. Instead of the use of scalpels, paper and paste used in most other areas of photocomposition, the entire process would be electronic. However, the technology didn't work well and Reed International struggled with the financial burden.[18] *The Times* newspaper group was next in line to attempt the switch to photocomposition, pushing ahead in defiance of attempted blockages by the NGA.

> Following a series of petty disputes, mainly over pay, the company announced in April 1978 that it wanted direct-input, photocomposition and new manning levels throughout the company, involving cuts of over 40 per cent, a new disputes procedure and new wage levels. If no agreement was reached by October 1978, the papers would be suspended and the staff dismissed.[19]

The bitter industrial dispute that followed shut down production of the paper from 1 December 1978 to 12 November 1979. Since there were no laws against secondary picketing, the unions stood firm, even utilising their power across the industry to re-employ striking production workers on casual contracts at other newspapers, thus softening the financial blow for those taking part in the action. A year later, under a new Conservative administration, the Employment Act withdrew immunity from legal action to participants in secondary strikes away from their own place of work, thus tipping the balance once again in favour of employers. The government also made concerted efforts to limit closed shop agreements, particularly in the design and print industries.

> Section 18 withdrew immunities from those who organised industrial action to enforce union membership on workers employed by a different employer or at different premises. The section was aimed at 'coercive recruitment' where the design union, SLADE, tried to pressure workers in art studios, instant print shops and advertising agencies, who were starting to take over the print union's traditional work, into joining the union which in 1982 became part of the NGA.[20]

The byzantine structure of the print unions had by this time led to a tightly controlled set of working practices, with the National Graphical Association and affiliated unions wielding significant control over the production and distribution of printed material. Many of the union's more than a hundred thousand working members were employed in small groups of often less than a dozen operators in typesetting or design studios. Historically, small groups of printing craftsmen had organised together in chapels (so termed because of early links between printing and the Church). These were initially overseen by Parliament and the Guilds, but when that system began to break down in the eighteenth century, the individual chapels began to reach out to each other, collaborating to protect their rights and to control access to the printing industry, leading eventually to the formation of a union.

> In the general field of printing and graphic reproduction, production functions tended to be aligned to very specific job roles. Each involved a particular training, historically in the form of apprenticeships, was represented by a different trade union or sections within trade unions and as such had their own job identities, hierarchical status and wage scales. The boundaries of job roles were reinforced by the protectionist regulations and practices of the print and graphic trade unions that had developed over the decades.[21]

A vital principle that eventually filtered down to the NGA rulebook itself was the banning (or 'blacking') of acceptance of any work from a non-unionised workplace or any chapel currently in dispute with management, effectively cementing secondary picketing as a universal code of conduct. Because of the fragmented nature of the printing industry, a chain of service providers (print estimators, artworkers/paste-up artists, typesetters, film planners, camera operators, platemakers, press operators, print finishers, distributors) was necessary to complete most jobs, and any attempt to restructure conditions in one chapel would lead to a refusal to take on the work across the rest of the industry.

> I remember the suited and booted union reps coming round to one studio for a meeting with all the freelancers, threatening all sorts of doom and destruction if we didn't all sign up. It was like a visit from the Krays.[22]

By the late 1970s, closed shop agreements restricting access to print production for independent designers were becoming untenable, while at the same time workers at the major newspaper print operators were fighting a top-down restructuring of their entire industry. New technologies, the advent of cheap colour offset lithoprinting and computerised composition and typesetting tools, combined with a government-led agenda to break the power of the unions, resulted in strike action and violent clashes, particularly in the newspaper industry centred around its historic centre, Fleet Street in London. While union influence varied widely across the print industry, those representing workers at the prominent mainstream newspapers held a formidable reputation regarding not just the national press but magazine publishing and local print media across the country. Labour practices agreed by the unions representing workers in the national press exerted a disproportionate influence on smaller print studios further down the chain. In the spring of 1980, a strike by IPC members of the National Union of Journalists directly impacted the British music press, with both the *NME* and *Melody Maker* forced to cease publication for six weeks between the end of April and early June. A new independent paper, *New Music News*, was launched in May 1980 by entrepreneur Felix Dennis, purely to take advantage of the temporary gap in the market. While the paper survived for fifteen issues, even in the face of the return of its competitors after the strike action ended, it was forced to close in August 1980 due to insufficient funding from creditors.[23]

The Society of Lithographic Artists, Designers, Engravers and Process Workers (SLADE) was one of several unions covering the design and print industries, though its core focus was on commercial artists and graphic designers. While the long-standing system of apprenticeships and tightly controlled closed shops was starting to decline, the NGA preserved the hierarchy between craft and non-craft workers in the design and print industries. During the 1970s, the NGA swept up several other craft-based associations including the Association of the Correctors of the Press, before finally taking over SLADE in 1982. Tensions at the NGA were further exacerbated by the arrival of the Electrical, Electronic, Telecommunications and Plumbing Union (EETPU) on the scene, which represented electricians and technical operators in the new phototypesetting arenas.

> The political and legal changes since 1979 have seriously curtailed that union power and transferred the whip hand to radically emboldened employers. The shift has taken longer to percolate through to Fleet Street than elsewhere in British industry, but the shake-out now gathering pace in the national newspaper industry marked by the shedding of labour, the introduction of new processes and the smashing of old conventions of industrial relations, is in a line of descent from the disputes in the steel industry (1980), British Leyland (1981), British Telecom (1983) and the mining industry (1984–85).[24]

An entrepreneur new to the newspaper industry, Eddie Shah had faced union disruption in response to his attempts to modernise production at a local paper in Manchester, *The Warrington Messenger*, between July 1983 and May 1984, but ultimately defeated the unions in that dispute. In March 1986, Shah went on to launch a completely new national newspaper, *Today*, using the same new technologies that required less operators and produced more contemporary, full-colour, news media. Sidelining the NGA by forging a deal with the EETPU, Shah implemented a no-strike clause, while in return the union agreed not to insist on a closed shop. *Today* ultimately failed to live up to Shah's ambition, though it did set a precedent for many of the changes to technology, working practices and labour relations that were to transform the British newspaper industry over the following decade.

Drawing inspiration from Shah's successful intervention in a notoriously conservative and hierarchical industry, Rupert Murdoch's News International seized the opportunity to secretly install advanced printing technology at a new headquarters in Wapping, East London. The management then issued redundancy notices to many former printing staff at their Fleet Street base and relaunched all four papers from the new site on 26 January 1986, with a new print workforce not affiliated to the NGA or SOGAT, but to the EETPU. At the same time, relations were becoming more strained between the NGA and the National Union of Journalists (NUJ), whose members were set to gain from the transition to direct input. The management's action led to major protests and an attempted blockade of the Wapping production site which ran from January 1986 to February 1987.[25] National newspapers had traditionally been despatched by rail, with an agreement between the rail unions and the NGA to block any attempt to distribute papers from non-union approved sources. Murdoch brought in an Australian road haulage firm, TNT, and set up a completely new system that could deliver direct to regional distribution hubs, bypassing the potential for disruption.[26] News International eventually managed to defeat the combined powers of the NGA chapels, along with secondary pickets from the members of the Transport and General Workers Union who were responsible for distribution of the papers, opening the door for other national newspaper proprietors to follow.[27]

Punk autonomy and the closed shop

The closed shop agreements preserved long-standing, established hierarchies in the print industry, many centred around specialist craft skills that were rigidly demarcated. However, it also limited the ability of new, non-union affiliated designers to access print production. Experiences varied, with some punk-related designers finding it easier to navigate entry to the profession than others. In some instances, ease of entry depended on the status of the artist or label the designer was working for and the economic potential of the job at hand. Chris Morton recalls few problems in navigating the design and print profession at Stiff Records.

> We didn't have any problems with unions or printers; on the contrary, the union smoothed the way to quickly make me 'Father of the Chapel' (I think that was the official nomenclature) so that our ads could be printed in the music press. The printers were very quickly elbowing each other out of the way to print our record covers – especially big LP cover runs.[28]

Others were less fortunate and were forced to find alternative ways to have their work approved and signed off to print. Like many other independent and do-it-yourself punk graphic designers, Mike Coles faced some difficulties and had to play a strategic game. It helped that he was working in pre-press departments as a paste-up artist, since that put him in direct contact with senior designers – who were also, importantly, union members – who could help him find a way around the tight regulations.

> I had two personas in the 70s/early 80s. One was doing paste-up and finished art for various studios, which paid well but was frustrating. The other was the Malicious Damage design stuff, which didn't pay at all, but I could do whatever I liked and satisfy my creative urges. A lot of artwork in those days had to have a union stamp on the back, but I had a very accommodating studio manager at one of the studios who'd stamp the back of my jobs so that they went to print ok.[29]

The post-punk DIY and independent record boom of the late 1970s saw many bands and designers keen to exercise a level of autonomy and control of their output throughout the whole production process, putting them in potential conflict with long-standing collective agreements and working practices in the printing industry. Near the end of the decade, tensions were building between individual designers keen to produce work on their own terms, bypassing some of the conventions and restrictions of the industry and the labour institutions that had been set up explicitly to protect print workers' interests. Malcolm Garrett asserts that he didn't encounter any problems with the print unions until he moved from Manchester to London.

> I had been working in Manchester and doing all the Buzzcocks and Magazine stuff. By and large, I sent off artworks to the record company art departments and they would then send stuff off to press. So I didn't encounter any union issues. But then when I came to London, I started to work for Radar Records. So I was now at the record company, effectively, and when I sent off a piece of artwork it was rejected because there was no union sticker on it. Something that had been oblivious to them became an issue.[30]

To address the problem, Garrett decided to join a trade union that was affiliated to the design and print professions: SLADE, the Society of Lithographic Artists, Designers and Engravers. The Radar Records office was on Parker Street, near Covent Garden, and SLADE was based just up the road in Red Lion Square. Neville Brody had followed a similar path when he began working with commercial clients outside the design studios where he had started his career.

> I joined the union very early on – I signed up with SLADE, as you couldn't send an artwork off to be printed without the sticker on the back. They would literally not print it, destroy it, or send it straight back. They had an iron grip on any printing.[31]

The Thatcher government attempted to curtail some of the more underhand activities of the unions through section 18 of the Employment Act 1980, introduced by Jim Prior. Not only did the Act withdraw immunity from civil action for those engaged in secondary picketing, but it also targeted the model of 'coercive recruitment' that had been widely utilised in the design and print industries, whereby workers in art studios, print shops and advertising agencies were pressurised to join the union. Either way, widespread closed shop agreements curtailed any opportunity for independent and non-affiliated designers to submit work within tightly controlled areas of the printing industry, particularly the music press.

> I had to go over to Red Lion Square and pay my twenty quid dues or whatever. When I came back, there was some sort of problem which meant that I couldn't join because I wasn't professional. I seem to remember having to stamp on the back of the piece of artwork, so I had a rubber stamp made up and it said, 'membership applied for' and then SLADE, and that would allow my artwork in. The only issue was the press, like newspaper adverts. If I wanted to get an advert into *New Musical Express*, it had to be stamped properly because the unions were heavy in the press and magazine industry, but it was much easier to get record sleeves printed.[32]

Meanwhile, the print profession was changing, with opportunities opening up for a new generation of small, independent operators. Murray Arbiter started a company called First Impression in 1986 with a single-colour Kord press. Prior to that he was an apprentice platemaker, learning lithographic reproduction, colour retouching and those skills he still uses today as a printer and a commercial artist, while also being heavily involved in the unlicensed and unregulated flyposting business.

> The early 1980s was like the Wild West. The union stranglehold was diminishing. Contrary to the political beliefs of many of the designers of the time, Thatcher's deregulation of the market led to what you might call an aspirational working class. Printers like me were free to take on work from whoever we wanted, we didn't have to have the SOGAT sticker on the back of the artwork and we could operate our businesses on our own terms.[33]

Post-punk graphic design sits in an awkward place in relation to significant disruptions in print technology and labour relations. While punk's natural anti-authoritarian ideals would seem to place it as a natural ally to the protesters fighting industrial change, the unlocking of closed shop practices to allow individual designers to access print without the authorising signature of a union official or the requirement to employ a team of pre-press artworkers for typesetting and composition reflects its 'anyone can do it' ideals.

The desire for autonomy as a reflection of punk agency and authenticity – moving deliberately away from the traditional practices of the established music industry – could be better facilitated through small studios and independent designers who took on pre-press roles themselves. In many ways, this development was a precursor to what would come next, with the desktop publishing revolution pushing designers towards more autonomous, but at the same time more atomised, practices. Dramatic changes in the print studios were now impacting further back in the creative process, with graphic designers taking on more technical roles that would previously have been passed to a specialist team. The drivers for this change were as much economic and political as they were technological, of course, and the transition towards the roles and practices we recognise more closely today will be discussed in the next two chapters, 'Parallel lines: into the eighties' and 'Retro-spective: influence and legacy'

Notes

1. Jesse Adams Stein (2017), *Hot Metal: Material Culture and Tangible Labour*, Manchester: Manchester University Press, pp. 5–6.
2. O'Connor (2023), email interview, 18 October.
3. Garrett (2020), online interview, 30 April.
4. For further information see TUC Library Collections, London Metropolitan University.
5. Bestley, '"I tried to make him laugh, he didn't get the joke …"'.
6. The best summary of this event and the ensuing media reaction is detailed in Savage, *England's Dreaming*. A transcript of the exchange has been reproduced many times, including in Kugelberg et al., *God Save Sex Pistols*.
7. Mumford (2024), online interview, 7 February.
8. François Bédarida (1991), *A Social History of England*, Abingdon: Routledge, p. 317.
9. Trevor Blackwell and Jeremy Seabrook (1996), *Talking Work: An Oral History*, London: Faber & Faber, p. 162.
10. Beckett, *When the Lights Went Out*, pp. 177–182.
11. Krista Bonello Rutter Giappone (2018), *The Punk Turn in Comedy: Masks of Anarchy*, London: Palgrave Macmillan.
12. Baines, 'Democratising print?', p. 102.
13. John Gennard and Peter Bain (1995), *A History of the Society of Graphical and Allied Trades*, Abingdon: Routledge, p. 588.
14. Stein, *Hot Metal*, p. 108.
15. See Cynthia Cockburn (1991), *Brothers: Male Dominance and Technological Change*, London: Pluto Press.
16. By the mid-1970s, as photocomposition was beginning to become more widely implemented in Britain, more than 80 per cent of US newspapers were set in cold type. The number of hot-metal line casters in the US newspaper industry fell from 10,290 in 1970 to 194 in 1980. Goodhart and Wintour, *Eddie Shah and the Newspaper Revolution*, p. 166.
17. Stein, *Hot Metal*, p. 105.
18. Reed International was eventually forced to sell the Mirror Group titles to entrepreneur Robert Maxwell in July 1984.
19. Goodhart and Wintour, *Eddie Shah and the Newspaper Revolution*, p. 60.
20. Goodhart and Wintour, *Eddie Shah and the Newspaper Revolution*, p. 63.
21. Baines, 'Democratising print?', p. 133.
22. Mike Coles (2016), email correspondence with the author, 22 September.

23 Paul Gorman (2022), *Totally Wired: The Rise and Fall of the Music Press*, London: Thames & Hudson, pp. 222–224.
24 Goodhart and Wintour, *Eddie Shah and the Newspaper Revolution*, p. xiii.
25 Stewart, *Bang!*, p. 366.
26 McSmith, *No Such Thing as Society*, p. 221.
27 The motives behind the actions of the print unions at Wapping are, naturally, contested. Many historians present technological change as inevitable, with the NGA and its affiliates standing in the way of change to protect long-standing (and hard won) privileges for their members. John Gennard and Peter Bain present an alternative case, however, arguing that the dispute was not about a group of workers resisting the implementation of a new technology that was already widely in use outside the national newspapers. Instead, they argue, the dispute centred on 'management authority and the continuation of effective trade unionism'. Gennard and Bain, *A History of the Society of Graphical and Allied Trades*, p. 621.
28 Bestley, '"Fuck Art, Let's Dance"', p. 370.
29 Coles (2016), email correspondence, 22 September.
30 Garrett (2020), online interview, 30 April.
31 Brody (2024), online interview, 5 March.
32 Garrett (2020), online interview, 30 April.
33 Murray Arbiter (2024), online interview with the author, 26 April.

7

Parallel lines: into the eighties

By the late 1970s, the original punk scene in the United Kingdom had been largely commercialised through the rebranding of new wave and post-punk, casting many musicians, writers, editors and designers by the wayside, while at the same time elevating some of the movement's more successful exponents within a revised and updated professional arena. The entrepreneurial spirit of punk had also afforded entry to the fields of journalism, popular music, film, photography and design for those who chose to take the opportunity and run with it. Barriers were breaking down and punk's 'no future' philosophy provided a blank sheet for artists and designers to make their mark on their own terms, at least temporarily. Radical changes in branding, youth style and design during the early 1980s reflected a new dynamism along with opportunities wrought by new technologies and dramatic changes in labour relations in the design and print industries. Those changes impacted everything from traditional music graphics (record covers, promotional material) to magazines (*iD*, *The Face*, *Smash Hits*), national newspapers (*Today*, *The Independent*) and television channels (Channel 4, TV-am, MTV). The work of Malcolm Garrett, Neville Brody, Russell Mills, Alex McDowell, Peter Saville, Vaughan Oliver and Rob O'Connor in music graphics, typography, magazine design, branding, advertising, television and even fashion, helped shape the new visual styles of the 1980s, while myriad anonymous designers behind the scenes in the growing post-punk subculture were shaping the further evolution of a punk-inspired underground. The design aesthetic also reflected the aspiration of a new decade. There were new ways to do things and a bright, colourful, futuristic style quickly became almost ubiquitous in fashion, publishing and commercial graphic design.

The critical and commercial success of punk's DIY mission also led to a significant growth in independent labels. By the early 1980s, sales of independent post-punk records were booming. Even the smallest label could secure distribution through the new Cartel network[1] and hope to return a profit – or at least not too great a loss. In some areas, this led to a greater sense of experimentation and innovation, rather than stagnation, blending styles and inspiring new fashions. It also generated significant profits for some of the more successful labels such as Rough Trade, Factory, 4AD and Mute Records, in turn impacting production budgets for both music and design. Mirroring the high-quality designs of the major label new wave coterie, big name independent artists were packaged in sophisticated, expensive, high-gloss, full-colour record covers, with designers such as Peter Saville and Vaughan Oliver given a free hand – and a substantial budget – to employ flamboyant materials, metallic inks, die-cuts, spot varnishes and inserts that mirrored the excesses of an earlier age of music packaging. To some critics, it was like punk had never happened.

A deliberately DIY post-punk scene continued in parallel, not least through the proliferation of home-recorded cassettes by artists who chose the medium as a cheap and convenient way to bypass professional music production entirely. The simplicity and relative cheapness of tape-to-tape technology also allowed compilers of compilation tapes to support numerous causes, from the promotion of fanzines to political campaigns. Mix tapes allowed friends to exchange music recorded directly from records, or the radio. The major labels responded to what they saw as a commercial threat with a campaign centred on the phrase 'home taping is killing music'. Rather ironically, given his role in supporting the independent new wave scene, it was Chris Morton who won the resulting logo competition with his iconic skull and crossbones cassette design (Figure 7.1).[2]

A by now stereotypical model of punk in the United Kingdom wasn't about to quietly fade away either, despite the proliferation of new styles and the fragmentation of post-punk in myriad new directions. Heavily influenced by the hardcore scene emerging in the United States, a new breed of younger groups and fans attempted to go back to basics, while at the same time creating something of a revised and updated punk visual aesthetic. New punk specialist independent labels – Riot City, No Future, Rondelet, Clay Records – developed their own visual and musical styles and achieved a degree of commercial success, while others including Bluurg and Corpus Christi tapped into the growth of the anarcho-punk scene centred around Crass and Poison Girls. There was also at least a measure of stylistic development in parts of the scene. Discharge, a group from Stoke-on-Trent, with roots going back several years, reworked their musical approach into a full-on aural assault for their debut EP, *Realities of War*, in 1980. The sleeve was equally brutal – a high contrast image of the back of a heavily studded leather jacket with the band name painted at the bottom, backed by a live shot of the band in extremely high contrast along

7.1 *Home Taping is Killing Music* logo, 1980. Courtesy Chris Morton.

with typewritten song titles and handwritten notes (Figure 7.2). The band's sound and visual style were to be highly influential on hardcore punk around the world, with the scene eventually merging more closely with metal as the 1980s wore on. At the same time, Discharge's lyrics picked up on some of the themes central to the anarcho-punk movement, particularly regarding passivism and the threat of nuclear war, and amplified them to the extreme. Along with sections of the anarcho-punk scene, the new groups following in the footsteps of hardcore scene leaders Discharge and The Exploited seemed fixated on death, destruction and war, with little of the humour or self-awareness of the previous punk generation.

Like the evolving dress styles, many of the new punk designers associated with what would become known as UK82 punk were also less creative and imaginative than their forebears. A marked shift towards horror and war themes, shocking images, badly drawn skeletons and illustrations of stereotypical 'punk' figures replete with studded leather jackets and mohican hairstyles helped to establish a set of generic graphic conventions that unfortunately still resonates across global punk scenes today. Unlike the first wave of punk designers, who quickly moved on from what were fast becoming stereotypical visual symbols – such as the swastika, safety pin and razor blade – this punk generation seemed stuck in a time loop (or doom loop) of its own making.

Meanwhile, competition from other media was beginning to impact directly on the printing industry. Digital media as we currently know it was still some way off, though technological advances in video and television were to make significant inroads in the music industry through the 1980s.

Parallel lines: into the eighties 203

7.2 Discharge (1980), *Realities of War*, 7" vinyl EP, United Kingdom: Clay Records. Design by Martin H. Collection of the author.

VHS and Betamax home video systems, together with the short-lived LaserDisc, helped facilitate popular music's shift to a moving image rather than purely audio experience, while the launch of MTV in the United States in August 1981 swiftly changed the way pop music would be consumed as the decade wore on. The introduction of pre-recorded compact discs in the autumn of 1982, followed by several other initiatives that ultimately failed to gain traction (digital audio tape, mini disc), revitalised a flagging music industry.[3] The design and print professions were also deeply affected by the opportunities provided by electronic information systems.

> The industry faced a big threat from the growth of an alternative communications industry based on electronic devices. Electronic information systems, such as Oracle, Ceefax and Prestel, offered an alternative way of communicating information ... Publishers of books and magazines were attracted to these new systems and, in particular, to desktop publishing.[4]

At this point, of course, desktop publishing was more of a futuristic ambition. Home computers such as the BBC Micro (launched in December 1981) were expensive, with relatively few functions beyond word processing and rudimentary educational tools. Early gaming-focused machines such as the

Commodore 64 and ZX Spectrum (both launched in 1982, followed by the British-made Amstrad CPC 464 a year later) proved more popular, though again their desirability reflected an interest in leisure and entertainment rather than creative practices such as design. The American-built Apple II (launched in the United States in 1977) provided more opportunities, though it was very expensive and its functionality as a creative tool was limited. Apple's Macintosh computers eventually started to make inroads into graphic design studios in the mid-1980s, while computer-based processing systems had already started to impact the print profession, albeit in a limited fashion, since the late 1970s.

Music and style magazines

Around the turn of the decade, punk and post-punk dress styles shifted away from the early prevalence of defaced school uniforms, dead men's suits, military surplus and workwear to the more flamboyant and expressive end of the dressing up box. At the same time, journalists and critics in the mainstream music press, photographers and stylists began to focus on a wider range of pop cultural practices, beyond simply the music, the bands and the records. The punk 'revolution' was to prove largely ineffective in its ambition to move away from pop music traditions and long-standing business practices, with many artists and labels falling into line as the industry took control. There had always been a direct relationship between the way an artist looked and the marketing and promotion of their music, and selling the new wave was no different. Many female punk performers, for instance, were still marketed as (often reluctant) sex symbols, with both the music press and mainstream media exploiting the seductive image of Debbie Harry, Siouxsie Sioux, Chrissie Hynde, Pauline Murray, Gaye Advert and many others to sell newspapers (Figure 7.3). Harry's band, Blondie, issued badges stating 'Blondie is a Group' on their 1978 tour, while The Adverts were publicly critical of their label, Stiff Records, for choosing a close-up photograph of their female bassist, rather than the whole group, for the front cover of their debut single, 'One Chord Wonders' (1977) (Figure 7.4). To a lesser extent, male punks were also exploited for their image: glossy colour pin-up photographs of Billy Idol, Paul Weller, Jean-Jacques Burnel, The Clash, Buzzcocks, Eater and The Rich Kids, among others, featured in weekly magazines aimed at teenage girls such as *Oh Boy!* and *Blue Jeans*. Sensing the winds of change, Sex Pistols vocalist Johnny Rotten quit the band at the end of a disastrous North American tour in January 1978. Going back to his real name, John Lydon, he quickly established a new group, Public Image Ltd., with the explicit intention to turn the image of the rock performer upside down and to critique the exploitative practices of the music industry from the inside.

7.3 'Wouldn't you like to rip her to shreds?' advertisement, *New Musical Express*, November 1977. Collection of the author.

7.4 The Adverts (1977), 'One Chord Wonders', 7″ single, United Kingdom: Stiff Records. Design by Barney Bubbles © Stiff Records Art Department – All Rights Reserved.

Image and style were becoming increasingly important, however. The dress codes, hairstyles and photogenic qualities of artists, musicians – and fans – were refracted through a wide range of visual media, from posters and record covers to an evolving style media whose interest centred on looks as well as music. Cameras turned to document the dress codes of subcultural participants – not just iconic pop stars positioned as style leaders. In the popular music arena, the military surplus, Dr. Martens boots and dour trench coats of post-punk gave way to the sartorial flamboyance, make-up and ostentatious hairstyles of the New Romantics. A new generation of multicoloured swap shop punks followed suit, diving into the Crazy Colour hair dye and jewellery box, while retaining the slightly more restrained – though increasingly self-decorated and personalised – attire of biker jackets, jeans and boots. Competing scenes went some way beyond the punk canon, reflecting parallel evolutionary paths that spanned a range of precursors from heavy rock, glam, rock'n'roll, mod, ska, disco and dance music. The New Wave of British Heavy Metal (NWOBHM), the Mod revival, the rockabilly revival, Two Tone and synth pop offered a much broader range of pop scenes, each reflected in its own set of dress codes and stylistic conventions. Post-punk's natural eclecticism embraced many of these competing genres, forming crossovers and hybrid styles that expanded its reach. Each of these developments reflected a turn back to a more spectacular form of youth cultural expression. While many post-punk distinctions of the late 1970s had been largely musical and stylistic – between Gang of Four and PIL or between Killing Joke and Joy Division, for instance – these new scenes reflected a return to fashion and dress as key indicators of tribal affiliation.

The new post-punk scenes moved away from focusing purely on music and lyrics to far more visual expressions of style and taste, along with a wider range of philosophical and aesthetic concerns, ranging from film to fashion, literature to fine art. This spectrum of cultural interests was reflected – and, in part, driven – by sections of the music press. Journalists at the *NME* adopted a cynical view of punk rock's failed revolution. Paul Morley and Ian Penman introduced oblique – and increasingly pretentious – references to postmodern theory in their reviews and interviews, driving discussion away from what they saw as a tired and outdated focus on the artist and their music towards a broader artistic palette fit for a new age of pop cultural importance. Musicians were asked about books or films that inspired them and treated as part of an intellectual avant-garde rather than the dull rock stars of old. Meanwhile, a wider range of individuals and groups became the focus of articles and interviews, from film directors to photographers, contemporary philosophers, politicians, visual artists and screenwriters. Even a small coterie of designers was featured, though they were presented as media personalities and their work was reduced to sweeping stylistic gestures and a barrage of sometimes less than informative art historical references.

Another key driver behind the bold (typo)graphic styles emerging in the early 1980s came in the shape of a new, weekly listings magazine in London. Formed by a group of journalists who had broken away from the long-established *Time Out* magazine following an industrial dispute, *City Limits* adopted a more overtly left-wing political stance. Front covers featured bold, upper-case typography, heavy grid lines, graphic arrows, lightning bolts, dynamic angles and bright, solid colours courtesy of art director David King, while the editorial pages continued the theme with bold lines and large photographs set against a prominent grid. King had previously helped to create the ground-breaking visual style of the *Sunday Times Magazine* between 1965 and 1975 (along with art director Michael Rand) and had designed posters, banners and other graphic material for Rock Against Racism and the Anti-Nazi League, both of which closely intersected with sections of the punk movement.[5]

The changing times and the wealth of new marketing opportunities were also reflected in a range of glossy new style magazines. Neville Brody had worked in the field of post-punk record sleeve design before taking on the design brief for Rod Pierce's Fetish Records and collaborating with Sheffield avant-garde, electronic post-punks Cabaret Voltaire.[6] In 1981, he began contributing to a new monthly music and style magazine, *The Face*, as a freelance editorial designer and typographer.[7] *The Face* had been launched by former *NME* editor Nick Logan in May 1980, building on the success of his previous magazine venture *Smash Hits*, a fortnightly glossy magazine launched in 1978 that centred on colour photographs and pull-out posters of contemporary pop stars along with transcribed lyrics of their hit songs. *Smash Hits* was published by EMAP (East Midlands Allied Press, the large publishing corporation behind the *NME*), but they declined to invest in his new venture, leaving Logan to set up on his own.[8]

> I went to see Nick Logan at *Smash Hits* and showed him my portfolio. He said my work wasn't appropriate for that magazine but kept my contact details. When he moved on to set up *The Face*, he called me and asked me to try out on a few spreads, which eventually led to the redesign and creative direction of the whole magazine.[9]

In direct contrast to *Smash Hits*, *The Face* combined photographs by leading rock and pop photographers – including Sheila Rock, Anton Corbijn, Chalkie Davies, Derek Ridgers, Jill Furmanovksy and Pennie Smith – with an editorial scope that extended into film, fashion and the arts and was aimed at a more style-conscious readership. The magazine also featured reflective features on contemporary music graphics by Jon Savage, along with profiles of two of the leading lights of the new generation of post-punk designers, Malcolm Garrett and Peter Saville.[10] The interviews were largely centred on the designers as personalities. While Garrett discusses his personal tastes and motivations along with a scattering of generic art historical references to Dada, Surrealism, Constructivism, the Bauhaus and Pop Art, Steve Taylor's interview with Saville does at least reveal something of the background process behind the designer's work for Factory Records and his early sleeve designs for Orchestral Manoeuvres in the Dark. A select few designer names (Bubbles, Reid, McDowell, Brody, Garrett, Saville) had by now become recognised in the music and style press as important contributors to contemporary culture, though they were largely still unknown to the wider public.

Printed in high-quality full colour, *The Face* also benefitted from Logan's business-savvy approach to marketing and distribution. A deal with West London-based Comag, an independent distributor established in 1977 to break the dominance of the publishing giants, allowed access to large high street retailers such as WH Smith as well as newsagents across the country. As Jon Wozencroft argues, 'Brody found himself in a unique position to break new ground, helped by the changing focus away from the newsprint music press to glossy magazines that qualitatively had more in common with Sunday supplements than with Punk's harbinger, the *New Musical Express*'.[11]

Brody took on the full redesign of *The Face* in June 1982, extending some of the radical typographic experiments that he had been exploring in feature articles to the grid of the entire magazine. Shifting the layout from a static four-column grid to a more flexible and dynamic two- and three-column approach, Brody introduced hand-rendered lettering, a mixture of different type styles on the same page – or even in the same heading – along with line work and typographic symbols to guide the reader in their navigation of contents. He was also commissioned to redesign *City Limits* in an attempt to reach a new readership.

> I ended up doing around two hundred covers for them over four years, trying to get them to be more competitive with *Time Out* but using a more raw, underground language.[12]

The wider availability of customised phototypesetting and the advent of digital type enabled other designers to follow suit, with a clear trend towards more dynamic and less standardised visual composition along with a greater use of the colour palette in keeping with contemporary fashions and popular culture more broadly. Some designers embraced the opportunities the new technology offered, though others – like Rob O'Connor – were a little more sceptical.

> There was loads of that faddy stuff going on around the time with, you know, experimental typography in so many new magazines, all that kind of stuff. We did try to avoid doing that, but occasionally I think we fell into the trap. Right next door to us [in Edgware Road] there was a headline typesetter which was all photographic, which was also very useful. You would pay them to literally expose one letter at a time to make a headline, or even small amounts of body text.[13]

Hot on Logan's heels, Terry Jones, along with his wife Tricia, designer Alex McDowell of Rocking Russian and arts graduate Perry Haines, founded *iD*, a quarterly magazine centred explicitly on fashion and style, rather than music. The first issue was published in October 1980. Utilising black and white photography that reflected the style of Jones' 1978 publication *Not Another Punk Book*, initial issues of *iD* were printed at Better Badges and retained many of the DIY design elements of the later punk fanzines – typewritten text, marks and corrections left on the page – along with an unusual landscape format and stapled binding for the first few issues, before reverting to a more standardised glossy magazine in 1983.[14] *iD* retained a measure of independence, since Jones' continuing demand as a senior art director for Fiorucci, German *Vogue* and *Sportswear International* allowed him to sidestep the major backers behind many of his competitors.

Other designers followed a similar path. Malcolm Garrett's Assorted Images studio, which had been responsible for the graphic identities of

Buzzcocks, The Members, Magazine and The Yachts among others, went on to score major success with the hugely successful pop groups Duran Duran and Culture Club in the early 1980s. Garrett's desire for control of the whole design and branding package, developed through his earlier experiences with Buzzcocks at United Artists, was at least partly resurrected in the process. In collaboration with his business partner, Kasper de Graaf, and funded by EMAP, Garrett art directed a new full-colour, glossy music and fashion magazine, *New Sounds New Styles*, which was launched in March 1981 and focused on the emerging New Romantic movement, with a heavy emphasis on his new clients, Duran Duran. In an increasingly crowded market, *New Sounds New Styles* was ultimately to be short-lived, ceasing publication after just thirteen issues in July 1982, though Garrett's typographic and editorial design interventions were to prove prescient.

> Malcolm did *New Sounds New Styles*, which was a mad, short-lived explosion, and it was great. In some ways, that magazine had arguably more of an influence on the design industry than his record covers, some of which, like the sleeves for the bands Magazine and Buzzcocks, were spectacularly influential – the use of those Letraset symbols was mind-blowing.[15]

Brody, Jones and Garrett's stylistic approaches would become instrumental across the graphic design profession over the following decade, particularly in the field of magazine design, fashion and branding centred on the growing youth market.

Another attempt to jump the bandwagon, *Blitz* magazine, was founded in 1980 by Oxford students Simon Tesler and Carey Labovitch – both of whom had family connections high up in the British media and politics. Designed by Jeremy Leslie, *Blitz* quickly moved from a quarterly to a monthly glossy magazine and shared many of the same interests as *The Face*, *iD* and *New Sounds New Styles*. Though it ultimately lacked the impact of those titles, *Blitz* did manage to continue publishing right through to the early 1990s.[16] At the same time, the publishers of *Flexipop!*,[17] Colourgold Ltd., attempted to infiltrate the *Smash Hits* market with a full-colour title printed on cheap paper, with few design attributes to celebrate and a tongue-in-cheek editorial approach to the celebration of pop cultural ephemera.[18] It did, however, include a free flexidisc single on the cover of each issue, featuring original recordings by some of the chart stars featured inside, ranging from Blondie to The Jam, Spandau Ballet and Bucks Fizz, leading to a measure of commercial success before the novelty wore off and *Flexipop!* was forced to close in 1983.

During this time, *Smash Hits* continued to go from strength to strength, reaching a circulation of around half a million copies every fortnight by 1984 and going on to nearly double that by the end of the decade. One other significant competitor in the pop magazine market, *No.1* (subsequently rebranded as *Number One*), was launched by IPC in

May 1983 as a new, weekly rival to *Smash Hits*. Initiated by former *NME* deputy editor Phil McNeill, the magazine occupied similar ground to both *Smash Hits* and *Flexipop!*, successfully running through to the early 1990s but never significantly challenging the domination of *Smash Hits* in circulation figures.[19]

The inkies (the traditional weekly music press) – *Melody Maker*, *New Musical Express*, *Sounds* and *Record Mirror*) – were finding it increasingly hard to keep up with these new trends. The oldest title, *Melody Maker*, founded by the International Publishing Corporation (IPC) in 1926, had taken some time to shift from its traditional focus on jazz and folk music to embrace more contemporary (and challenging) rock genres, while *New Musical Express* (known as the *NME*, also from IPC, founded in 1952) and *Sounds* (initiated by former *Melody Maker* journalists through a new parent company, Spotlight Publications, in 1970) were quicker to latch on to the long tail of the 1960s counterculture and the subversive promise of punk. *Record Mirror* had pioneered the use of colour in the 1960s, while maintaining an editorial stance that was closer to the pop charts than their often more 'serious' rivals, but still saw the need to rebrand as a glossy colour magazine from 1982, in direct competition with *Smash Hits*. Meanwhile, *Melody Maker*, *NME* and *Sounds* retained their newspaper formats but shifted away from their traditional monochrome and two-colour reproduction to a greater use of full colour on both covers and editorial pages.

At the same time, the expansion in music publishing and the impact of cheap printing technologies afforded a proliferation of colour magazines dedicated to niche style groups and scenes. It also facilitated the transition of some former punk fanzines to national magazines. Through a distribution deal with Seymour Press, Tony Fletcher's *Jamming!* made the leap to high street status (and a print run of fifty thousand copies) in 1983, sitting alongside long-standing specialist music titles like *ZigZag* on newsagents' shelves, together with the new style magazines and the by now declining inkies. Meanwhile, Tom Vague, Charlie Chainsaw and Mick Mercer adopted more professional standards of production at *Vague*, *Chainsaw* and *Panache* respectively, spanning the perceived divide between fanzines and the commercial magazine market.

Ever trying to keep on top of new trends, the established music press publishers attempted to develop their own magazine titles. *Sounds* editor Alan Lewis published the dubiously entitled *Punk's Not Dead* (which ironically lasted for just one issue) in 1981. A year later, *Record Mirror* journalist Alf Martin launched the monthly *Punk Lives!*, which ran for eleven issues between 1982 and 1983 and included noted former fanzine contributors Mick Mercer, Richard Cabut and Tony Drayton among its regular team. *Record Mirror* were also behind the launch of another fortnightly new title, *Noise!*, an attempt to bridge the space between 1980s punk and wider rock and pop markets (a total of sixteen issues published across six months in 1982). Reflecting a stronger brand concept and targeting a less well-served readership, specialist heavy metal magazine *Kerrang!* was established by *Sounds* editor Alan Lewis and staff writer Geoff Barton in 1981.

Breaking with convention

While some of the more successful young designers entering the profession were forced to step into line with the demands and long-standing conventions of the mainstream music industry, Malcolm Garrett felt that his generation of punk-inspired and punk-informed designers were able to reinvent, or at least circumvent, the design rule book.

> It was a new generation of designers who used DIY technologies. Why go through accepted channels just for the sake of it? You know, let's use new channels. Let's use different technologies. We can use photocopies, we can use fax machines, we can use felt pens, we can use whatever we want and just do stuff in different ways. And that's a big step because the print industry was so conservative, so tied to their processes – they were technicians by and large and they'd been taught the tools of a particular trade. And people like me, pesky whippersnappers, would be just kind of eating into that.[20]

Digital production methods were also impacting the graphic design industry. In something of a parallel evolution to the dissemination of photographic processes two decades earlier, many of the initial developments took place at the printers, rather than in design studios, with the (very expensive) new technologies employed for processing and reproduction work at the prepress stage, rather than as creative tools. Chris Morton recalls using the early digital Paintbrush system – a precursor to Photoshop – for the cover of a Siouxsie and the Banshees album, *Peepshow*, in 1988 (Figure 7.5). At that point, designers would seldom encounter – or be allowed access to – these new technologies. Describing the machine as a 'sealed, dust-free, double-glazed room the size of a small conservatory in the middle of the main print production room that cost a small fortune!',[21] Morton notes that 'it was something to be used by pre-press artworkers for digitally preparing artwork and photographs for printing; part of the print manufacturing process, as opposed to a tool for creatives to design with'.[22] For the single released to promote the album, 'Peek-A-Boo', Morton resorted to simpler methods. Photographing stills from a video of a masked performer on an old colour television (Figure 7.6), he developed a range of alternative designs for different versions of the release, including card masks and a three-dimensional, pop-up gatefold single cover.

Typesetting technology was also changing rapidly at this point, with specialist agencies and new service providers established to service both the design and print industries. The limited range of typefaces available

Parallel lines: into the eighties   213

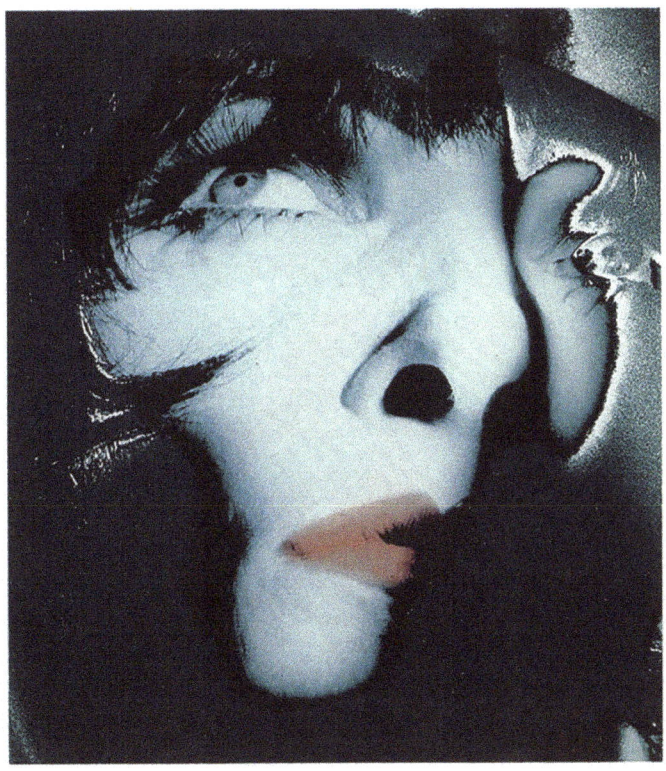

7.5 Siouxsie & The Banshees (1988), *Peepshow*, vinyl album, United Kingdom: Polydor. Original artwork, courtesy Chris Morton.

from phototypesetters, or through the Letraset catalogue, expanded dramatically with the ability to digitally adapt and modify letterforms.

> In the mid-80s typesetters were a bit slow on the uptake when it came to digital and we ended up starting to use a new company, Galley Slaves – a one-man band who bought the very first digital type compositors. And we were using him all the time; we were one of his biggest clients for some reason, and it was fantastic. Obviously, it was early digital so the actual quality of it when you looked through an eyeglass was a little bit 'jaggy', but at the same time the opportunity to modify, expand it, italicise it, stretch it …[23]

The shift to digital typesetting went beyond this expansion in the choice of typefaces and styles, also allowing for greater experimentation and modification at the design stage. The turnaround time was rapid in comparison with phototypesetting and designers could try alternative approaches before finalising the layout.

> Digitising typography was like a revelation really because it was quick. Yeah, try things and then have it changed without it costing a fortune. Whereas

7.6 Siouxsie & The Banshees (1988), 'Peek-A-Boo', 7" single, United Kingdom: Polydor. Original artwork, courtesy Chris Morton.

> literally, if someone gave us the copy and it was six pages like that, you'd have to sit there and mark it all up in the margins, you know, 'six-on-seven-point Meridian Italic' and so on ... And literally, you could spend three, four hours just doing that.[24]

However, as with the compression of job roles in other areas of design and print, digital type service providers were to be short-lived, with desktop computer technology rapidly evolving to give designers control over many more areas of their work, including typesetting. Independent designers and smaller studios began to invest in the revolutionary new Apple Macintosh computers, allowing them greater control of type and image manipulation while cutting out their reliance on expensive agencies. Mike Coles made the leap for economic, as well as creative, reasons.

> One of the deciding factors in jumping into the desktop publishing pit in the late 80s was because of the huge, unionised typesetting costs. Minimum charges, union rates, triple time with a minimum of two guys to work on a weekend. The typesetters were making millions, but the dawn of the Apple Mac revolutionised that completely.[25]

It wasn't just the methods and practices of design that were changing. The print industry witnessed a significant growth in small, independent and specialist studios servicing new markets and agencies such as ARTOMATIC, established by Tim Milne, offered bespoke services to the evolving music and style industry of the early 1980s.

> We started ARTOMATIC around 1981. Malcolm Garrett coined the name, because the year before he had done a catalogue for an exhibition by Peter Phillips that featured a painting entitled *Art-O-Matic Cudacutie* (1972). I had done a bit of paste-up work for Malcolm in his old studio in Denmark Street and the first ARTOMATIC studio was downstairs from his new place in Curtain Road. We specialised in screen printing and did a variety of music-related work for Malcolm, along with John Warwicker who was working for A&M at that time, Al McDowell at Rocking Russian and Peter Saville.[26]

A new group of record labels – both independents and larger, more established corporations – began to move away from the accepted conventions of the music business. Creativity did not lie just in the recording studio or the innovations of packaging designers and branding teams, but in the approach to business by managers, investors and stakeholders. There was a clear distinction between these emerging new record labels and their established counterparts in the music industry. Malcolm Garrett recalls working with the team at Virgin Records and the contrast between that outfit and his previous experience at United Artists. Despite Virgin being by now a leading player in the popular music business, to the extent that it was regarded as a major label alongside other large, international independents such as A&M and Island, its approach to business and management structure remained progressive and leftfield, at least in comparison with the likes of EMI, CBS and Polydor. Jill Mumford recalls a similar experience at Virgin, after leaving the more tightly controlled environment of the Polydor art department.

> Polydor was a very controlling environment, with procedures to follow for commissioning artwork and job orders. There was an A&R department and even a press office who organised all the interviews and publicity. Siouxsie was trying to bring in her own designers, but the Polydor contract specified that they had to use us for all publicity material and artwork. Virgin was completely different – I don't think we even had orders. It was like a holiday.[27]

Even the arch Situationist behind punk's original graphic provocations, Jamie Reid, found a creative home in the mid-1980s, taking up the offer of a studio at Assorted Images to develop his art practice. While Reid never did make the leap to the commercial graphic design industry, he did continue to collaborate with musicians, artists, filmmakers and political activists, embracing the potential of new print reproduction tools to create a new aesthetic.

> The big shift came with a call in 1985 from Malcolm Garrett to join the team at Assorted iMages on Curtain Rd, where he was to be a kind of talisman, with a studio and his own colour Ricoh four-colour copier with flatbed scanner to

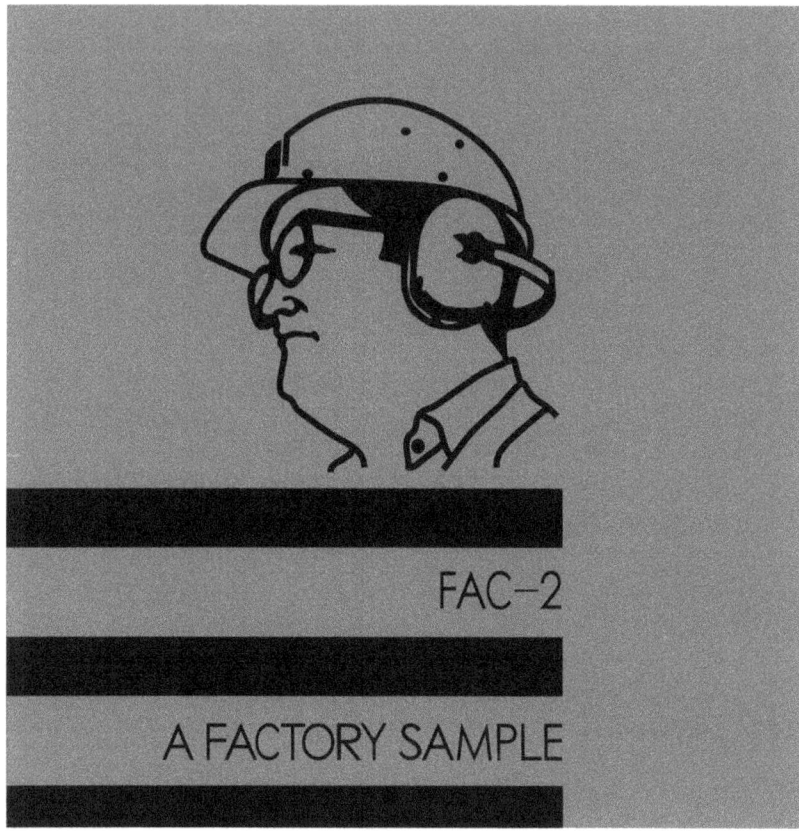

7.7 Various Artists (1978), *A Factory Sample*, double 7" vinyl EP, United Kingdom: Factory Records. Design by Peter Saville, collection of the author.

> play with … This is where Jamie refined his use of the colour copier, adjusting or 'dodging' the original on the copy bed between colour passes (black, red, green or blue) to add visual confusion and a three-dimensional quality.[28]

Other aspects of the music industry were also changing rapidly. Factory Records had started out as an extension of a series of live gig events promoted by Tony Wilson and Alan Erasmus at the Russell Club in 1978. Dubbed The Factory, the irregular nightclub showcased local post-punk and avant-garde artists. Peter Saville, at that point still a student at Manchester Polytechnic, offered to design posters for the club and was subsequently employed to create the label identity and covers for record releases by Factory Records. The label was set up by Wilson and Erasmus, along with Joy Division manager Rob Gretton and in-house producer Martin Hannett. Factory Records launched in December 1978 with a double EP featuring artists that had played at the club: The Durutti Column, Joy Division, Cabaret Voltaire and comedian John Dowie (Figure 7.7). All artefacts associated with Factory were assigned a catalogue number, from the first Saville poster (FAC 1) to Factory notepaper (FAC 7), an egg timer (FAC 8) and a film (FAC 9).[29] After Hannett left to set up his own recording studio, Wilson, Erasmus and Gretton formed Factory Communications Ltd. With funding from the success of post-Joy Division group New Order, Factory Communications branched out to establish a nightclub in central Manchester, The Haçienda (FAC 51), which opened its doors in May 1982. Reflecting a kind of industrial chic, further emphasised by the club's interior design by Ben Kelly and the continuation of Factory's graphic branding by Saville, The Haçienda proved to be much more of a critical than a commercial success.[30]

The club did, however, catch a wave with the resurgence of nightclubs and DJ culture in the 1980s, moving steadily away from traditional gigs centred on live bands to encompass a diversity of events spanning house music, film screenings, performance art and comedy. Similar changes were happening across Europe and the United States, and these had a direct impact on the evolution of both Factory Records and The Haçienda. The experience of the musicians in New Order and their entourage at house music clubs in Chicago fed directly into their music and their ambitions for the club, with Manchester becoming a central location for the emergence of techno and acid house later in the decade.

Electronically yours

The debut single by Daniel Miller, 'T.V.O.D.', issued under the guise of The Normal in February 1978 on Miller's own Mute Records label, was recorded in Miller's bedroom on a four-track studio. The sound was hard, dry, repetitive, explicitly electronic and synthetic and helped to set the scene for an entire musical movement that was to follow. Miller's label went on to release a successful catalogue of electronic music by a range of artists including Fad Gadget and Depeche Mode. The sleeves for many of these electronic music pioneers were a further development from the technical/machine aesthetic pioneered on earlier punk cover designs that blended a modernist graphic style with an ironic appropriation of advertising imagery and clean, clinical, highly technical images.[31] Letraset architectural figures provided easily replicated illustrations which utilised a clean use of line, and these were adopted by sleeve designers with a sardonic wit. Stylised illustrations of modern living from the 1960s and early 1970s were incorporated into the reverse sleeve design of Miller's debut single, designed by Simone Grant.[32] The figures – a man and woman exiting a car (from Letraset Art Sheet AA15) and a man watching television (Letraset Art Sheet AA130) (Figure 7.8) were set against a white background and within ruled boxes with rounded corners, mirroring the frame of a television screen (Figure 7.9). The front sleeve, meanwhile,

7.8 Letraset Figures, dry transfer sheet AA130.

harked back to a long-standing punk obsession with the mechanical and non-human. A still photograph taken from a car crash test features two dummies, strapped into car seatbelts, about to be thrown forward at the point of impact, with the image credited to the Motor Industry Research Association (Figure 7.10). The Mute Records logo, still going more than forty-five years on, was a simple geometrical Letraset figure of a man walking, viewed from above (from Letraset sheet ASH1055).

Similar illustrated Letraset figures were used by Sheffield electronic pop pioneers The Human League in their early artwork, designed by Martyn Ware in collaboration with Bob Last. The cover of the group's debut single, 'Being Boiled', released in June 1978 on Last's Fast Product label, shows a dancing couple in 1960s party clothes (from Letraset Art Sheet AA115) (Figure 7.11) set against a towering cityscape (in fact, the Manhattan skyline, from Letraset Art Sheet AA134) (Figure 7.12). The skyscrapers are used to denote a musical scale, with stylised notation terms including *a tempo*, *legato* and *staccato*, offset against the skyline. Ware had sent Last an original cover design – a black and white layout featuring the dancing couple together with many other visual elements – and Last chose to strip the design back to its key fundamental parts, then to add a flat salmon-pink background (Pantone 7416C) to emphasise the two figures, knocked out against the white card base. The reverse sleeve reflects a

Parallel lines: into the eighties 219

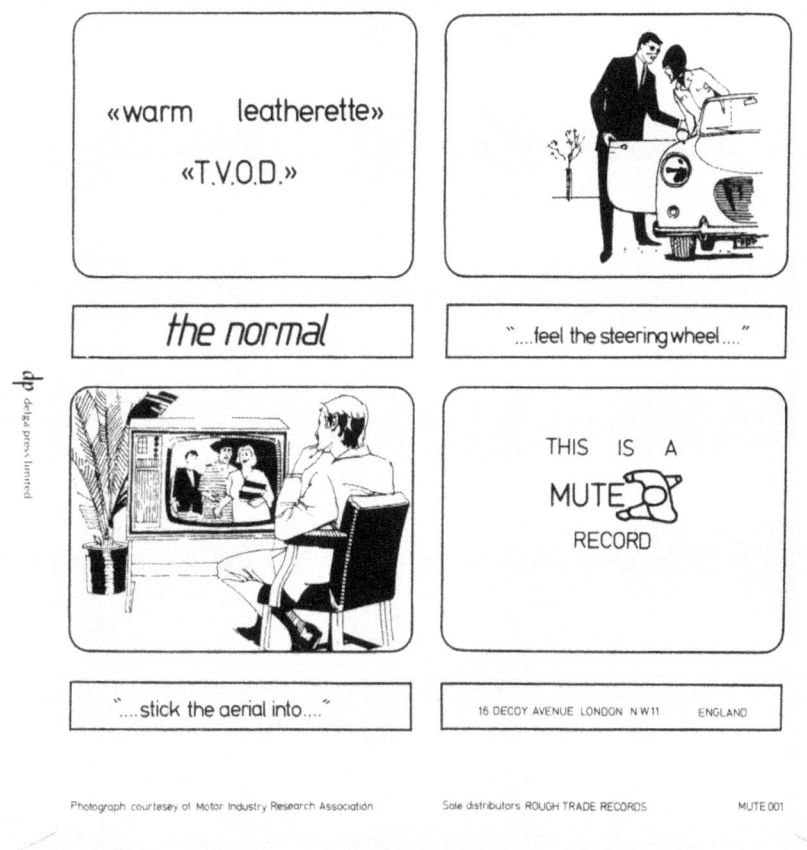

7.9 The Normal (1978), 'T.V.O.D.', 7" single, United Kingdom: Mute. Back cover. Design by Simone Grant. Collection of the author.

similar graphic approach, this time using Egyptian pyramids (again taken from Letraset Art Sheet AA134) surrounded by musical time signatures and symbols, including crotchets and quavers (Figure 7.13). Beside this, a modernist building (from Letraset Art Sheet AA122) sits above a selection of other, seemingly randomly selected, Letraset human figures. The ironic strapline 'electronically yours' accompanies the name of the group on the front and reverse of the sleeve, further emphasising the machine-made aesthetic, while parodying the advertising language of the 1950s and 1960s record industry.

Other electronic artists embraced the 'machine aesthetic' of technical drawing, ruled line work and the visual language of technical instruction manuals. The second single by Fad Gadget, 'Ricky's Hand', another release on the Mute Records label, incorporates a sequence of crudely

7.10 The Normal (1978), 'T.V.O.D.', 7" single, United Kingdom: Mute. Front cover. Design by Simone Grant. Collection of the author.

hand-drawn line images (with halftone film 'shading') of a hand being shredded in a liquidiser. The front cover is bordered by red and yellow striped 'warning tape' and both front and reverse use typography from the Letraset catalogue. The record featured Mute Records founder Daniel Miller on additional synthesiser, along with Fad Gadget's use of 'synthesiser, voice*, tapes*, Black & Decker V8 double speed electric drill*' and a label on the reverse sleeve proudly declares that 'only synthetic sound sources have been used in the making of this disc (excluding*)'.

Similar visual styles were adopted by other groups and artists who were developing their own synthesised and electronic music. Cabaret Voltaire, an experimental group founded in Sheffield as far back as 1973, signed to Rough Trade records in 1978, releasing a series of increasingly 'electronic' singles and albums in the ensuing years. Early singles such as

7.11 Letraset Figures, dry transfer sheet AA115.

the *Extended Play* EP (November 1978) and 'Nag Nag Nag' (June 1979) combined heavily distorted guitars with synthesisers and drum loops, forging a new direction in avant-garde post-punk. The group's record sleeves paralleled their development musically, from raw, amateur, DIY punk-influenced origins towards a more sophisticated machine aesthetic. The reverse sleeve of their debut *Extended Play* EP, with artwork credited to the group, includes stencil, Letraset and hand-rendered typography, along with simple shading produced by masking and spray painting. The overall effect is raw and immediate (Figure 7.14). By the time of the group's fourth single release, 'Seconds Too Late' (November 1980), more complex photomontage effects were evident and the sleeve was printed in two colours, in contrast to the simple black and white sleeves of earlier releases (Figure 7.15). Typography was still rub-down Letraset and was still poorly registered, but an aesthetic development was evident. By 1981, the group had begun to work with graphic designer Neville Brody and a dramatic shift in the visual style of their records ensued.[33] Alongside the shift towards more complex, full-colour, professionally designed sleeves, the group's sound moved more into funk and dance grooves.

Crossovers also emerged between avant-garde post-punk and the disco scene – the release of Donna Summer's 'I Feel Love' in 1977, the

7.12 The Human League (1978), 'Being Boiled', 7″ single, United Kingdom: Fast Product. Front cover. Reproduced courtesy of Holdings Ecosse Ltd.

first hit song recorded with an entirely synthesised backing track, had blended the machine aesthetic with dance rhythms. Produced by Giorgio Moroder, the song inspired mainstream rock artists such as David Bowie as well as influencing later groups as diverse as Blondie, Joy Division and Killing Joke. Journalist Simon Reynolds even asserts that the song, along with Kraftwerk's 'Trans-Europe Express', had been the most significant single release of that year in relation to the post-punk scene to come.[34]

Parallel shifts occurred across the nascent electronic music scene. Following the underground success of their first two singles, The Human League signed to Virgin Records and began a highly successful chart career, their sleeves documenting the transition from abrasive post-punk to the mainstream pop market, where glossy full-colour photographs

7.13 The Human League (1978), 'Being Boiled', 7" single, United Kingdom: Fast Product. Back cover. Reproduced courtesy of Holdings Ecosse Ltd.

of the group wearing the latest outfits were more important than arty visual rhetoric. A similar fate beset Liverpool electronic duo Orchestral Manoeuvres in the Dark (OMD) – their debut single, 'Electricity', was released by Factory Records in May 1979, with a special 'black on black' thermographic sleeve designed by Peter Saville.[35] Following some good airplay and critical acclaim for the record, they then signed to the new Virgin subsidiary DinDisc, reissuing the single in a revised format – with a white reversed out of black cover – and going on to achieve chart success with their debut album and a string of very successful pop singles in the early 1980s. Like The Human League, the group saw their success reflected in a rebranding for the pop market and a move away from the earlier visual and musical simplicity that had allied them to the post-punk electronic field.

7.14 Cabaret Voltaire (1978), *Extended Play*, 7" vinyl EP, United Kingdom: Rough Trade. Back cover. Design by Cabaret Voltaire, collection of the author.

Other artists produced electronic and experimental records in a similar style to The Normal and The Human League but chose not to adopt the visual conventions of the developing genre. Whether this was a conscious choice, an unawareness of the developing visual aesthetic or even simply the result of expediency and a lack of available tools, it is difficult to know. The first single by Thomas Leer, 'Private Plane', recorded like so many others in a small home studio and issued on his own Oblique label in November 1978, followed similar musical directions to the new electronic experimentalists, but retained much of the visual style of the earlier punk DIY movement, replete with ransom note typography (Figure 7.16). Leer's friend, Robert Rental, recorded his debut single at the same time and followed a similar path: setting up his own label, Regular, Rental issued the single 'Paralysis' in the autumn of 1978 and later went on to record an

7.15 Cabaret Voltaire (1980), 'Seconds Too Late', 7" single, United Kingdom: Rough Trade. Design by Cabaret Voltaire, collection of the author.

album with Mute Records founder Daniel Miller. Both Leer's and Rental's debut singles can be placed firmly within the post-punk DIY milieu – many of the sounds on the records were produced by electronically processing sounds from traditional instruments, rather than generated by a synthesiser. The sleeve artwork for both singles was based on a raw, black and white photocopy style, more in keeping with the punk legacy than the new electronic age. In many ways, these aspects mirrored other crossover groups such as Cabaret Voltaire and it was not until the early 1980s that a widely recognised generic visual style for electronic music became dominant.

Prior to the development of a specific electronic pop market in the early 1980s, the most successful of the early electronic artists was Gary Numan, who helped to establish the music within the mainstream, opening the way

7.16 Thomas Leer (1978), 'Private Plane', 7" single, United Kingdom: Oblique. Design by Thomas Leer, collection of the author.

for many successful electronic pop acts to follow. A multi-instrumentalist who recorded much of his music as a solo artist, he recruited other musicians to play live. Numan was formerly a member of London punk group Mean Street, whose 'Bunch of Stiffs' was included on the *Live at The Vortex* compilation in November 1977. He released three singles and an album under the guise of his follow-up project, Tubeway Army, on the Beggars Banquet label between February 1978 and March 1979, all of which used suitably android-like and futuristic imagery, before hitting the national number one spot with 'Are 'Friends' Electric?' in May 1979. The accompanying album, *Replicas*, also hit the top of the charts, as did Numan's next single, 'Cars' – now credited to the solo artist Gary Numan – and album, *The Pleasure Principle*, the following autumn. The earlier records had featured a blend of standard rock instrumentation (electric guitars, live drums) with synthesisers, but by this time Numan was moving into a far heavier use of electronic composition. His chart career was to see diminishing returns from 1982 onwards, as other groups such as Depeche Mode, Yazoo, Soft Cell and The Human League came to the fore.

Another electronic pioneer to come directly from the early London punk scene, John Foxx (Dennis Leigh, formerly of prog rockers Tiger Lily) had originally led art-punk group Ultravox! between 1976 and 1979. Ultravox! were heavily influenced by Roxy Music and David Bowie, with former Roxy Music keyboardist and electronic music pioneer Brian Eno brought in to co-produce their self-titled debut album alongside Steve Lillywhite. Driven by the singer's interest in the machine aesthetic, the group moved away from their glam punk roots and further towards electronic sounds, culminating in their third album, *Systems of Romance*, in 1978. However, commercial success evaded them and Foxx left to pursue a solo career early in 1979 at the end of a disastrous North American tour. Rather ironically, Ultravox (having dropped the exclamation mark) continued with a new singer, former Slik and Rich Kids frontman Midge Ure, and achieved international acclaim as pioneers of synth pop in the early 1980s, while Foxx pursued a more leftfield direction in electronic and ambient music, closer in style to early Kraftwerk and the work of his mentor and original inspiration, Brian Eno.

The 1980s new pop and electronic dance remix culture, led by New Order, Depeche Mode, Soft Cell, Frankie Goes to Hollywood and The Human League, drew heavily from synthetic musical styles. It was in the field of electronic music that the strongest impact of new technologies and the machine age was felt: the introduction of cheap programmable synthesisers in the late 1970s fed directly into the home-recording and DIY record industry. Drum loops and synthesised bass and keyboard sounds could be synchronised together to create musical arrangements and controlled by one or two musicians. While the original punk DIY pioneers such as The Desperate Bicycles and Buzzcocks had used commercial studios to record their songs, a new generation of musicians could take the entire recording and production process in-house, alongside the graphics and packaging. The only area left that could not be self-produced was record cutting and pressing, which could be accessed via the numerous small manufacturing services that had begun to advertise in the music press. The home-recorded DIY cassette scene offered an alternative even there.

The success of new pop in chart terms in the early 1980s meant that post-punk, DIY approaches were short-lived but still highly influential – the machine aesthetic became a visual trope in the sleeve design of the new electronica which continues to this day within techno and EDM recordings and label identities, albeit in a more sophisticated visual form. During the mid-1980s, the crossover from early handmade styles to computer-generated forms (designed by professional designers) mirrored the shift in musical production from the home studio to the major labels: the ragged, handmade nature of early DIY electronic graphics reflected the home studio approach to music making and recording, and the more complex and glossy image which followed was in keeping with the highly polished musical production of artists such as The Art Of Noise and Trevor Horn's ZTT label. At a time when independent labels were booming, Mute Records proved highly successful through the following decades, retaining its signature style and original Letraset logo, while the visual signifiers of technology and machine-made or computer output remained in place across a broad range of sleeve artwork.[36] These themes were to become more sophisticated with the advent of desktop publishing and the Apple Macintosh as a design tool, but certain codes persisted and can be traced back to a pre-computer age.

This is the postmodern world

The concept of postmodernism impacted architecture in the late 1960s and early 1970s and the term was applied to approaches that were eclectic, hybrid, decorative or witty, a deliberate counterpoint to the *form follows function* austerity of contemporary modernism. Since the 1960s, writers including Roland Barthes, Jacques Derrida and Michel Foucault had been exploring the notion of authorship and communication, emphasising the importance of the reader as an individual with their own personal biases, interests and perspectives. The argument that texts may have multiple readings suggested a rejection of modernism's rationality and universality, leading to shifts in popular culture, the visual arts and literature. A decade later, some graphic designers and typographers were starting to reject the established conventions of Swiss Modernism as a sell-out of its original, radical ideals to corporate stakeholders, branding and marketing departments and capitalist excess. Dramatic cultural and political changes were also underway, from the hippie counterculture and the Vietnam War to the May 1968 Paris riots and the activities of the Situationist International in Europe.[37]

From a graphic design perspective, at least some of the new aesthetic 'revolution' brought about by punk could be situated within a broader history of the modernist – and postmodernist – project. Bob Last even recalls a similarly aligned critical appraisal of his design for the debut release by Gang of Four, *Damaged Goods*, in a high-end New York fashion magazine: 'I remember the Gang of Four sleeve was hailed as a significant postmodern design milestone in *Harpers & Queen* at the time!'[38] In some respects, changes in the graphic design profession were already pre-empting (or at least paralleling) some punk design developments, particularly at the more commercial end of the spectrum: for instance, the work of Barney Bubbles and Chris Morton for Stiff and Radar Records and Alex McDowell at Rocking Russian. These trends within the graphic design industry would seem to indicate that at least *some* visual approaches adopted by punk designers, and subsequently viewed as core punk aesthetics, were evolving more widely in other commercial and professional arenas.

The visual identities of major punk and new wave groups, reproduced on a large scale and marketed to consumers, also reflected, to an extent, some of the 'new wave' professional graphic design styles evolving contemporaneously in Europe and the US.[39] However, the two convergent themes should not be conflated, particularly given their visual similarities and ostensibly overlapping terminology. Certainly, the mid-1970s design and typography of Wolfgang Weingart and Hard Werken[40] in the Netherlands, along with visual work produced by Dan Friedman and April Greiman in the United States later in the same decade, does not look out of place alongside much of the graphic design produced by designers for major punk and new wave groups and labels, but its roots are in a different place. That isn't to say that some contemporary, European avant-garde work was not influential on the British punk and post-punk designers, including the illustration styles of the Bazooka collective in France.[41]

> I was really influenced by the underground magazines in Paris, particularly the work of Bazooka and their publication *Bulletin Periodique*. In France, the main cultural inspiration coming out of punk wasn't music, it was radical comic books, illustrations, magazines ... it heavily influenced Barney Bubbles too and it started to appear in some of his work.[42]

Noting Weingart's radical graphic experimentation and the evolution of what were termed 'Swiss punk' styles, design historian Rick Poynor suggests that the British 'new wave' in graphic design differed from its US and European counterparts, in part because of the different context of modernism to which it was responding.

> Modernism had never been the dominant force in British graphic design that it was in Europe, or that it was, in a more corporate sense, in the United States. Much more than in the US, Britain's new wave was identified with youth culture and popular music and these designers tended to position themselves outside of design's professional mainstream, a quest for identity that could be read as a postmodern gesture in itself.[43]

We also need to consider the changing nature of design discourse, particularly in academia, away from the restrictions of professional practice. Notions of graphic design and visual communication practice changed enormously in the second half of the twentieth century, impacted by new technologies and a repositioning of the discipline away from purely trade or vocation. In the United Kingdom, the late 1980s and early 1990s saw many traditional art schools merged with technical colleges and polytechnics under the banner of new universities. As a result, discourse around visual communication took on more theoretical or philosophical positions, with art and design students encouraged to interrogate the critical, cultural and historical context of their practice. Graphic design – or visual communication, as it was commonly known – was late to the table in relation to many of its creative arts peers, but a new form of publishing sprang up to engage with the new theories and design took a turn towards a problematic combination of critical self-reflection and visual complexity.

The apparent overlap between post-punk and new wave graphic styles and the approaches of leading design professionals can, then, be theorised and mapped historically. Graphic design and commercial art have a long-standing relationship with both advances in technology (ranging from print to screen) and artistic or cultural trends. While this book has argued that much punk graphic design was heavily impacted – or even driven – by access to materials and technology, punk's visual provocations clearly also had antecedents in Dada, Surrealism and the Situationist International, together with Pop Art and its inherent critique of the distinction between fine art and the commercial arena, both in the United States (Andy Warhol, Roy Lichtenstein) and the United Kingdom (Richard Hamilton, Peter Blake, The Independent Group). But those connections were often indistinct, serendipitous and stylistic, rather than formal – and the same can be said of the similarities between post-punk or new wave music graphics and the new styles emanating from American and European designers in response to postmodernism.

Even the material form of the work overlapped at times. While Neville Brody, Malcolm Garrett and Terry Jones were engaged in the reconstruction of the pop culture magazine, Andy Warhol and John Wilcock's *Interview* had been running along similar lines in New York since 1969. At the same time, Leonard Koren's California-based *WET* magazine (subtitled *The Magazine of Gourmet Bathing*) ran between 1976 to 1981 and covered a wide range of contemporary cultural themes, alongside photography, illustration and design by celebrated professionals including Moshe Brakha, Gary Panter and April Greiman. In the Netherlands, the design group Hard Werken published a self-titled magazine between 1979 and 1982, drawing upon punk graphic styles as one element among many in their critically acclaimed design innovations.[44] Meanwhile, the Dutch *Vinyl* magazine made the leap from a music-centred publication to a lifestyle magazine featuring music, fashion, art, literature and film, paralleling UK magazines such as *i-D* and *The Face*, blending contemporary design with post-punk content and wider cultural interests.[45]

As all these converging themes illustrate, the historical relationships between punk, art history and design are highly complex, with punk and post-punk graphic approaches drawing upon earlier visual conventions while they themselves helped to inspire a new generation of design professionals working outside of the subculture. Whether that fits the model of postmodernist theory or not is something of a moot point, since punk's historical moment intersects so closely with wider changes in the arts, media and politics that it is almost impossible to separate causes from consequences. This has led to something of a retrospective re-evaluation of punk and post-punk art and design, however, and we will return to this theme in this book's final chapter, 'Retro-spective: influence and legacy'.

Notes

1. The Cartel was established by Rough Trade in the late 1970s to support the distribution of independent labels through regional centres. Partners in the group included Backs (Norwich), Fast Forward (Edinburgh), Nine Mile (Leamington Spa), Probe (Liverpool), Revolver (Bristol), Red Rhino (York) and Rough Trade (London).
2. Bestley, '"Fuck Art, Let's Dance"', p. 371.
3. Greg Milner (2010), *Perfecting Sound Forever: The Story of Recorded Music*, London: Granta.
4. Gennard and Bain, *A History of the Society of Graphical and Allied Trades*, p. 38.
5. Rick Poynor (2020), *David King: Designer, Activist, Visual Historian*, New Haven, CT and London: Yale University Press.
6. Wozencroft, *The Graphic Language of Neville Brody*.
7. The original identity for *The Face* was created by Steve Bush and Nick Logan, with Brody taking up the position of art director and redesigning the entire magazine in 1982.
8. Paul Gorman (2017), *The Story of The Face: The Magazine that Changed Culture*, London: Thames & Hudson, pp. 16–17.
9. Brody (2024), online interview, 5 March.
10. See Jessamy Calkin (1982), 'Image maker', *The Face*, March, pp. 44–45; Steve Taylor (1982), 'Industrial manoeuvres in the art', *The Face*, May, pp. 50–55.
11. Wozencroft, *The Graphic Language of Neville Brody*, p. 95.
12. Brody (2024), online interview, 5 March.
13. O'Connor (2023), email interview, 18 October.
14. Jones, *Smile i-D*.
15. Brody (2024), online interview, 5 March.
16. See www.blitzmagazine.co.uk/ for visual examples of covers and spreads (Accessed 14 February 2025).
17. Barry Cain and Neil Matthews (2015), *Flexipop! The Book*, London: Colourgold Ltd.
18. Trowell, 'Digging up the dead cities'.
19. Gorman, *Totally Wired*, p. 249.
20. Garrett (2020), online interview, 30 April.
21. Bestley, '"Fuck Art, Let's Dance"', p. 375.
22. Bestley, '"Fuck Art, Let's Dance"', p. 375.
23. O'Connor (2023), email interview, 18 October.
24. O'Connor (2023), email interview, 18 October.
25. Coles (2016), email correspondence, 22 September.
26. Milne (2024), online interview, 30 April.
27. Mumford (2024), online interview, 7 February.
28. John Marchant in Reid, *Rogue Materials*, p. 3.
29. Matthew Robertson (2007), *Factory Records: The Complete Graphic Album*, London: Thames & Hudson. Also known as FAC 461.
30. The Haçienda closed in 1997 and the building was demolished shortly afterwards.
31. Garrett adapted Letraset architectural figures (from Letraset sheet ASH1054) for the sleeve of the Buzzcocks single 'Love You More', released in June 1978, as well as the Entertaining Friends tour poster, May/June 1978.

32 Terry Burrows and Daniel Miller (2017), *Mute: A Visual Document*, London: Thames & Hudson.
33 Wozencroft, *The Graphic Language of Neville Brody*.
34 Reynolds, *Rip it Up and Start Again*.
35 Thermographic printing utilises heat-sensitive inks that expand through an oven-baking process to form raised marks or letters on the page. Saville had seen the effect at Manchester Polytechnic and chose to print a pattern of raised dots and lines in black against a black card background for the OMD sleeve.
36 Burrows and Miller, *Mute*.
37 Sadie Plant (1992), *The Most Radical Gesture: The Situationist International in a Postmodern Age*, London: Routledge.
38 Bob Last (2024), email conversation with the author, 6 February.
39 Andrew Blauvelt (2021), 'Riding a new wave', in Krivine, *Reversing into the Future*, pp. 100–117.
40 Ian Horton and Bettina Furnée (2018), *Hard Werken: One for All: Graphic Art & Design 1979–1994*, Netherlands: Valiz.
41 A creative collective brought together by Kiki and Loulou Picasso (Christian Chapiron and Jean-Louis Dupré) and Olivia Clavel in the mid-1970s. See also Michelle Scatton-Tessier (2019), 'Côté punk: Marc Caro', *Punk & Post-Punk* 8:3, pp. 343–362.
42 Brody (2024), online interview, 5 March. For a notable example of Bubbles' connection to Bazooka, see the 1979 album *Armed Forces* by Elvis Costello and the Attractions, which featured a fold-out cover centred around a collage of images created in collaboration with the French group.
43 Poynor, *No More Rules*, p. 32.
44 Russ Bestley and Tony Credland (2018), 'Fanzines and self-publishing in the 1970s', in Horton and Furnée, *Hard Werken*, pp. 168–171.
45 Richard Foster (2017), 'Moderne muziek: Vinyl magazine and the Dutch post-punk movement', *Punk & Post-Punk* 6:1, pp. 7–20.

8
Retro-spective: influence and legacy

The connections between form and content, materials and technology, marketing and consumption, labour relations and the economy are all important drivers of design and visual communication. Punk and post-punk design operated within that complex framework and the graphic history of punk needs to be viewed through the lens of craft, materials, technology, labour relations and the act of making. This book has attempted to recognise the central role of craft practices in punk graphic design and, particularly, print. Pre-press production teams and agency artworkers worked in the space between the creative director or graphic designer and the press operator, though their roles were changing rapidly in the late 1970s and early 1980s through the implementation of new technologies and working practices. Punk's new designers were forced to navigate this terrain, pursuing the path of complete control and radical autonomy at the heart of the subculture while facing resistance in the form of traditional ways of working and the professional establishment.

No more heroes

Popular music has changed irrevocably in the past forty years. Compact discs offered a level of rejuvenation to the recorded music industry in the 1980s, claiming better quality, resilience and ease of use (at a price – the 'upgrade' in quality was matched by significant profiteering and price hikes).[1] A boom in profits resulted from music fans investing in the new technology and replacing their old, redundant vinyl records and cassettes with compact discs, while the major labels shifted production of all new music to the format. However, over time, CD player technology developed to allow high-quality duplication on recordable discs and, like the cassette before it, the CD came under fire for enabling music piracy. The monopoly that was originally derived from the production of physical formats was finally (nearly) broken by digital file duplication, the internet and illegal peer-to-peer sharing in the late 1990s.[2] The corporations fought back, utilising legal injunctions, acquisitions and licensing deals with service providers, eventually beating the pirates at their own game by shifting away from physical media to online streaming and subscription services. In the twenty-first century, once again it is the ownership and control of the medium and the player, rather than the physical format (let alone the recording artist), that holds the power. Stand up and take a bow, Sony, Apple, Spotify and YouTube.

Many of the larger record companies also sought to diversify, to take advantage of changing technologies and new licensing and marketing opportunities, with dozens of smaller labels bought out by multinational media and entertainment businesses.[3] This model of amalgamation – and predatory capitalism – had always been a feature of the industry, but it started again in earnest in the early 1980s, a precursor to the corporate takeover and consolidation of the music industry in the ensuing decade. The Decca label, a major force in the pop music industry since the 1960s with high-profile signings including the Rolling Stones and the Small Faces, was sold off to the PolyGram group in January 1980 after several months of negotiation between the chairman, Sir Edward Lewis, and potential investors, including EMI and WEA. The pop and rock side of the Decca label was subsequently run down, though the classical music label continued. United Artists and Liberty were taken over by EMI in early 1980, along with specialist jazz label Blue Note. Meanwhile, Pye Records, which had been a strong player in the singles market since the 1960s (though it chose to move into the disco and pop markets rather than punk in the late 1970s), was bought out by Philips as part of a deal to sell off its electronics wing and the decision was made to change the label name to PRT in 1980, resulting in a steady decline and eventual collapse in 1989.

Within five years, the entire record market would be dominated by a small group of major players; EMI, PolyGram, WEA, CBS and RCA. With the collapse of the independent distributor Pinnacle Records in 1984, shortly followed by the Cartel network, the scene was set for the dominance of the corporate entertainment empires from the 1990s onwards. Things got even worse after the turn of the century, with the 'Big Five' eventually reduced to three. Whereas, up to the early 1980s at least, an assortment of major labels, large independents and DIY outfits offered a semblance of choice to music fans and a measure of internal market competition, a small number of global corporations came to dominate the global music and entertainment industries in the twenty-first century.

> Just three major companies – the Universal Music Group (UMG), Sony Music Entertainment (SME), and the Warner Music Group (WMG) – combine to

monopolize the global market for recorded music. The publishing arms of the same three major companies hold sway in the global music publishing market. When it comes to the live music industry, just two operators – Live Nation Entertainment (LNE) and the Anschutz Entertainment Group (AMG) dominate the landscape. In short, each of the three core sectors of the global music industries is dominated by a very small number of very large organizations.[4]

The function – and cultural centrality, for many fans – of popular music also shifted, first with music video and the crossover to more visual forms of entertainment, then through the impact of competing leisure pursuits and pastimes, from gaming to 'movies' (a term adopted from the US that perhaps more than most demonstrates the reach and impact of global consumerism), social media and 24-hour television. The notion of music as a core element of personal identity and (sub)cultural capital seemed to fall away in the 1990s, a process that accelerated in the new Millennium. In the postmodern consumer era, younger fans could pick from a variety of music genres, offering freedom of choice at the expense of a shared, communal identity. The lifestyle and fashion magazines that emerged in the early 1980s came to dominate the market, merging pop music with a range of other interests, from film to fashion, celebrity culture, sports, literature and the arts. A combination of new competition and revitalised or rebranded older magazines – *Vogue*, *GQ*, *Dazed & Confused*, *Arena*, *Wired* – threatened the established titles.[5]

The traditional music press inkies, already in terminal decline by the mid-1980s, eventually curled up and died in the 1990s.[6] While some music criticism shifted online (*Pitchfork*, *The Quietus*) or was incorporated in the glossy lifestyle magazines and newspaper colour supplements as one element of a wider spectrum of interests, the notion of music journalism as a form of cultural gatekeeping and taste-making in the printed form largely fell by the wayside, beyond a few glossy monthly magazines with a musical bent, often centred on 'serious' artists and targeted at middle-aged, financially well off consumers (*The Word*, *Uncut*, *Q Magazine*, *Mojo*). Pop music as simply a form of light entertainment or background noise came back into fashion, driven as much by marketing and promotion teams within the entertainment industry as it was by consumer demand. The public wants what the public gets. Rock music was also in decline, a process accelerated by banal television 'talent' shows and the return of the pop music Svengali in the odious form of Simon Cowell.

At the same time, punk became recuperated, at least in its commercial guise, through the cementing of a set of visual and musical tropes that could be picked up and regurgitated in the affectation – if not the performance – of a generic 'punk' identity. A revitalised form of pop punk became hugely successful in the United States in the mid-1990s, spreading around the world and embedding itself in popular culture from South America to South East Asia. Hardcore punk continued its global underground journey,[7] with smaller DIY scenes springing up in parallel, or in direct opposition, to punk's parent culture, though many suffered from a reliance on imitation rather than origination. Where the smaller scenes did move away from a hardcore/crust punk stereotype, it was often through closer association with 'indie', the bastardised offspring of the original independent post-punk scene, combined with a postmodern, sometimes ironic and often conceited form of self-reflection in musical approach, dress style and design. The early 2000s even witnessed something of a post-punk revival – or commercial pastiche – with highly successful groups adopting some of the gestures and signature styles of their late 1970s forebears, though often with little of the wit or intelligence. Style, rather than substance, was the name of the game.

In many ways running counter to these developments – including the hollowing out of punk as a subculture and the decline of rock music in general – the vinyl revival, centred around 'classic album' reissues and marketing initiatives such as Record Store Day (RSD)[8] has reinvigorated public interest in music graphics. Sadly, this interest is often linked to home decor and interior styling, with 'album art' displayed on bookshelves or in purpose-made frames hung on the wall – a marker of the owner's cool taste and cultural capital, rather than an object with a function and purpose. Limited edition, coloured vinyl re-pressings of big-name albums are paralleled with retrospective box sets by an increasingly obscure selection of long-forgotten artists, including many from the punk canon. Many feature booklets, posters and associated graphic ephemera sourced from archives and personal collections, sometimes in collaboration with the original designer. In part this reflects a growing market of middle-aged fans with disposable income and a nostalgia for their youth, with a more mainstream, parallel market established in major supermarket chains, selling classic reissues alongside soap powder and ready meals to buyers who don't frequent record shops. It's not purely nostalgia for the older generation, however. The tactility and visual presence of album art also appeals to a younger generation who have grown up through the graphic wilderness of iTunes, Spotify and online playlists.

> The big record labels learnt very quickly that they couldn't defeat punk, or underground culture, but they could emulate it without the danger and eventually replace it. This cycle of reaction and adoption just keeps happening. It's not even about revolution and counter-revolution, it's about the way differences end up being absorbed within society, through emulation.[9]

Live performance has also shifted in favour of these new consumer markets. Retrospective, themed gigs and festival weekends are geared towards comfort, convenience and the leisure package. Fifties rock'n'roll, sixties pop, seventies glam rock and Northern Soul and eighties New Romantic weekends take place regularly at off-season holiday camps and large entertainment venues, with indoor stages, catering, bars and accommodation all available in-house. An increasing array of 'alternative' events, spanning punk, new wave, synth pop, indie, goth and metal have sprung up in parallel, with crumbling Butlins holiday camps and traditional English seaside resorts the unlikely beneficiaries of an influx of weekend nostalgia hunters.[10] The annual Rebellion Festival in Blackpool[11] is approaching its thirtieth year, a gathering of the punk masses spanning five days and featuring several hundred live bands that attracts multiple generations of fans from around the world.

The Rebellion Festival followed in the bootsteps of the Vans Warped Tour[12] in the United States, a multivenue extravaganza of 'alternative' music that helped cement the already close relationship between punk and consumerism for a younger generation of fans. Perhaps a more direct equivalent is the Punk Rock Bowling[13] festival, established in 1999 and held in Las Vegas in the late Spring every year, which has grown from a small gathering of like-minded groups to a major, three-day outdoor event featuring more than one hundred bands, many of them also playing at Rebellion later in the year. Summer 2023 also saw the grand opening of The Punk Rock Museum in Las Vegas, a massive former warehouse building in the Arts District, now dedicated to preserving the history and heritage of punk rock while offering guided tours led by ageing pop punk musicians, a gift shop and a facsimile of a punk dive bar.

In the shadows

Punk's visual conventions, in turn, were appropriated, mimicked and blatantly copied by a rampant branding and marketing industry that is always on the lookout for material that might communicate an elusive sense of authenticity and agency. From trainers to power tools, credit cards to hamburgers, punk graphic conventions have been milked for all they are worth in the pursuit of profit. Like Milton Glaser's I [heart] New York logo, Arturo Vega's classic graphic identity for The Ramones has been replicated on countless millions of t-shirts, bags and patches, to be sold to unsuspecting teenagers in low-budget fashion stores and supermarkets from the United States to South East Asia. Meanwhile, identikit, cosplay 'punks' around the globe adopt outfits lifted directly from the stylistic dead end of 1980s hardcore punk, in a desperate search for subcultural legitimacy. The longevity of a generic global punk style could be taken as positive proof of its effectiveness, though the diversity and eclecticism of the original punk and post-punk scenes seems to have been jettisoned in favour of a universally recognised uniform. A narrow set of graphic codes is endlessly repeated on record covers, band identities, logos, clothing, flyers and posters for a self-sustaining marketplace that often seems to mindlessly repeat the 'alternative' rhetoric while disavowing its inherent contradictions.

Punk, and post-punk, graphic design needs to be evaluated and understood in relation to more than simply visual style or retro nostalgia. There is much more to it beneath the surface, beyond stylistic gestures and visual tropes. It is something of a self-evident truth that the history of visual communication is closely entwined with the history of print technology.[14] The visual presentation of punk's sometimes inarticulate concepts was driven by the knowledge, enthusiasm, dedication and willingness to *have a go* of the early punk do-it-yourself designers. It was also clearly shaped and delineated by the technology available to its proponents. The graphic conventions of early punk fanzines, for instance, were as much a product of the mark-making capacity of the typewriter, marker pen, biro and photocopier as they were the creative vision of their producers. Even though the fanzines were a central driver of punk graphic style, influencing professional design teams behind the scenes at the record companies and spilling into the mainstream music press and marketing campaigns, fanzine producers have been largely noted for their writing, or as editors and critical commentators, but seldom acknowledged as (albeit amateur and untrained) graphic designers. At the same time, the design process and technical production elements of the equation have often been overlooked or ignored in favour of a surface reading of the visual artefact. Like the style-without-substance pillaging of a punk aesthetic, punk fanzines have become fetishised and removed from their historical and cultural moment.

This codification of concepts purely through their visual qualities leads to a misguided presumption that those codes are intrinsically tied to meaning. In the case of punk graphics, this way of thinking suggests that the scruffy, distressed, awkward style of the early fanzines was a natural reflection of the do-it-yourself concept and therefore something that is endlessly replicable as a reflection of an authentic DIY avant-garde, even in the context of twenty-first century digital technologies. Zine-making workshops in colleges, community centres and museums are often seen as a simple way to engage the public in a kind of transparent ritual of do-it-yourself activism, tied to an aesthetic drawn directly from punk's distant past. Stripped of historical context or communal understanding, the visual elements become purely stylistic, empty gestures without content, function or purpose.

The dawning of a new era

The graphic design and print professions also underwent significant change in the late 1980s and 1990s. Impacted directly by the digital revolution, design followed behind the print industry in its radical restructuring and changes to technology and labour practices. As a result, the winds of change began to impact more keenly on individual designers.

The punk and post-punk designers' embrace of Letraset, the photocopier, the Grant projector, PMT camera and alternative tools and materials helped establish a new creative approach, while the original punk philosophy of DIY autonomy and independence spread through a wide range of creative practices.

> The whole independent record industry thing really fuelled the rebirth of British graphic design.[15]

The digital design revolution was yet to come, but the seeds of the modern design practitioner's role were sown during this period. It also marked the first big steps in the transition away from conception, specification, planning and project management (the traditional role of the art director) to a designer-maker model, which was to lead eventually to digital systems, desktop publishing and WYSIWYG in the 1990s.[16]

> The print and, more specifically, the pre-press sector was one of the first to feel the winds of change breeze through it in the 1980s. Where we are now used to disruptive technologies, all this happened before any real understanding of 'digitisation' took hold. We all gawped in amazement at how a million-pound Scitex scanner could rotate an image through 90 degrees (overnight, mind) and the arrival of the first Macintosh computers meant that pre-press inevitably moved into the domain of the designers. Though it had the initial effect of cheapening four-colour printing, leading to the high-water mark for print industry output by the mid-nineties, it cemented its ultimate decline thereafter.[17]

These changes, and the subsequent compression of roles and responsibilities in the hands of the designer, were not just empowering – they also carried a downside. Where the graphic designer had once been part of a longer chain of expertise between the brief and the product, with a focus on planning, strategy and project management, they were increasingly expected to absorb all elements of process and craft, from the creation of a draft layout through to the construction of print-ready artwork.

> It's hard to overstate the revolution when the Apple computers came in and started to bring all the stuff that had been the prerogative of the retouchers and the repro houses into the hands of the designers. Prior to that point the designers might have been able to have a go at explaining what they wanted to the repro house, but it was largely pointless because they weren't going to get it.[18]

At the same time, many steps in the design process have shifted to the direct control of the designer, though in recent years this itself has led to ethical questions regarding access.

> The democratic liberation of technology has ended up putting us in the most non-democratic communication space we've ever been in. When you look at restrictions nowadays, it's not the unions any more, it's subscription-based software that is shutting out amateur designers.[19]

The now almost ubiquitous Adobe PDF system has also shifted responsibility even further into the hands of the designer, with proofing and colour calibration sometimes left to luck, or trust, and 'wet proofs' a thing of the past.

> I remember thinking, it seemed logical to me, that the idea of a journalist being able to type up their own column ready to go into a newspaper made a lot of sense, though the compositor is going to be more fine-tuned towards proof-reading, identifying typos and what have you. Whereas the idea of a graphic designer becoming a repro person never made any sense to me and I'm still a little bit nostalgic about the craft that used to go into pre-press, because some of those guys really took your artwork and made it a hell of a lot better. And now if anything, it's the other way around.[20]

While many of the design and production stages remained largely in place – typesetting, image preparation, colour specification – they were condensed and rendered invisible, particularly to clients who no longer felt they needed to pay a craftsman for each step of the process. Printer Murray Arbiter recognised early on that the shift in design education and skillsets was potentially storing up problems for the future.

> The Mac was the second big revolution of the 1980s in terms of design and print. In the early 2000s there was a widespread assumption that print was dead, but I wrote a paper at that time suggesting that all the skilled workers – the bookbinders, the press operators – would still be needed in the future. Now, we find that that knowledge and expertise is required once again.[21]

The flexibility afforded by digital technology and a single designer in control of the whole project meant that record labels felt empowered to request multiple, additional changes to artwork for different media formats and merchandise such as t-shirts and posters, treating the extra tasks as part of the same brief. In 1988, the government introduced the Copyright, Designs and Payments Act, which in effect gave the author or creator of a written piece, an art piece, a photograph or film total control of the rights for its use or reproduction. Agreements to license the rights to these works needed to be negotiated and signed by both the creator and the client or buyer. In response, the record companies very quickly produced blanket agreements which would effectively give them all rights to all designs and artworks produced by creative studios and individuals to exploit and amend as they wished without further payment. Following informal discussions between several key players, a group of music graphics professionals eventually banded together to form a new support group, AMID (Figure 8.1).[22]

> We eventually set up this thing called AMID, the Association of Music Industry Designers. And we had something like a hundred or more members at one point – it wasn't really a union, but it was a great excuse to meet up. Unfortunately, in those days, geography was a hindrance to many of the great

8.1 AMID logo, 1988. Design by Keith Breeden, courtesy Rob O'Connor.

design companies who weren't based near London, but we did send out membership handbooks and newsletters to everyone to keep them updated, this being before the age of the internet.[23]

Of course, even though many of the earlier stages of production had been absorbed into the remit of the designer, record covers and other complex forms of design often involved multiple creators, such as photographers, illustrators and digital artworkers, but the group felt empowered to push back against the more exploitative practices they were facing. AMID members agreed to abide by a set of guidelines, including acknowledgement and recognition of those partner services, and devised a standard form that could be used in contractual agreements with the major labels. Regular meetings also provided an opportunity for peer recognition and support, including discussions with some of the older generation of senior designers and art directors.

> People would pay a subscription, so we had a bit of money to book a meeting room, generally at the ICA, or wherever it was. The very first meeting was at the Groucho Club in Soho – there was Martin Atkinson from T&CP, Malcolm [Garrett], Peter [Saville], about ten people altogether. And we soon persuaded Roger Dean and Storm Thorgerson – these godfather figures of record sleeve design – to come to a couple of meetings, which was great. It was actually very useful. We used the group not just as a professional forum, but also as a negotiating body to sit down with some of the business affairs departments of record companies like Warners, Sony and Arista to figure out alternatives to these untenable blanket agreements.[24]

The digital revolution created both winners and losers in the graphic design profession. While desktop publishing afforded opportunities for individual designers to take control of many pre-press activities for the first time, their previous reliance on specialists at various stages was jettisoned and they were forced to become expert in a greater range of craft skills and practices. With autonomy comes responsibility. Typesetting and layout were much quicker, however, and the ability to make changes on the fly, to try out a range of variations and to step backwards without incurring a great deal of additional time or expense, was truly ground-breaking. That kind of flexibility appears self-evident nowadays, from the perspective of forty years of desktop publishing history, with digital interfaces in virtually every home and workplace and the ability to type, arrange, rescale, edit and instantly erase commonplace features of twenty-first century life. But in the 1970s and 1980s such technology was in its infancy, and the gradual transition for designers from the position of one link in a long chain of producers to (almost) complete control of the whole print production process took time and a great deal of learning. The print industry was also changing rapidly during this period, in part driven by new technologies but also through government and business development strategies.

> The big change in the printing industry came when asset-based financing allowed printers to buy new presses through leasing agreements. In the late 1970s and 1980s, manufacturers like Heidelberg stepped up production and you started to see lots of four-colour printing houses, all with CMYK logos and the word 'colour' in their business name. Since that high-water mark around the late 1980s and early 1990s, print has been on a slow, steady decline and is now much more of a luxury good.[25]

Eventually, the ubiquitous computer and a concurrent shift away from manufacturing to the provision of services led to huge changes in design as well as print. While designers were temporarily able to retain a sense of professional control, even when working increasingly as computer operators on the direct instructions of clients, the advent of more sophisticated templates, the internet and, more recently, artificial intelligence as a supposedly creative tool, undermined the entire industry. The early twenty-first century witnessed a boom in client and customer-facing service industries, not least in the print on demand sector.

> The advent of print on demand and the type of machinery that businesses are now using – where you can print onto almost anything – has completely changed the industry, along with the level of service that these companies have realised they need to deliver. Printing has gone from an entirely B2B [business-to-business] industry, with nothing consumer-facing at all, to a few big, successful companies who have figured out how to do this stuff with a level of customer service. I marvel at how they have turned a medium of infinite variables into a set of rules that normal people can follow.[26]

The period of flux that impacted both music and graphic design production through the 1980s and 1990s saw many in the punk-related cohort either moving on to other things or taking up positions within the established industry. Few, however, became household names.

> Weirdly, there's a whole generation of designers who never managed to move on to wider commercial success in the mainstream. None of the main protagonists went on to something else – fashion or corporate branding or whatever. People of the same generation, who went to the same art schools, like David Davis or Michael Peters, went on to make big fortunes. The gravy train went straight past the music graphics designers. I never really understood it.[27]

Most of the fanzine producers moved on to new scenes and new directions, with the majority ceasing production after a brief spell in the limelight. Some higher profile fanzine writers stepped into mainstream journalism, often via the weekly music press or the new breed of specialist music and style magazines. Jon Savage, Richard Cabut, Mick Mercer, Tony Drayton and others retained a measure of underground, countercultural cachet in the process, while for others a longer and more lucrative career eventually tarnished punk-related reputations: Garry Bushell, Paul Morley and John Robb, among others, pursued a career in popular journalism that went some way beyond their less than auspicious roots.

> Look closely and future photographers, journalists, musicians, costume designers, writers, illustrators, politicos, band/label managers, academics and authors appear in earlier guises contributing to youthful labours of love, be it Kevin Cummins, Jane Suck, Mike Scott, Rebecca Hale, Paul Morley, Steve McGarry, John McTernan, Richard Boon, Shirley O'Loughlin or Philp Hoare.[28]

Some from the incoming generation of punk designers moved into a broader art practice – major solo exhibitions by Gee Vaucher,[29] Linder Sterling[30] and Jamie Reid[31] have been mounted in contemporary art galleries in recent years, and they have belatedly been acknowledged as important contributors to the cultural landscape of the late twentieth century. Reid's passing in August 2023 also led to a re-evaluation of his life and work,[32] with museums and galleries affording him greater recognition as a cultural and political pioneer. Barney Bubbles had passed away forty years earlier, in November 1983, his incredible visual legacy only being re-evaluated nearly three decades later in Paul Gorman's *Reasons To Be Cheerful*.[33] Chris Morton left Stiff in 1983 to form c-more-tone studios and created iconic graphics for Theatre of Hate, Spear of Destiny, Siouxsie and the Banshees, The Beat, Stray Cats, Dave Edmunds, John Otway, Feargal Sharkey, Scott Walker and Philip Glass, among many others. He still works with Theatre of Hate and Spear of Destiny through his design practice in Newcastle.

Vaughan Oliver carried on as in-house designer for 4AD Records, moving on to establish a new studio, V23, with Chris Bigg after his former partner Nigel Grierson left 23 Envelope in 1988. Major success with Pixies, Cocteau Twins, This Mortal Coil and The Breeders elevated the label, along with the designer's artwork, to critical and commercial prominence in the late 1980s and early 1990s, and Oliver was celebrated as an important figure in the graphic design profession of the postmodern era.[34] Oliver passed away in December 2019,[35] his stunning visual legacy having been celebrated in print by Tony Brook and Adrian Shaughnessy a year earlier.[36] Chris Bigg continues to produce work for 4AD and other clients in music and the arts. Peter Saville's work with New Order in the 1980s and 1990s and the commercial success of Factory led to critical acclaim and a partnership at Pentagram, before moving on to work in branding and advertising for high-profile clients including Selfridges, Burberry, Stella McCartney and Calvin Klein. He also worked closely with avant-garde Belgian fashion designer Raf Simons, reproducing much of his Factory imagery on their hugely expensive Autumn/Winter 2003 collection.[37] In 2020, Saville was appointed Commander of the Order of the British Empire (CBE) for services to design. Malcolm Garrett worked with Duran Duran, Culture Club, Simple Minds and Peter Gabriel in the 1980s, expanding his clientele at Assorted iMaGes to the design and production of exhibition and television graphics, before moving into interactive media at AMXstudios and linking back up with his former business partner Kasper de Graaf in 2013 to establish IMAGES&Co. Garrett was elected Master of the Faculty of Royal Designers in November 2013 and appointed Member of the Order of the British Empire (MBE) in 2020 for services to design. Neville Brody also moved away from both music packaging and magazine design in the late 1980s, seeking new challenges in type design and interaction through the FUSE project collaboration with Jon Wozencroft and his own Research Studios.

> I stopped doing record covers when the whole thing shifted, post-New Romantics, when every cover would just have a photo of the singer and the design job just involved choosing a photographer, a font, a hairdresser, a stylist and a make-up artist. Similar stuff happened with printed magazines – there was a lot of innovation, but after a while it hit a dead end. It was done.[38]

Bob Last closed Fast Product at the height of the label's success, going on to establish another short-lived but critically acclaimed independent label, Pop Aural, then moving into artist management with The Human League, Heaven 17 and ABC, before making his way into the film industry. In the 1990s he worked as a music supervisor, subsequently achieving commercial success in the early twenty-first century as a producer for films, including the 2010 Oscar-nominated animation *The Illusionist*. Alex McDowell had made a similar journey following the success of his design group Rocking Russian, which he had established with former Sex Pistols bassist Glen Matlock in 1978. After working on album covers for The

Rich Kids, Siouxsie and the Banshees and The Clash, McDowell moved to Los Angeles and became involved in music video production for clients including The Cure, Queen, Madonna and Michael Jackson, along with the creation of advertising commercials for Nike, Coca-Cola, Chanel and other high-profile international corporations. McDowell eventually went into production design for Hollywood studios, creating award winning visual narrative design for films including *The Crow* (1994), *Fight Club* (1999) and *The Terminal* (2004). Mike Coles, meanwhile, continued to work with Malicious Damage and a range of commercial clients. He stepped away from the label's leading group, Killing Joke, for a period in the late 1980s and early 1990s before being reunited for a prolonged period of creative partnership, through to the death of guitarist Geordie Walker in 2023. Coles also worked closely with electronic ambient house pioneers The Orb, moving into the realm of live video projections as well as printed graphics alongside his own art practice.

Many of the former in-house art directors also established their own independent practices. Jill Mumford decided to step away from music graphics in the mid-1980s, moving into scenic art for film and video. Her former colleague at Polydor, Bill Smith, set up his own studio, BSS, in 1978 and continued to work within the industry through to 2019, creating graphic identities and album covers for Genesis, Kate Bush, the Rolling Stones, Led Zeppelin and Mike Oldfield. Rob O'Connor established his own studio, Stylorouge, in 1981.[39] He created album artwork for high-profile artists including Blur, Enya, Squeeze and Crowded House, along with the film posters and graphic branding for the film *Trainspotting* (1996), and continues to work with music industry partners and clients alongside video production, corporate identity work and exhibition design.

By way of a conclusion

We have explored the various, sometimes contradictory, strands of what might be termed punk visual aesthetics and made a distinction between punk's broadly conceptual themes (including the twin notions of *do-it-yourself* and *anyone can do it*) and the acts of making that followed. At its best, the punk DIY message was more than rhetorical – it was a call to arms that not only encouraged others to take up the baton for themselves but offered guidance on how to do so, albeit implicitly, through its form. Self-referential and explicit making practices included cut-and-paste, appropriation, parody and satire, collage and an embrace of distortion, disruption and decay – punk's roughly torn edges were fundamental to its message.

Although punk was a broad church, bringing together cultural provocateurs alongside bandwagon-jumpers and opportunists, experienced countercultural radicals and kids still in school, its core values of autonomy, authenticity and empowerment were widely repeated (if not always acted upon). The punk diaspora across the regions of the United Kingdom embraced stereotypical punk conventions, sometimes received through the mainstream media without direct contact to 'authentic' points of origin, but also enabled myriad new directions and the evolution of post-punk styles. Punk-inspired designers were also entering a professional establishment that was facing an impending storm brought about by new technologies and radical changes to working practices. With the commercial success of the new wave, experienced designers and art directors in the established creative studios continued to work to their brief, adopting punk's overt signs of distress as visual code for the new pop music scene.

Technology is essential to graphic design history, from the use of tools for origination of artwork to pre-press modification and print reproduction. Punk designers could make use of simple tools and techniques that fitted perfectly with its rough and ready visual aesthetic, from cut-and-paste and collage techniques to Letraset, stencils and crude mark-making, utilising the new photocopier technology for simple and effective reproduction, if only in very limited quantities. For longer print runs, they ran the gauntlet of the print industry, accessing services from small, high street lithographic printing studios or via print cooperatives – a legacy of the 1960s counterculture in some of the bigger cities. In the bigger commercial design studios, PMT cameras and halftone screens came into the hands of designers, affording more control of pre-press processes, swiftly followed by computer-based tools for type design, typesetting and image manipulation – the precursor to the desktop publishing revolution of the 1990s. Changes to traditional job roles and reduction in the commercial print workforce led to significant disruption, led by the major unions in the national press and publishing industries. Punk and post-punk designers were largely bystanders in that dispute, but its knock-on effects combined with the entrepreneurial aspects of punk's call for autonomy were to impact the field of music graphics enormously over the following decade.

It would be a mistake, however, to limit punk's impact to a technological or professional context. Punk was a social and cultural movement and its facilitation of a sense of identity and the empowerment of participants – *anyone can do it* – brought about significant changes in design, as well as the broader arts, media and cultural industries. Punk blurred the distinction between amateur and professional: punk fans could be their own media, and its visual styles could be copied and reproduced with cheaply accessible tools. In parallel with the restructuring of the print industry, punk's have-a-go mission of autonomy and complete control enabled new creative practices and the growth of small, specialist design studios that contrasted with the corporate model that had dominated the music industry for decades.

This book couldn't possibly provide a fully detailed account of the entirety of punk-related practice in the design and print industries. It does, however, offer an insight into the complex relationships that existed between punk as a concept and its manifestation in printed material, from fanzines to record covers, posters to music magazines and adverts in the mainstream press. Interview extracts from conversations with a few design pioneers of the era are not intended to function as authentic oral histories, nor are they without post-rationalisation and bias, as all retrospective accounts are likely to be. However, with graphic designers operating largely anonymously, if not invisibly, behind the scenes of a cultural phenomenon, there are few contemporaneous accounts of the creative process from the perspective of those doing the work. Even the small number of published interviews in the early 1980s tended to centre on the personalities, tastes and lifestyles of a few higher profile designers alongside opaque references to their art historical influences and lacked any meaningful analysis of their design process.

The graphic styles of early UK punk – from dayglo colour palettes to ransom note lettering and gritty, distressed photographs – have become commonplace tropes in the marketing of sportswear, youth clubs, style magazines, fashion brands and pop music. Punk and post-punk aesthetics continue to inspire up-and-coming designers and fleece consumers in the twenty-first century, though the more brutal, basic DIY template created by punk's determinedly combative non-professionals still evades mainstream commercial reappropriation. Viewed from a contemporary vantage point, 'spectacular subcultures' such as punk, that centred on tribal affiliations and subtle (or not so subtle) visual tropes, appear to have come from another age. The internet, personal blogs, influencers, social media and search engines have redefined modes of discovery, criticism and taste-making.

The almost ubiquitous computer shapes our visual landscape while limiting the choices available to us, including the opportunity to learn by our mistakes or through engagement with physical materials. Perhaps the time lag between punk's original autonomous ambition of doing-it-yourself and the widespread availability of technologies that allow full artistic control from inception to reception has softened the pioneering spirit of contemporary musicians, artists, writers and designers. Punk's disruptive impact can only be fully understood in its historical and cultural context. The manifestos, messages of empowerment and direct calls to arms of the early punk generation were embodied in the struggle to communicate within the restrictions of the medium and the technologies of the time – they were a push-back against limitations and conventions, an engagement with process as much as with product. That struggle was in many ways the driver of creativity and innovation. A new visual aesthetic of punk graphic design was the result.

Notes

1. Milner, *Perfecting Sound Forever*.
2. Launched in June 1999, Napster specialised in the distribution and peer-to-peer sharing of digital MP3 audio files. Following a succession of high-profile lawsuits, the service was shut down in July 2001.
3. Louis Barfe (2005), *Where Have All the Good Times Gone?: The Rise and Fall of the Record Industry*, London: Atlantic Books.
4. Murphy and Rogers, *Sounds Irish, Acts Global*, p. 42.
5. *iD* managed to retain its place in the market, though *The Face* folded in 2004.
6. Following the restructuring of parent company United Newspapers, *Sounds* and *Record Mirror* both folded in 1991. *Melody Maker* merged with the *New Musical Express* in January 2001. The *NME* had already by this time switched from newsprint to a glossy magazine format, though it was forced to shift to a free publication in 2015 and eventually ceased printing in 2018.
7. Russ Bestley, Mike Dines, Alastair Gordon and Paula Guerra (eds) (2021), *Trans-Global Punk Scenes: The Punk Reader Vol. 2*, Bristol: Intellect. See also Russ Bestley, Mike Dines, Matt Grimes and Paula Guerra (eds) (2021), *Punk Identities, Punk Utopias: Global Punk & Media*, Bristol: Intellect.
8. Record Store Day was launched in the United States in 2007 as a marketing initiative to support independent record stores, with limited edition releases only available in store. The event now takes place annually on the third Saturday of April each year around the world. Despite its positive impact on the vinyl revival, RSD faces a great deal of criticism from commentators and long-standing collectors for its crass commercialism.
9. Brody (2024), online interview, 5 March.
10. Simon Reynolds (2012), *Retromania: Pop Culture's Addiction to its Own Past*, London: Faber & Faber.
11. Formerly Holidays in the Sun (Blackpool and Morecambe, 1996–2003) and Wasted (Morecambe, 2004–2006). The festival promoters also established parallel events in Germany, the USA, Japan, Ireland, Belgium, the Netherlands, Australia, Italy and Austria between 2000 and 2018.
12. The Vans Warped Tour ran across the United States between 1995 and 2019.
13. Established by former Los Angeles hardcore punk musicians Shawn and Mark Stern in 1999.
14. Richard Hollis (1994), *Graphic Design: A Concise History*, London: Thames & Hudson.
15. Brody (2024), online interview, 5 March.
16. WYSIWYG: 'What you see is what you get', computer screen-based design processes.
17. Tim Milne (2023), email conversation with the author, 2 August.
18. Milne (2024), online interview, 30 April.
19. Brody (2024), online interview, 5 March.
20. Rob O'Connor (2020), online interview with the author, 30 April.
21. Arbiter (2024), online interview, 26 April.
22. AMID committee members included Keith Breeden (DKB), Andrew Ellis (Icon), Kasper de Graaf (Assorted Images), Bruce Gill (Green Ink), Rob O'Connor (Stylorouge), Nigel Proktor (Might) and Bill Smith (Bill Smith Studio).
23. O'Connor (2020), online interview, 30 April.
24. O'Connor (2023), email interview, 18 October.
25. Milne (2024), online interview, 30 April.
26. Milne (2024), online interview, 30 April.
27. Milne (2024), online interview, 30 April.
28. Worley, '"If I had more time it could be better, but the new wave's about spontaneity, right?"', p. 226.

29 Rebecca Binns (2017), 'Gee Vaucher: Introspective, Firstsite, Colchester, 12 November 2016–19 February 2017', Punk & Post-Punk 5:3, pp. 329–338.
30 Rebecca Binns (2018), 'The House of Fame: An Exhibition Convened by Linder, Nottingham Contemporary Gallery, UK, 24 March–24 June 2018', Punk & Post-Punk 7:3, pp. 479–486.
31 Ian Trowell (2019), 'XXXXX: 50 Years of Subversion and the Spirit, Humber Street Gallery, Hull, 12 October 2018–6 January 2019', Punk & Post-Punk 8:2, pp. 305–316.
32 Rebecca Binns (2023), 'Jamie Reid, legendary artist, rebel and campaigner: 16 January 1947–8 August 2023', Punk & Post-Punk 12:3, pp. 379–388.
33 Gorman, Reasons to be Cheerful.
34 Poynor, Vaughan Oliver.
35 Russ Bestley (2020), '"This monkey's gone to heaven": Vaughan Oliver 1957–2019', Punk & Post-Punk 9:1, pp. 121–126.
36 Brook and Shaughnessy, Vaughan Oliver.
37 Calum Gordon (2017), 'A history of Raf Simons' collaborations with Peter Saville', Another Man, 17 July. www.anothermanmag.com/style-grooming/9956/a-history-of-raf-simons-collaborations-with-peter-saville (Accessed 19 March 2024).
38 Brody (2024), online interview, 5 March.
39 O'Connor, Delicious.

Bibliography

Ades, Dawn (1976), *Photomontage*, London: Thames & Hudson.
Arbiter, Murray (2024), online interview with the author, 26 April.
Averill, Steve (2023), online conversation with the author, 1 December.
Bain, Peter and Shaw, Paul (1998), *Blackletter: Type and National Identity*, New York: Princeton Architectural Press.
Baines, Jessica (2016), 'Democratising print? The field and practices of radical and community printshops in Britain 1968–98', PhD thesis, London School of Economics and Political Science.
Balls, Richard (2014), *Be Stiff: The Stiff Records Story*, London: Soundcheck Books.
Barfe, Louis (2005), *Where Have All the Good Times Gone? The Rise and Fall of the Record Industry*, London: Atlantic Books.
Barker, Hugh and Taylor, Yuval (2007), *Faking It: The Quest for Authenticity in Popular Music*, London: Faber & Faber.
Bech Poulsen, Henrik (2005), *'77: The Year of Punk and New Wave*, London: Helter Skelter.
Beckett, Andy (2009), *When the Lights Went Out: Britain in the Seventies*, London: Faber & Faber.
Beckett, Andy (2015), *Promised You a Miracle: UK 80–82*, London: Allen Lane.
Bédarida, François (1991), *A Social History of England*, Abingdon: Routledge.
Bestley, Russ (2012), 'From "London's Burning" to "Sten Guns in Sunderland"', *Punk & Post-Punk* 1:1, pp. 41–71.
Bestley, Russ (2013), 'Art attacks and killing jokes: The graphic language of punk humour', *Punk & Post-Punk* 2:3, pp. 231–267.
Bestley, Russ (2013), '"I tried to make him laugh, he didn't get the joke …" – taking punk humour seriously', *Punk & Post-Punk* 2:2, pp. 119–145.
Bestley, Russ (2015), '(I want some) demystification: Deconstructing punk', *Punk & Post-Punk* 4:2/3, pp. 117–127.
Bestley, Russ (2016), 'Big A little a: The graphic language of anarchy', in Matthew Worley and Mike Dines (eds), *The Aesthetic of Our Anger: Anarcho-Punk, Politics, Music*, New York: Autonomedia, pp. 43–65.

Bestley, Russ (2016), '"I wonder who chose the colour scheme, it's very nice …": Mike Coles, Malicious Damage and Forty Years in the Wilderness', *Punk & Post-Punk* 5:3, pp. 311–328.
Bestley, Russ (2018), 'Design it yourself? Punk's division of labour', *Punk & Post-Punk* 7:1, pp. 7–24.
Bestley, Russ (2018), 'Holiday in Cambodia: Punk's acerbic comedy', in Krista Bonello Rutter Giappone, Fred Francis and Iain MacKenzie (eds), *Comedy and Critical Thought: Laughter as Resistance*, London: Rowman & Littlefield International, pp. 165–183.
Bestley, Russ (2018), 'Still fighting the cuts: An interview with Mekons 77', *Punk & Post-Punk* 7:1, pp. 103–115.
Bestley, Russ (2019), 'Anarchy in Woolworths: Punk comedy and humour', in Thomas M. Kitts and Nick Baxter-Moore (eds), *The Routledge Companion to Popular Music and Humor*, New York: Routledge, pp. 76–84.
Bestley, Russ (2020), 'Art on my sleeve: An interview with Steve Averill, graphic designer', *Punk & Post-Punk* 9:3, pp. 549–566.
Bestley, Russ (2020), '"This monkey's gone to heaven": Vaughan Oliver 1957–2019', *Punk & Post-Punk* 9:1, pp. 121–126.
Bestley, Russ (2023), '"Fuck Art, Let's Dance": An interview with Chris Morton', *Punk & Post-Punk* 12:3, pp. 353–377.
Bestley, Russ and Binns, Rebecca (2018), 'The evolution of an anarcho-punk narrative (1978–84)', in Subcultures Network (eds), *Ripped, Torn and Cut: Pop, Politics and Punk Fanzines from 1976*, Manchester: Manchester University Press, pp. 129–149.
Bestley, Russ and Burgess, Paul (2018), 'Fan artefacts and doing it themselves: The home-made graphics of punk devotees', *Punk & Post-Punk* 7:3, pp. 317–340.
Bestley, Russ and Credland, Tony (2018), 'Fanzines and self-publishing in the 1970s', in Ian Horton and Bettina Furnée (eds), *Hard Werken: One for All: Graphic Art & Design 1979–1994*, Netherlands: Valiz, pp. 168–171.
Bestley, Russ, Dines, Mike, Gordon, Alastair and Guerra, Paula (eds) (2021), *Trans-Global Punk Scenes: The Punk Reader Vol. 2*, Bristol: Intellect.
Bestley, Russ, Dines, Mike, Grimes, Matt and Guerra, Paula (eds) (2021), *Punk Identities, Punk Utopias: Global Punk & Media*, Bristol: Intellect.
Bestley, Russ and McNeil, Paul (2022), *Visual Research*, London: Bloomsbury.
Bestley, Russell and Noble, Ian (1999), 'Punk uncovered: An unofficial history of provincial opposition', *Eye* 33, pp. 66–75.
Bestley, Russ and Ogg, Alex (2012), *The Art of Punk*, London: Omnibus Press.
Binns, Rebecca (2017), '*Gee Vaucher: Introspective*, Firstsite, Colchester, 12 November 2016–19 February 2017', *Punk & Post-Punk* 5:3, pp. 329–338.
Binns, Rebecca (2018), '*The House of Fame: An Exhibition Convened by Linder*, Nottingham Contemporary Gallery, UK, 24 March–24 June 2018', *Punk & Post-Punk* 7:3, pp. 479–486.
Binns, Rebecca (2022), *Gee Vaucher: Beyond Punk, Feminism and the Avant-Garde*, Manchester: Manchester University Press.
Binns, Rebecca (2023), 'Jamie Reid, legendary artist, rebel and campaigner: 16 January 1947–8 August 2023', *Punk & Post-Punk* 12:3, pp. 379–388.
Blackwell, Trevor and Seabrook, Jeremy (1996), *Talking Work: An Oral History*, London: Faber & Faber.
Blake, Mark (ed.) (2006), *Punk: The Whole Story*, London: Dorling Kindersley.

Blauvelt, Andrew (2021), 'Riding a new wave', in Andrew Krivine, *Reversing into the Future: New Wave Graphics 1977–1990*, London: Pavilion, pp. 100–117.

Blazwick, Iwona (ed.) (1989), *An Endless Adventure … An Endless Passion … An Endless Banquet: A Situationist Scrapbook*, London: ICA Publications.

Boot, Adrian and Salewicz, Chris (1996), *Punk: The Illustrated History of a Music Revolution*, London: Penguin Studio.

Brody, Neville (2024), online interview with the author, 5 March.

Brook, Tony and Shaughnessy, Adrian (eds) (2016), *Action Time Vision: Punk and Post-Punk 7" Record Sleeves*, London: Unit Editions.

Brook, Tony and Shaughnessy, Adrian (eds) (2017), *Letraset: The DIY Typography Revolution*, London: Unit Editions.

Brook, Tony and Shaughnessy, Adrian (eds) (2018), *Vaughan Oliver: Archive*, London: Unit Editions.

Burrows, Terry and Miller, Daniel (2017), *Mute: A Visual Document*, London: Thames & Hudson.

Butt, Gavin (2022), *No Machos or Pop Stars: When the Leeds Art Experiment Went Punk*, Durham, NC: Duke University Press.

Butt, Gavin, Eshun, Kodwo and Fisher, Mark (eds) (2016), *Post-Punk Then and Now*, London: Repeater Books.

Cain, Barry and Matthews, Neil (2015), *Flexipop! The Book*, London: Colourgold.

Calkin, Jessamy (1982), 'Image maker', *The Face*, March, pp. 44–45.

Cannon, Brian (1989), *Going Nowhere: The Art and Design of Punk and New Wave*, London: Omnibus Press.

Cherry, David (1976), *Preparing Artwork for Reproduction*, London: BT Batsford.

Cockburn, Cynthia (1991), *Brothers: Male Dominance and Technological Change*, London: Pluto Press.

Colegrave, Stephen and Sullivan, Chris (2001), *Punk*, London: Cassell & Co.

Coles, Mike (2016), interview with the author, 22 August.

Coles, Mike (2016), email correspondence with the author, 22 September.

Coles, Mike (2016), email correspondence with the author, 26 September.

Coles, Mike (2016), *Forty Years in the Wilderness: A Graphic Voyage of Art, Design & Stubborn Independence*, London: Malicious Damage.

Coles, Mike (2024), email conversation with the author, 24 March.

Connell, John and Gibson, Chris (2003), *Sound Tracks: Popular Music, Identity and Place*, Abingdon: Routledge.

Connerty, Michael (2023), '"Teddy boy, he's got them all": An interview with Ted Carroll about Rock On, Chiswick and Ace Records', *Punk & Post-Punk* 12:3, pp. 327–352.

Coon, Caroline (1977), *1988: The New Wave Punk Rock Explosion*, London: Hawthorn.

Czezowski, Andrew and Carrington, Susan (2016), *The Roxy: Our Story*, London: Carrczez Publishing.

Davis, Julie (1977), *Punk*, London: Millington.

de Ville, Nick (2003), *Album: Style and Image in Sleeve Design*, London: Mitchell Beazley.

Dempsey, Michael and Ridgers, Derek (1978), *100 Nights at the Roxy*, London: Big O Publishing.

Diboll, Mike (2016), email interview with the author, 18 December.

Drayton, Tony (2016), email interview with the author, 18 December.

Drayton, Tony (2018), *Ripped & Torn: 1976–79: The Loudest Punk Fanzine in the UK*, London: Ecstatic Peace Library.
Duncombe, Stephen (2008), *Notes from Underground: Zines and the Politics of Alternative Culture*, Portland: Microcosm.
Elborough, Travis (2008), *The Long-Player Goodbye: The Album from Vinyl to iPod and Back Again*, London: Sceptre.
Elliott, David (2020), *1984: British Pop's Dividing Year*, London: York House Books.
Eno, Brian and Mills, Russell (1986), *More Dark Than Shark*, London: Faber & Faber.
Fletcher, Tony (2021), *The Best of Jamming!: Selections and Stories from the Fanzine That Grew Up, 1977–86*, London: Omnibus Press.
Foster, Richard (2017), 'Moderne muziek: Vinyl magazine and the Dutch post-punk movement', *Punk & Post-Punk* 6:1, pp. 7–20.
Frith, Simon and Goodwin, Andrew (1990), *On Record*, London: Routledge.
Frith, Simon and Horne, Howard (1987), *Art into Pop*, Abingdon: Routledge.
Garrett, Malcolm (2018), email interview with the author, 6 November.
Garrett, Malcolm (2020), online interview with the author, 30 April.
Gennard, John and Bain, Peter (1995), *A History of the Society of Graphical and Allied Trades*, Abingdon: Routledge.
Giappone, Krista Bonello Rutter (2018), *The Punk Turn in Comedy: Masks of Anarchy*, London: Palgrave Macmillan.
Gibbs, Alvin (1996), *Destroy: The Definitive History of Punk*, London: AK Press.
Goodhart, David and Wintour, Patrick (1986), *Eddie Shah and the Newspaper Revolution*, London: Coronet.
Gordon, Calum (2017), 'A history of Raf Simons' collaborations with Peter Saville', *Another Man*, 17 July. www.anothermanmag.com/style-grooming/9956/a-history-of-raf-simons-collaborations-with-peter-saville (Accessed 19 March 2024).
Gorman, Paul (2010), *Reasons to be Cheerful: The Life and Work of Barney Bubbles*, London: Adelita Ltd.
Gorman, Paul (2017), *The Story of The Face: The Magazine That Changed Culture*, London: Thames & Hudson.
Gorman, Paul (2022), *Totally Wired: The Rise and Fall of the Music Press*, London: Thames & Hudson.
Gravelle, Peter (2016), *The Death of Photography: The Shooting Gallery*, London: Carpet Bombing Culture.
Griffin, Brian (2017), *Pop*, London: GOST Books.
Hall, Stuart and Jefferson, Tony (eds) (1976), *Resistance Through Rituals: Youth Subcultures in Post-War Britain*, London: Hutchinson.
Harker, Dave (1980), *One For The Money: Politics and Popular Song*, London: Hutchinson & Co.
Hebdige, Dick (1979), *Subculture: The Meaning of Style*, Abingdon: Routledge.
Hebdige, Dick (1988), *Hiding in the Light*, London: Routledge.
Hennessy, Val (1978), *In the Gutter*, London: Quartet Books.
Hollis, Richard (1994), *Graphic Design: A Concise History*, London: Thames & Hudson.
Home, Stewart (1995), *Cranked Up Really High: Genre Theory & Punk Rock*, London: Codex.
Horton, Ian and Furnée, Bettina (2018), *Hard Werken: One for All: Graphic Art & Design 1979–1994*, Netherlands: Valiz.

Howard, Andrew (2016), email interview with the author, 12 December.
Jahangiri, Nadi (2005), email interview with the author, 14 March.
John, Lynn (1988), *Preparing Design for Print*, Oxford: Phaidon.
Jones, Terry (2001), *Smile i-D: Fashion and Style: The Best from 20 Years of i-D*, Los Angeles, CA: Taschen America.
Jones, Terry and Anscombe, Isabelle (1978), *Not Another Punk Book*, London: Aurum Press.
Jones, Terry and McDermott, Catherine (1990), *Wink: Manual of Instant Design*, London: Architecture Design and Technology Press.
Kent, Nick (1976), 'Meet the new Col. Tom Parker', *New Musical Express*, 27 November.
King, Emily (ed.) (2003), *Designed by Peter Saville*, London: Frieze.
Krivine, Andrew (2020), *Too Fast to Live Too Young to Die: Punk & Post Punk Graphics 1976–1986*, London: Pavilion.
Krivine, Andrew (2021), *Reversing into the Future: New Wave Graphics 1977–1990*, London: Pavilion.
Kugelberg, Johan (2012), *Punk: An Aesthetic*, New York: Rizzoli.
Kugelberg, Johan, Savage, Jon and Terry, Glenn (2016), *God Save Sex Pistols*, New York: Rizzoli.
Laing, Dave (1985), *One Chord Wonders: Power and Meaning in Punk Rock*, Milton Keynes: Open University Press.
Last, Bob (2024), email conversation with the author, 6 February.
Last, Bob (2024), telephone interview with the author, 9 February.
Latimer, Henry C. (1977), *Preparing Art and Camera Copy for Printing: Contemporary Procedures and Techniques for Mechanicals and Related Copy*, New York: McGraw-Hill.
Lazell, Barry (1997), *Indie Hits: The Complete UK Independent Charts 1980–1989*, London: Cherry Red Books.
Livingston, Alistair (2016), email interview with the author, 4 December.
Lycett, Kevin (2000), email interview with the author, 4 February.
Lycett, Kevin (2007), email interview with the author, 2 February.
Lycett, Kevin (2018), email interview with the author, 25 January.
MacFie, Joly (2016), email interview with the author, 4 December.
MacIntyre, Douglas and McPhee, Grant (2022), *Hungry Beat: The Scottish Independent Pop Underground Movement (1977–1984)*, London: White Rabbit.
Marcus, Greil (1989), *Lipstick Traces: A Secret History of the Twentieth Century*, Cambridge, MA: Harvard University Press.
McDermott, Catherine (1987), *Street Style: British Design in the 80s*, London: Design Council.
McNeil, Paul (2023), in conversation with the author, 21 November.
McSmith, Andy (2011), *No Such Thing as Society: A History of Britain in the 1980s*, London: Constable.
Milne, Tim (2023), email conversation with the author, 2 August.
Milne, Tim (2024), online interview with the author, 30 April.
Milner, Greg (2010), *Perfecting Sound Forever: The Story of Recorded Music*, London: Granta.
Morton, Chris (2024), in conversation with the author, 5 February.
Mott, Toby (2016), *Oh So Pretty: Punk in Print 1976–1980*, London: Phaidon.

Muggleton, David (2000), *Inside Subculture: The Postmodern Meaning of Style*, Oxford: Berg.
Muggleton, David and Weinzierl, Rupert (2003), *The Post-Subcultures Reader*, Oxford: Berg.
Muirhead, Bert (1983), *Stiff: The Story of a Record Label*, Poole: Blandford Press.
Mumford, Jill (2024), online interview with the author, 7 February.
Murphy, Michael Mary and Rogers, Jim (2023), *Sounds Irish, Acts Global: Explaining the Success of Ireland's Popular Music Industry*, Sheffield: Equinox.
O'Connor, Rob (2001), *Delicious: The Design and Art Direction of Stylorouge*, Berlin: Die Gestalten Verlag.
O'Connor, Rob (2020), online interview with the author, 30 April.
O'Connor, Rob (2023), email interview with the author, 18 October.
Ogg, Alex (2006), *No More Heroes*, London: Cherry Red.
Ogg, Alex (2009), *Independence Days: The Story of UK Independent Record Labels*, London: Cherry Red Books.
Ogg, Alex (2013), 'For you, Tommy, the war is never over', *Punk & Post-Punk* 2:3, pp. 281–304.
O'Neill, Sean and Trelford, Guy (2003), *It Makes You Want to Spit! The Definitive Guide to Punk in Northern Ireland*, Dublin: Reekus.
Pawson, Mark (1989), *MaPk nAbCoH*, London: Mark Pawson.
Perry, Mark (2000), *Sniffin' Glue: The Essential Punk Accessory*, London: Sanctuary.
Piller, Eddie and Rowland, Steve (2021), *Punkzines: British Fanzine Culture from the Punk Scene 1976–1983*, London: Omnibus Press.
Plant, Sadie (1992), *The Most Radical Gesture: The Situationist International in a Postmodern Age*, London: Routledge.
Powell, Aubrey (2014), *Hipgnosis Portraits*, London: Thames & Hudson.
Powell, Aubrey (2017), *Vinyl. Album. Cover. Art: The Complete Hipgnosis Catalogue*, London: Thames & Hudson.
Poynor, Rick (2000), *Vaughan Oliver: Visceral Pleasures*, London: Booth-Clibborn Editions.
Poynor, Rick (2003), *No More Rules: Graphic Design and Postmodernism*, London: Laurence King.
Poynor, Rick (2020), *David King: Designer, Activist, Visual Historian*, New Haven, CT and London: Yale University Press.
Punk Rock (1976), [episode, TV documentary series], dir. Bruce Macdonald, *The London Weekend Show* (28 November, London Weekend Television).
Punk Rock (1977), [episode, TV documentary series], dir. Roger Casstles and Derek Towers, *Brass Tacks* (3 August, BBC Television).
Raposo, Ana and Bestley, Russ (2020), 'Designing fascism: The evolution of a neo-Nazi punk aesthetic', *Punk & Post-Punk* 9:3, pp. 467–498.
Raposo, Ana and Sabin, Roger (2017), 'New visual identities for British neofascist rock (1982–1987): White noise, "vikings" and the cult of Skrewdriver', in N. Copsey and M. Worley (eds), *Tomorrow Belongs to Us: The British Far Right Since 1967*, London: Routledge, pp. 132–149.
Rees, Paul (ed.) (2006), 'Punk '76', *Q Magazine*, March, pp. 57–87.
Reid, Jamie (2003), *The Illustrated Ape: Fuck Forever*, Dearborn, MI: Carhartt.
Reid, Jamie (2018), *XXXXX*, London: L-13 Light Industrial Workshop.
Reid, Jamie (2021), *Rogue Materials: 1972–2021*, London: L-13 Light Industrial Workshop.

Reid, Jamie and Savage, Jon (1987), *Up They Rise: The Incomplete Works of Jamie Reid*, London: Faber & Faber.

Reynolds, Simon (2005), *Rip it Up and Start Again: Post Punk 1978–84*, London: Faber & Faber.

Reynolds, Simon (2012), *Retromania: Pop Culture's Addiction to its Own Past*, London: Faber & Faber.

Rhodes, Graham A. (2016), *The View from Inside the Punk Monster*, Scarborough: Templar Publishing.

Rider, Alan (2016), email interview with the author, 18 December.

Rider, Alan (2021), *Adventures in Reality: The Complete Collection*, Krakow: Fourth Dimension.

Robb, John (2006), *Punk Rock: An Oral History*, London: Ebury Press.

Robertson, Matthew (2007), *Factory Records: The Complete Graphic Album*, London: Thames & Hudson.

Robinson, Lucy (2023), *Now That's What I Call a History of the 1980s: Pop Culture and Politics in the Decade That Shaped Modern Britain*, Manchester: Manchester University Press.

Rock, Sheila (2020), *Young Punks*, London: Omnibus Press.

Rose, Cynthia (1980), 'Search and decoy', *New Musical Express*, 1 November, p. 29.

Rose, Cynthia (1991), *Design After Dark*, London: Thames & Hudson.

Ryde, Robin and Bestley, Russ (2016), 'Thinking punk', *Punk & Post-Punk* 5:2, pp. 97–110.

Sabin, Roger (ed.) (1999), *Punk Rock: So What?*, Abingdon: Routledge.

Sandbrook, Dominic (2010), *State of Emergency: Britain, 1970–1974*, London: Allen Lane.

Sandbrook, Dominic (2012), *Seasons in the Sun: Britain, 1974–1979*, London: Allen Lane.

Sandbrook, Dominic (2019), *Who Dares Wins: Britain, 1979–1982*, London: Allen Lane.

Savage, Jon (1983), 'The age of plunder', *The Face*, January, pp. 44–49.

Savage, Jon (1983), 'Guerilla graphics: The tactics of agit prop art', *The Face*, October, pp. 26–31.

Savage, Jon (1991), *England's Dreaming: Sex Pistols and Punk Rock*, London: Faber & Faber.

Savage, Jon (2009), *The England's Dreaming Tapes*, London: Faber & Faber.

Savage, Jon and Baker, Stuart (eds) (2013), *Punk 45: The Singles Cover Art of Punk 1976–80*, London: Soul Jazz Records.

Scatton-Tessier, Michelle (2019), 'Côté punk: Marc Caro', *Punk & Post-Punk* 8:3, pp. 343–362.

Shaw, Greg (1978), *New Wave on Record: England & Europe, 1975–8*, Burbank, CA: Bomp Books.

Skov, Marie Arleth (2020), 'The 1979 American Punk Art dispute: Visions of punk art between sensationalism, street art and social practice', *Punk & Post-Punk* 9:3, pp. 443–466.

Skov, Marie Arleth (2023), *Punk Art History: Artworks from the European No Future Generation*, Bristol: Intellect.

Smith, Bill (2021), *Cover Stories: Five Decades of Album Art*, London: Red Planet.

Smith, Bill (2024), online interview with the author, 13 February.

Spencer, Herbert (1969), *Pioneers of Modern Typography*, London: Lund Humphries Publishers.
Stein, Jesse Adams (2017), *Hot Metal: Material Culture and Tangible Labour*, Manchester: Manchester University Press.
Stevenson, Ray (1978), *Sex Pistols File*, London: Omnibus Press.
Stewart, Graham (2013), *Bang!: A History of Britain in the 1980s*, London: Atlantic Books.
Stolper, Paul and Wilson, Andrew (2004), *No Future: Sex, Seditionaries and the Sex Pistols*, London: Hospital Group.
Strange, Simon (2022), *Blank Canvas: Art School Creativity from Punk to New Wave*, Bristol: Intellect.
Subcultures Network (ed.) (2018), *Ripped, Torn and Cut: Pop, Politics and Punk Fanzines from 1976*, Manchester: Manchester University Press.
Subcultures Network (ed.) (2020), *Hebdige and Subculture in the Twenty-First Century*, London: Palgrave Macmillan.
Sussman, Elisabeth (ed.) (1991), *On the Passage of a Few People Through a Rather Brief Moment in Time: The Situationist International 1957–1972*, Boston, MA: MIT Press.
Taylor, Steve (1982), 'Industrial manoeuvres in the art', *The Face*, May, pp. 50–55.
Thompson, Stacy (2004), *Punk Productions: Unfinished Business*, New York: State University of New York Press.
Treweek, Chris and Zeitlyn, Jonathan with the Islington Bus Co. (1983), *The Alternative Printing Handbook*, Harmondsworth: Penguin.
Triggs, Teal (1995), 'Alphabet soup: Reading British fanzines', *Visible Language* 29:1, pp. 72–87.
Triggs, Teal (2006), 'Scissors and glue: Punk fanzines and the creation of a DIY aesthetic', *Journal of Design History* 19:1, pp. 69–83.
Trowell, Ian (2017), 'Digging up the dead cities: Abandoned streets and past ruins of the future in the glossy punk magazine', *Punk & Post-Punk* 6:1, pp. 21–40.
Trowell, Ian (2019), '*XXXXX: 50 Years of Subversion and the Spirit*, Humber Street Gallery, Hull, 12 October 2018–6 January 2019', *Punk & Post-Punk* 8:2, pp. 305–316.
Trowell, Ian (2020), 'Counter-realities and conflicted place: Gee Vaucher's *The Feeding of the Five Thousand* in the punk art tradition', *Punk & Post-Punk* 9:3, pp. 397–424.
Trowell, Ian (2023), *Throbbing Gristle: An Endless Discontent*, Bristol: Intellect.
Turner, Alwyn W. (2008), *Crisis? What Crisis?: Britain in the 1970s*, London: Aurum Press.
Turner, Alwyn W. (2010), *Rejoice! Rejoice!: Britain in the 1980s*, London: Aurum Press.
Vaucher, Gee (1999), *Crass Art and Other Pre Post-Modernist Monsters*, Edinburgh: AK Press.
Vaucher, Gee (2018), *International Anthem*, London: Exitstencil Press.
Walker, John A. (1987), *Cross-Overs: Art into Pop and Pop into Art*, London: Routledge.
Webb, Pete and Vague, Tom (2023), *Vague Volume One: 1979–1984*, Bristol: PC Press.
Wilkinson, David (2016), *Post-Punk, Politics and Pleasure in Britain*, London: Palgrave.

Williams, Paul (2022), *The US Graphic Novel*, Edinburgh: Edinburgh University Press.
Worley, Matthew (2012), 'Shot by both sides: Punk, politics and the end of "consensus"', *Contemporary British History* 26:3, pp. 333–354.
Worley, Matthew (2017), *No Future: Punk, Politics and British Youth Culture, 1976–1984*, Cambridge: Cambridge University Press.
Worley, Matthew (2020), '"If I had more time it could be better, but the new wave's about spontaneity, right?": Finding meaning in Britain's early punk fanzines (1976–77)', *Punk & Post-Punk* 9:2, pp. 223–245.
Worley, Matthew (2024), *Zerox Machine: Punk, Post-Punk and Fanzines in Britain, 1976–88*, London: Reaktion Books.
Worley, Matthew and Copsey, Nigel (2017), 'White youth: The far right, punk and British youth culture, 1977–87', in N. Copsey and M. Worley (eds), *Tomorrow Belongs to Us: The British Far Right Since 1967*, London: Routledge, pp. 113–131.
Worley, Matthew and Dines, Mike (eds) (2016), *The Aesthetic of Our Anger: Anarcho-Punk, Politics and Music*, New York: Autonomedia.
Wozencroft, Jon (1988), *The Graphic Language of Neville Brody*, London: Thames & Hudson.
The Year of Punk (1978), [episode, TV documentary series], dir. Bruce Macdonald, *The London Weekend Show* (1 January, London Weekend Television).
Young, Hugo (1989), *One of Us: A Biography of Margaret Thatcher*, London: Macmillan.
Zuleika, Beavan, O'Dair, Marcus and Osborne, Richard (2019), *Mute Records: Artists, Business, History*, London: Bloomsbury.

Discography

Adam and the Ants (1978), *Dirk Wears White Sox*, vinyl album, United Kingdom: Do It.
The Adicts (1979), *Lunch with The Adicts*, 7" vinyl EP, United Kingdom: Dining Out.
The Adverts (1977), 'One Chord Wonders', 7" single, United Kingdom: Stiff Records.
The Adverts (1978), *Crossing the Red Sea*, vinyl album, United Kingdom: Bright Records.
Alternative TV (1977), 'How Much Longer', 7" single, United Kingdom: Deptford Fun City Records.
Anti-Nowhere League (1981), 'So What', 7" single, United Kingdom: WXYZ Records.
Anti-Social (1982), *Made in England*, 7" vinyl EP, United Kingdom: Beat The System.
The Atoms (1979), 'Max Bygraves Killed My Mother', 7" single, United Kingdom: Rinka Records.
The Banned (1977), 'Little Girl', 7" single, United Kingdom: Harvest Records.
Blank Students (1980), 'We Are Natives', 7" single, United Kingdom: Dexter Records.
Blitzkrieg Bop (1977), 'Let's Go', 7" single, United Kingdom: Lightning Records.
The Boomtown Rats (1978), *A Tonic for The Troops*, vinyl album, United Kingdom: Ensign.
Buzzcocks (1977), *Spiral Scratch*, 7" vinyl EP, United Kingdom: New Hormones.

Buzzcocks (1977), 'Orgasm Addict', 7" single, United Kingdom: United Artists.
Buzzcocks (1978), *Time's Up*, bootleg vinyl album, United Kingdom: Voto.
Buzzcocks (1978), *Another Music in a Different Kitchen*, vinyl album, United Kingdom: United Artists.
Buzzcocks (1978), 'What Do I Get?', 7" single, United Kingdom: United Artists.
Buzzcocks (1978), 'I Don't Mind', 7" single, United Kingdom: United Artists.
Buzzcocks (1978), 'Love You More', 7" single, United Kingdom: United Artists.
Buzzcocks (1979), *Love Bites*, vinyl album, United Kingdom: United Artists.
Cabaret Voltaire (1978), *Extended Play*, 7" vinyl EP, United Kingdom: Rough Trade.
Cabaret Voltaire (1979), 'Nag Nag Nag', 7" single, United Kingdom: Rough Trade.
Cabaret Voltaire (1980), 'Seconds Too Late', 7" single, United Kingdom: Rough Trade.
Chron Gen (1981), *Puppets of War*, 7" vinyl EP, United Kingdom: Gargoyle Records.
The Clash (1977), 'White Riot', 7" single, United Kingdom: CBS Records.
The Clash (1977), *The Clash*, vinyl album, United Kingdom: CBS Records.
The Clash (1977), *Take It Or Leave It!*, bootleg vinyl album, United Kingdom: Wise/P.F.P. Company Ltd.
The Clash (1978), 'Clash City Rockers', 7" single, United Kingdom: CBS Records.
Clay Fav (1979), 'Air Lakeland', 7" single, United Kingdom: Clay Fav Records.
Cockney Rejects (1980), 'I'm Forever Blowing Bubbles', 7" single, United Kingdom: Zonophone.
Cocteau Twins (1982), *Lullabies*, 12" vinyl EP, United Kingdom: 4AD.
The Cortinas (1977), 'Fascist Dictator', 7" single, United Kingdom: Step Forward Records.
The Cortinas (1977), 'Defiant Pose', 7" single, United Kingdom: Step Forward Records.
Crass (1978), *The Feeding of the Five Thousand*, vinyl album, United Kingdom: Small Wonder.
Crass (1980), 'Bloody Revolutions', 7" single, United Kingdom: Crass Records.
Crass (1984), 'You're Already Dead', 7" single, United Kingdom: Crass Records.
Cult Maniax (1981), *Frenzie*, 7" vinyl EP, United Kingdom: Next Wave.
The Cure (1978), 'Killing An Arab', 7" single, United Kingdom: Small Wonder Records.
The Cure (1979), 'Boys Don't Cry', 7" single, United Kingdom: Fiction Records.
The Cure (1979), 'Jumping Someone Else's Train', 7" single, United Kingdom: Fiction Records.
The Cure (1979), *Three Imaginary Boys*, vinyl album, United Kingdom: Fiction Records.
The Cure (1979), 'A Forest', 12" single, United Kingdom: Fiction Records.
The Cure (1980), *Seventeen Seconds*, vinyl album, United Kingdom: Fiction Records.
The Damned (1976), 'New Rose', 7" single, United Kingdom: Stiff Records.
The Damned (1977), *Damned Damned Damned*, vinyl album, United Kingdom: Stiff Records.
The Damned (1977), 'Neat Neat Neat', 7" single, United Kingdom: Stiff Records.
The Damned (1977), *Music For Pleasure*, vinyl album, United Kingdom: Stiff Records.
Das Schnitz (1979), *4AM*, 7" vinyl EP, United Kingdom: Ellie Jay.

The Desperate Bicycles (1977), 'Smokescreen' / 'Handlebars', 7" single, United Kingdom: Refill Records.
The Desperate Bicycles (1977), 'The Medium Was Tedium' / 'Don't Back the Front', 7" single, United Kingdom: Refill Records.
Devo (1978), *Are We Not Men?*, vinyl album, United Kingdom: Virgin Records.
Discharge (1980), *Realities of War*, 7" vinyl EP, United Kingdom: Clay Records.
Disco Zombies (1980), 'Here Come the Buts', 7" single, United Kingdom: Dining Out.
Dr. Feelgood (1975), *Down by the Jetty*, vinyl album, United Kingdom: United Artists.
Dr. Feelgood (1976), *Stupidity*, vinyl album, United Kingdom: United Artists.
The Exploited (1980), 'Exploited Barmy Army', 7" single, United Kingdom: Exploited.
Fad Gadget (1980), 'Ricky's Hand', 7" single, United Kingdom: Mute.
The Fall (1978), 'Bingo-Masters Break Out', 7" single, United Kingdom: Step Forward Records.
Fifty Fantastics (1980), 'God's Got Religion', 7" single, United Kingdom: Dining Out.
Front (1978), 'System', 7" single, United Kingdom: The Label.
Gang of Four (1978), *Damaged Goods*, 7" vinyl EP, United Kingdom: Fast Product.
Gang of Four (1979), *Entertainment!*, vinyl album, United Kingdom: EMI.
Gang of Four (1980), 'Outside the Trains Don't Run on Time', 7" single, United Kingdom: EMI.
Generation X (1977), 'Your Generation', 7" single, United Kingdom: Chrysalis.
Headache (1977), 'Can't Stand Still', 7" single, United Kingdom: Lout Records.
The Human League (1978), 'Being Boiled', 7" single, United Kingdom: Fast Product.
The Jam (1977), 'In the City', 7" single, United Kingdom: Polydor.
The Jam (1977), *In the City*, vinyl album, United Kingdom: Polydor.
Killing Joke (1979), *Turn To Red*, 10" vinyl EP, United Kingdom: Malicious Damage.
Killing Joke (1980), *Killing Joke*, vinyl album, United Kingdom: Malicious Damage.
Killing Joke (1981), *What's THIS For ...!*, vinyl album, United Kingdom: Malicious Damage.
Killing Joke (1990), *Extremities, Dirt and Various Repressed Emotions*, vinyl album, Germany: Aggressive Rockproduktionen.
Thomas Leer (1978), 'Private Plane', 7" single, United Kingdom: Oblique.
The Lurkers (1977), 'Shadow', 7" single, United Kingdom: Beggars Banquet.
The Lurkers (1978), *Fullham Fallout*, vinyl album, United Kingdom: Beggars Banquet.
Magazine (1978), 'Shot By Both Sides', 7" single, United Kingdom: Virgin Records.
Magazine (1978), *Real Life*, vinyl album, United Kingdom: Virgin Records.
Manchester Mekon (1979), 'Not Forgetting', 7" single, United Kingdom: Newmarket.
The Maniacs (1977), 'Chelsea '77', 7" single, United Kingdom: United Artists.
The Mekons (1978), 'Never Been in A Riot', 7" single, United Kingdom: Fast Product.
The Mekons (1978), 'Where Were You?', 7" single, United Kingdom: Fast Product.
The Mekons (1979), *The Quality of Mercy is not Strnen*, vinyl album, United Kingdom: Virgin Records.
The Mekons (1980), *Devils, Rats & Piggies: A Special Message from Godzilla*, vinyl album, United Kingdom: Red Rhino.

The Mekons (1982), '1st Guitarist', *The Mekons Story*, vinyl album, United Kingdom: CNT Records.
Menace (1978), 'GLC', 7" single, United Kingdom: Small Wonder.
Newtown Neurotics (1979), 'Hypocrite', 7" single, United Kingdom: No Wonder Records.
999 (1977), 'I'm Alive', 7" single, United Kingdom: Labritain Records.
The Normal (1978), 'T.V.O.D.', 7" single, United Kingdom: Mute.
Nuclear Socketts (1980), *Honour Before Glory*, 7" vinyl EP, United Kingdom: Subversive.
Gary Numan (1980), *The Pleasure Principle*, vinyl album, United Kingdom: Beggars Banquet.
Orchestral Manoeuvres in the Dark (1979), 'Electricity', 7" single, United Kingdom: Factory Records.
The Panik (1977), *It Won't Sell*, 7" vinyl EP, United Kingdom: Rainy City.
The Partisans (1981), 'Police Story', 7" single, United Kingdom: No Future.
The Partisans (1982), '17 Years of Hell', 7" single, United Kingdom: No Future.
The Pigs (1977), *Youthanasia*, 7" vinyl EP, United Kingdom: New Bristol Records.
Plastic Bertrand (1977), 'Ça Plane Pour Moi', 7" single, Portugal: Vogue Records.
Public Image Ltd. (1978), 'Public Image', 7" single, United Kingdom: Virgin Records.
Public Image Ltd. (1978), *Public Image (First Issue)*, vinyl album, United Kingdom: Virgin Records.
Public Image Ltd. (1979), *Metal Box*, vinyl album, United Kingdom: Virgin Records.
PVC2 (1977), 'Put You in the Picture', 7" single, United Kingdom: Zoom Records.
Radiators From Space (1977), 'Television Screen', 7" single, United Kingdom: Chiswick.
Radiators From Space (1977), *TV Tube Heart*, vinyl album, United Kingdom: Chiswick.
Ramones (1976), *Ramones*, vinyl album, USA: Sire Records.
Ramones (1977), *Leave Home*, vinyl album, USA: Sire Records.
Ramones (1977), *Rocket to Russia*, vinyl album, USA: Sire Records.
Raped (1977), *Pretty Paedophiles*, 7" vinyl EP, United Kingdom: Parole Records.
Red Alert (1982), *In Britain*, 7" vinyl EP, United Kingdom: No Future.
Robert Rental (1978), 'Paralysis', 7" single, United Kingdom: Company Regular.
Resistance 77 (1983), 'Nottingham Problem', 7" single, United Kingdom: Riot City.
Resistance 77 (1984), 'You Reds', 7" single, United Kingdom: Resistance.
The Rings (1977), 'I Wanna Be Free', 7" single, United Kingdom: Chiswick Records.
Satan's Rats (1977), 'In My Love For You', 7" single, United Kingdom: DJM Records.
Scritti Politti (1978), *Skank Bloc Bologna*, 7" vinyl EP, United Kingdom: St Pancras Records.
Scritti Politti (1979), *Work in Progress: 2nd Peel Session*, 7" vinyl EP, London: Rough Trade.
Sex Pistols (1977), 'Anarchy in the UK', 7" single, United Kingdom: EMI Records.
Sex Pistols (1977), 'God Save The Queen', 7" single, United Kingdom: Virgin Records.
Sex Pistols (1977), 'Holidays in the Sun', 7" single, United Kingdom: Virgin Records.
Sex Pistols (1977), *Never Mind the Bollocks*, vinyl album, United Kingdom: Virgin Records.

Sex Pistols (1977), *No Future U.K.?*, bootleg vinyl album, United Kingdom: Blank Records.
Sex Pistols (1977), 'Pretty Vacant', 7" single, United Kingdom: Virgin Records.
Sex Pistols (1977), *Spunk*, bootleg vinyl album, United Kingdom: Blank Records.
Sex Pistols (1978), *Indecent Exposure*, bootleg vinyl album, United Kingdom: Rotten Records.
Sex Pistols (1979), *Flogging a Dead Horse*, vinyl album, United Kingdom: Virgin Records.
Sex Pistols (1979), 'The Great Rock'n'Roll Swindle', 7" single, United Kingdom: Virgin Records.
Sex Pistols (1979), *The Great Rock'n'Roll Swindle*, vinyl album, United Kingdom: Virgin Records.
Siouxsie and the Banshees (1978), 'Hong Kong Garden', 7" single, United Kingdom: Polydor.
Siouxsie and the Banshees (1978), *Love in a Void*, bootleg vinyl album, United Kingdom: Sioux Records.
Siouxsie and the Banshees (1978), *The Scream*, vinyl album, United Kingdom: Polydor.
Siouxsie and the Banshees (1979), *Join Hands*, vinyl album, United Kingdom: Polydor.
Siouxsie and the Banshees (1979), 'Mittageisen', 7" single, United Kingdom: Polydor.
Siouxsie and the Banshees (1988), 'Peek-A-Boo', 7" single, United Kingdom: Polydor.
Siouxsie and the Banshees (1988), *Peepshow*, vinyl album, United Kingdom: Polydor.
Six Minute War (1980), *Six Minute War*, 7" vinyl EP, United Kingdom: Six Minute War.
The Skroteez (1982), *Overspill*, 7" vinyl EP, United Kingdom: Square Anarchy.
Special Duties (1982), 'Colchester Council', 7" single, United Kingdom: Charnel House.
Stiff Little Fingers (1978), 'Alternative Ulster', 7" single, United Kingdom: Rough Trade.
The Stranglers (1977), '(Get A) Grip (On Yourself)', 7" single, United Kingdom: United Artists.
The Stranglers (1977), *Rattus Norvegicus*, vinyl album, United Kingdom: United Artists.
The Stranglers (1977), *No More Heroes*, vinyl album, United Kingdom: United Artists.
The Stranglers (1978), *London Ladies*, bootleg vinyl album, United Kingdom: RZM Productions.
The Stranglers (1978), *Black and White*, vinyl album, United Kingdom: United Artists.
The Straps (1982), 'Brixton', 7" single, United Kingdom: Donut.
Television Personalities (1978), '14th Floor', 7" single, United Kingdom: Teen 78.
Television Personalities (1978), *Where's Bill Grundy Now?*, 7" vinyl EP, United Kingdom: Kings Road.
Theatre of Hate (1980), 'Original Sin', 7" single, United Kingdom: SS Records.

Theatre of Hate (1982), *Westworld*, vinyl album, United Kingdom: Burning Rome Records.
Tubeway Army (1979), 'Are 'Friends' Electric?', 7" single, United Kingdom: Beggars Banquet.
Tubeway Army (1979), *Replicas*, vinyl album, United Kingdom: Beggars Banquet.
Ultravox! (1977), *Ultravox!*, vinyl album, United Kingdom: Island Records.
Ultravox (1978), *Systems of Romance*, vinyl album, United Kingdom: Island Records.
Various Artists (1978), *A Factory Sample*, double 7" vinyl EP, United Kingdom: Factory Records.
Various Artists (1978), *Vaultage '78*, vinyl album, United Kingdom: Attrix Records.
Various Artists (1979), *Vaultage '79*, vinyl album, United Kingdom: Attrix Records.
Various Artists (1980), *Vaultage '80*, vinyl album, United Kingdom: Attrix Records.
The Vibrators (1977), 'London Girls', 7" single, United Kingdom: Epic Records.
Victim (1977), 'Strange Thing By Night', 7" single, Northern Ireland: Good Vibrations.
Wire (1977), *Pink Flag*, vinyl album, United Kingdom: Harvest Records.
Wire (1978), 'Dot Dash', 7" single, United Kingdom: Harvest Records.
Wire (1978), 'I Am the Fly', 7" single, United Kingdom: Harvest Records.
X-Ray Spex (1978), *Germfree Adolescents*, vinyl album, United Kingdom: EMI International.
XTC (1978), *Go2*, vinyl album, United Kingdom: Virgin Records.

Index

4AD (record label) 123, 126, 138, 201, 243, 244
23 Envelope 13, 123, 138, 244
48 Thrills (fanzine) 124

Adam and the Ants (band) 55, 98, 178
Adventures in Reality (fanzine) 16, 124, 172, 173
The Adverts (band) 25, 144, 204
  Gaye Advert 33, 204, 206
Alternative TV (band) 25, 172
anarchism 51–52, 109–110
anarcho-punk 3, 6, 32, 83, 90, 104, 109–110, 112, 138, 173, 175, 201, 202
Angelic Upstarts (band) 110
Anti-Nazi League 51, 110, 207
appropriation 14, 19, 52, 62, 78, 86–87, 99, 217, 245
Arbiter, Murray 1, 197, 240
Association of Music Industry Designers (AMID) 240–241
Assorted Images 38, 56, 133, 168, 209, 215, 244
The Atoms (band) 75–76
authenticity 4–8, 25, 26, 37, 45, 58, 77, 103, 112, 115, 171, 178, 185, 197, 237, 245
autonomy 4, 8, 18, 19, 25, 26, 28, 37, 49, 51, 106, 107, 108, 142, 183, 185, 186, 195–197, 233, 239, 242, 245, 246
Averill, Steve 1, 156, 159–161

Bayley, Roberta 38, 147
Bazooka collective 229
Beal, Michael 2, 28, 143
Beckman, Janette 3
Beggars Banquet (record label) 118, 123, 226
Better Badges 32, 73, 173–175, 209
Blake, Peter 7, 230
Blauvelt, Andrew 17
Blitz (magazine) 210
Blitzkrieg Bop (band) 42, 43
Blondie (band) 43, 204, 205, 210, 222
Bondage (fanzine) 77, 124, 172
The Boomtown Rats (band) 98, 112, 115
Boon, Richard 46, 129, 131, 132, 243
Boot, Adrian 2
bootlegs 27–28
Brody, Neville 1, 3, 13, 58, 99, 128, 134–135, 167, 196, 200, 207–209, 210, 221, 230, 244
Bubbles, Barney 3, 7, 13, 28, 39, 40, 48, 98, 99, 126–128, 129, 134, 157, 167, 206, 208, 228, 229, 243
Burchill, Julie 51

Buzzcocks (band) 5, 28, 37, 38, 46, 55, 56, 66, 78–79, 105, 111, 123, 126, 129, 131–134, 136, 167, 168, 185, 188, 196, 204, 210, 227
Spiral Scratch 46, 55, 129, 131, 132, 136

Cabaret Voltaire (band) 57, 106, 134, 135, 208, 216, 220, 224, 225
Campaign for Nuclear Disarmament (CND) 109
Carrington, Susan 30
The Cartel 108, 201, 234
Centre for Contemporary Cultural Studies (CCCS) 103
Chainsaw, Charlie 3, 29, 124, 172, 211
Chainsaw (fanzine) 74, 124, 125, 158, 172, 174, 211
Christopherson, Peter 'Sleazy' 13, 90, 128, 129
Chron Gen (band) 42, 45
The Clash (band) 5, 12, 13, 24, 25, 28, 38, 64, 85, 94–96, 113, 116, 117, 121, 124, 135, 144, 147, 187, 188, 204, 245
Clay Records (record label) 118–120, 201, 203
Cocteau Twins (band) 139, 244
collage 3, 19, 37, 55, 62, 78, 80, 82, 87–92, 128, 136, 138, 140, 157, 160, 164, 245, 246
Coles, Mike 1, 3, 16, 126, 139–142, 161, 162, 196, 214, 245
Compact Disc (CD) 203, 233
Coon, Caroline 12, 51, 94
Copyright, Designs and Payments Act 1, 240
The Cortinas (band) 41, 42, 53, 88, 89, 91
Crass (band) 3, 32, 83, 84–85, 109–110, 126, 137, 201
Crass Records (record label) 137
The Cult Maniax (band) 116
The Cure (band) 144, 148, 149, 151, 245
cut-and-paste 62, 76–77, 87, 156, 245
Czezowski, Andrew 30

Dada 13, 14, 26, 35, 57, 84, 88, 146, 208, 230
The Damned (band) 5, 25, 38, 40, 41, 78, 98, 124, 126, 127, 163, 187
Das Schnitz (band) 85–86
Dean, Roger 7, 241
The Desperate Bicycles (band) 5, 46, 48, 49, 50, 55, 67, 108, 227
détournement 5, 37, 62, 78–79, 84, 86–88, 94, 157
Diboll, Mike 3, 124, 175
Discharge (band) 119, 120, 201–203
do-it-yourself (DIY) 1, 4, 5, 6, 8, 9, 16, 18, 19, 24, 27, 32, 37, 44–49, 57, 59, 60–77, 87, 94, 95, 103, 104, 106, 108, 109, 112, 121, 123, 136, 142, 151, 154, 157, 158, 163, 164, 166, 170–179, 184, 188, 196, 200, 201, 209, 212, 221, 224, 225, 227, 228, 234, 236, 238, 239, 245, 247
Dr. Feelgood (band) 40, 126, 143, 144
Drayton, Tony 3, 124, 172, 174, 176–178, 211, 243

Echenberg, Erica 3, 29
Eddie and the Hot Rods (band) 143, 187
Electrical, Electronic, Telecommunications and Plumbing Union (EETPU) 194, 195
The Exploited (band) 91, 114, 202

The Face (magazine) 3, 14, 100, 200, 208–209, 210, 230
The Factory (club) 134, 216
Factory Records (record label) 99, 126, 134, 201, 208, 216–217, 223, 244
Fad Gadget (band) 217, 219, 220
The Fall (band) 37, 55, 106, 111, 114
fanzine 3, 5, 16, 19, 25, 27, 29, 30–34, 44, 45–47, 50, 51, 55, 59, 64, 67, 70–73, 77, 90, 95, 110, 124, 125, 136, 137, 151, 154, 157, 158, 170–179, 211, 238, 243
Fast Product (record label) 64–68, 107, 123, 135–137, 218, 222, 223, 244
Fawcett, Diana 48, 49, 50
Fifty Fantastics (band) 74

Fletcher, Tony 3, 16, 73, 124, 172, 174, 211
Flexipop! (magazine) 210–211
Foxx, John 227
Friedman, Dan 17
Furmanovsky, Jill 2, 38, 42
Futurism 14, 98

Gabrin, Chris 2, 39
Gang of Four (band) 58, 65–69, 106, 118, 136, 207, 228
Garrett, Malcolm 1, 3, 13, 14, 16, 17, 28, 38, 55, 56, 58, 99, 123, 126, 129–134, 157, 167, 168, 185, 196, 200, 208, 210, 212, 215, 230, 241, 244
Generation X (band) 5, 98
Gestetner Cyclograph 71, 157, 173
Goddard, Martyn 147, 148, 149
Good Vibrations (record label) 79
de Graaf, Kasper 210, 244
Grant enlarger 169–170, 239
Grant, Simone 217, 219, 220
Gravelle, Peter (Kodick) 2, 14, 30, 40, 41, 93, 117
Greiman, April 17, 229, 230
Grierson, Nigel 13, 123, 138, 244
Griffin, Brian 2
Grunwick 187
Gun Rubber (fanzine) 124, 172

The Haçienda (club) 217
halftone process 40, 71, 73, 77, 87, 95, 128, 164, 165, 168, 169, 173, 182–183, 220, 246
Hamilton, Richard 7, 136, 148, 230
Hannett, Martin 216–217
Hard Werken 229
hardcore (punk) 6, 43, 90, 104, 112, 119, 201, 202, 235, 236, 237
Harry, Debbie 204, 205
Haworth, Jann 7
Headache (band) 42, 44
Hebdige, Dick 32–34, 52, 53, 54, 57, 78, 103, 115
Henry, Paul 3, 144
Heseltine, Michael 83
Hipgnosis 7, 87, 90, 128, 150
Hornsey College of Art 134, 135

The Human League (band) 136, 218, 222, 223, 224, 227, 244
iD (magazine) 32, 200, 209, 210
illustration 2, 3, 14, 84, 98, 118, 119, 127, 182, 229, 230
Impossible Dream (magazine) 32
In The City (fanzine) 124, 172, 178
Independent Chart 108–109
Ingham, Jonh 51, 88
International Anthem (magazine) 3, 32

The Jam (band) 5, 25, 38, 43, 58, 134, 144, 147, 148, 151, 188, 210
Jamming! (fanzine) 16, 73, 124, 172, 174, 211
Jeffery, David 3
Jones, Barry 30, 178
Jones, Terry 13, 14, 32, 129, 209, 210, 230
Joy Division (band) 12, 99, 106, 134, 207, 216, 217, 222

Kent, Nick 51
Kerrang! (magazine) 211
Kill Your Pet Puppy (fanzine) 74, 124, 172, 173, 176, 177
Killing Joke (band) 106, 140–142, 161, 162, 207, 222, 245
King, David 207

Last, Bob 1, 3, 64–68, 107, 123, 135–137, 218, 228, 244
Lazell, Barry 108
Leer, Thomas 224–226
Letraset 16, 34, 36, 56, 66, 82, 91, 131, 135, 140, 154, 156, 157, 158–165, 170, 172, 210, 213, 220, 221, 239, 246
  Letraset figures 217–219, 228
Lettrism 26
Linder 88, 89
Linotype 191
lithographic printing 68, 70, 71, 73, 171, 172, 173, 174, 175, 178, 181, 193, 197, 246
Livingston, Alistair 172, 173
Logan, Nick 208

London College of Printing (LCP) 135, 146
London's Burning (fanzine) 88, 124
London's Outrage (fanzine) 77, 88, 124, 172
Lycett, Kevin 64
Lydon, John (Johnny Rotten) 84, 92, 94, 105, 128, 204

MacFie, Joly 32, 73, 173–175, 178
McDermott, Catherine 13
McDowell, Alex 3, 14, 135, 200, 208, 209, 215, 228, 244–245
McLaren, Malcolm 5, 27, 35, 36, 51–52, 57, 62, 128
Magazine (band) 3, 5, 37, 105, 106, 111, 126, 196, 210
Malicious Damage (record label) 3, 126, 140–142, 162, 196, 245
Marcus, Greil 13, 57
The Mekons (band) 57, 58, 64–66, 67, 106, 136
Melody Maker (magazine) 12, 31, 51, 94, 106, 183, 194, 211
Mercer, Mick 3, 124, 211, 243
Miller, Daniel 16, 217, 220, 225
Mills, Russell 3, 13, 200
Milne, Tim 1, 166, 167, 171, 215
Mirowski, Jo 3, 28, 147, 149, 150
Moon, Tony 3, 46, 47, 124, 172
Morris, Keith 40
Morton, Chris (c-more-tone) 1, 3, 17, 28, 126–128, 129, 130, 135, 151, 157, 163, 167, 169, 170, 171, 195, 201, 202, 212, 213, 214, 228, 243
Mumford, Jill 1, 105, 145–146, 148, 149, 215, 245
Mute Records (record label) 201, 217–218, 219, 220, 225, 228

National Front 50, 110–111
National Graphical Association (NGA) 184, 190– 195
National Society of Operative Printers and Assistants (NATSOPA) 190
National Union of Journalists (NUJ) 194, 195
New Music News (magazine) 194

New Musical Express (*NME*) (magazine) 3, 31, 51, 52, 63, 96, 97, 106, 183, 194, 197, 205, 207, 208, 209, 211
New Order (band) 12, 99, 217, 227, 244
New Sounds New Styles (magazine) 210
new wave 5, 6, 17, 20, 24, 26, 27, 38, 40, 43, 45, 51, 63, 93, 98, 104, 106, 112, 119, 124, 126, 128, 134, 144, 145, 146, 148, 151, 187, 188, 200, 201, 204, 229, 230, 237, 246
New Wave of British Heavy Metal (NWOBHM) 206
Noise! (magazine) 211
The Normal (band) 217, 219, 220, 224
Nuclear Socketts (band) 116
Numan, Gary 225–227
Number One (magazine) 210

O'Connor, Rob 1, 3, 16, 58, 78, 138, 143, 148–151, 169–170, 182, 200, 209, 213, 214, 240, 241, 245
Oliver, Vaughan 3, 13, 99, 123, 126, 129, 138–139, 200, 201, 243–244
Orchestral Manoeuvres in the Dark (OMD) (band) 208, 223

Panache (fanzine) 124, 158, 172, 211
Pantone 164, 165, 218
parody 84–87, 94, 98, 100, 114, 157, 187, 245
Parry, Chris 147, 148, 151
Parsons, Tony 51
The Partisans (band) 42, 92
pastiche 84, 94, 157, 184, 236
Perry, Mark 3, 13, 16, 44–46, 70, 72, 91, 114, 124, 171, 172
photocomposition 1, 191–192
photocopier 16, 19, 34, 55, 68, 71–75, 77, 82, 87, 94, 135, 141, 155, 157, 158, 160, 167–173, 175, 178, 212, 225, 238, 239, 246
photography 2, 3, 4, 12, 26, 29, 30, 32, 37–40, 41, 42, 43, 65, 67, 71, 77, 84, 86, 87, 88, 92, 94, 95, 113, 115, 116, 117, 118, 119, 128, 129, 140, 141, 143, 147, 148, 155, 156, 182, 200, 204, 207, 208, 209, 212, 218, 222, 230, 240, 247

photolithography 167
photomontage 3, 221, 87–89, 98, 138, 167, 168
Photoshop 212
The Pigs (band) 88, 90
Plastic Bertrand (band) 28, 30
PMT (photomechanical transfer) camera 16, 131, 135, 138, 141, 156, 158, 166–170, 173, 174, 178, 239, 246
Pop Art 57, 73, 208, 230
post-punk 1, 2, 3, 6, 9, 11, 12, 13, 14, 17, 18, 19, 57, 58, 75, 99, 104–109, 112, 123, 128, 134, 137, 139, 142, 144, 155, 158, 163, 165, 174, 179, 188, 196, 197, 200, 201, 204, 206, 207, 208, 216, 221, 222, 223, 225, 227, 229, 230, 231, 233, 236, 237, 238, 239, 246, 247
Poison Girls (band) 32, 201
Polydor (record label) 31, 105, 107, 143, 144, 145–151, 155, 182, 184, 213, 214, 215, 245
Powell, Aubrey 7, 90, 128
Poynor, Rick 15, 17, 34, 80, 98, 99, 138, 229
Public Image Ltd. (band) 105, 106, 204
Punk Lives! (magazine) 211
Punk's Not Dead (magazine) 211

Radar (record label) 99, 126, 128, 196, 228
The Radiators From Space (band) 112, 115, 159–161
The Ramones (band) 5, 38, 40, 53, 71, 113, 121, 147, 237
ransom note typography 34–37, 77, 95, 157, 160, 224, 247
Rapidograph 127
razor blade 28, 35, 37, 202
Record Mirror (magazine) 31, 106, 183, 211
Reid, Jamie 1, 3, 5, 6, 7, 12, 13, 14, 16, 28, 34–37, 57, 79–82, 85, 88, 92, 100, 123, 124, 131, 157, 208, 215, 243
Reynolds, Simon 12, 104, 222
The Rezillos (band) 5, 112, 115–116, 136

Rhodes, Bernie 51, 52
Rider, Alan 3, 16, 124, 173
Ridgers, Derek 2, 30, 208
Rimbaud, Penny 137
The Rings (band) 117
Ripped & Torn (fanzine) 16, 77, 124, 158, 172–175, 178
Riviera, Jake 126, 128, 170
Robinson, Dave 126, 128, 135
Robinson, Lucy 10, 11
Rock, Sheila 2, 208
Rock Against Racism 51, 104, 109, 111, 158, 207
Rocking Russian 3, 135, 209, 215, 229, 244
Rough Trade (record shop) 108, 172–173, 178
  Rough Trade (record label) 123, 201, 220, 224, 225
The Roxy (club) 5, 29, 30, 178

Safety in Numbers (fanzine) 124, 172
safety pin 25, 28, 35, 37, 80, 202
The Saints (band) 55
Satan's Rats (band) 29
Savage, Jon 12, 14, 15, 51, 57, 77, 88, 99–100, 172, 208, 243
screen printing 75, 76, 215
Das Schnitz (band) 85, 86
Scritti Politti (band) 5, 58, 67, 68, 70, 108
Sex Pistols (band) 5, 12, 13, 15, 25, 27, 28, 34–37, 51, 57, 64, 79–82, 83, 84, 85, 88, 94, 105, 121, 123, 124, 128, 131, 134, 157, 158, 187, 188, 204, 244
Shah, Eddie 194–195
Sham 69 (band) 5, 25, 110, 145, 150
Sideburns (fanzine) 46, 47, 77, 172
Simon, Kate 2, 94
Siouxsie and the Banshees (band) 28, 37, 98, 105, 106, 134, 145, 149, 150, 182, 204, 212, 213, 214, 215, 243, 245
Situationist International 5, 13, 57, 78, 84, 100, 215, 228, 230
The Skids (band) 3, 99, 112, 145
Small Wonder (record label) 123, 148

Smash Hits (magazine) 200, 208, 210, 211
Smee, Phil 3
Smith, Bill 1, 3, 16, 28, 144, 146–148, 149, 155, 156, 169
Sniffin' Glue (fanzine) 13, 16, 44, 46, 70, 72, 77, 124, 158, 171–172, 173
Snow, George 'God' 3, 28, 144
Socialist Workers Party (SWP) 50, 51
Society of Graphical and Allied Trades (SOGAT) 190
Society of Lithographic Artists, Designers, Engravers and Process Workers (SLADE) 183
Sounds (magazine) 31, 51, 106, 109, 183, 211, 212
stencil 27, 71, 73, 94, 100, 109, 138, 154, 155, 156, 157, 158, 164–165, 168, 221, 246
Step Forward (record label) 31, 42, 91
Stevenson, Nils 1, 36
Stevenson, Ray 3
Stiff Records (record label) 5, 39, 99, 123, 126–128, 135, 163, 169, 170, 171, 195, 204, 206, 228, 243
Strangled (fanzine) 124, 172
The Stranglers (band) 25, 28, 38, 95, 97, 113, 134, 144, 188
Street-Porter, Janet 4, 5
Stylorouge 3, 151, 169, 245
Suburban Press 6, 35, 57
Suburban Studs (band) 28
Surrealism 14, 26, 57, 84, 99, 208, 230
swastika 28, 37, 52–54, 82, 202

The Table (band) 55
Tebbit, Norman 82
Television Personalities (band) 68, 70, 108, 113
Thatcher, Margaret 9, 10, 11, 14, 82–83, 84, 92, 173, 188, 189, 197
Theatre of Hate (band) 129, 130, 243
Thorgerson, Storm 7, 90, 128, 241
Throbbing Gristle (band) 13, 18, 106, 128–129
Toxic Grafity (fanzine) 124, 175
Trade Union and Labour Relations Act (TULRA) 186

Trick (magazine) 31, 32, 33
Tschichold, Jan 134
Tubeway Army (band) 226
typography 2, 32, 34, 35, 37, 41, 64, 66, 71, 88, 91, 95, 98, 99, 126, 127, 129, 134, 135, 138, 142, 148, 154, 156, 157, 158, 159, 160, 161, 163, 164, 165, 185, 190, 200, 207, 209, 210, 213, 220, 221, 224, 228, 229

Ultravox! (band) 106, 227

Vague, Tom 3, 16, 124
Vague (fanzine) 16, 124, 172, 175, 211
The Valves (band) 55
Vaucher, Gee 3, 15, 16, 17, 32, 83, 84, 85, 90, 126, 137–138, 142, 157, 243
Vega, Arturo 14, 237
The Velvet Underground (band) 7
The Vibrators (band) 25, 54, 78, 113, 187
Victim (band) 79
de Ville, Nicholas 3, 144
Virgin Records (record label) 11, 22, 31, 80, 82, 145, 146, 166, 187, 215, 222, 223
The Vortex (club) 5, 31, 226

Walton, Rik 2
Ware, Martyn 218
Warhol, Andy 7, 230
Weingart, Wolfgang 17, 229
Wellington-Lloyd, Helen 1, 28, 36
Westwood, Vivienne 5, 51–52, 62, 64
Winter of Discontent 9, 185
Wire (band) 3, 5, 37, 56, 105, 106
The Wombles (band) 95
Wright, Ian 3, 14, 58

Xerox 55, 71, 73, 74, 77, 173, 178
X-Ray Spex (band) 54, 55
XTC (band) 5, 86–87, 134, 145

ZigZag (magazine) 108, 170, 211

EU authorised representative for GPSR:
Easy Access System Europe, Mustamäe tee 50,
10621 Tallinn, Estonia
gpsr.requests@easproject.com

www.ingramcontent.com/pod-product-compliance
Lightning Source LLC
Chambersburg PA
CBHW041803230426
43749CB00037BA/942